A General Equilibrium Model for Tax Policy Evaluation

A National Bureau
of Economic Research
Monograph

A General Equilibrium Model for Tax Policy Evaluation

Charles L. Ballard
Don Fullerton
John B. Shoven
John Whalley

The University of Chicago Press

Chicago and London

Charles L. Ballard is Assistant Professor of Economics, Michigan
State University. Don Fullerton is Associate Professor of Economics, University of Virginia. John B. Shoven is Professor of
Economics, Stanford University. John Whalley is Professor of Economics, University of Western Ontario. The latter three authors
are also Research Associates of the National Bureau of Economic
Research.

The University of Chicago Press, Chicago 60637
The University of Chicago Press, Ltd., London

Library of Congress Cataloging in Publication Data
Main entry under title:

A General equilibrium model for tax policy evaluation.

(A National Bureau of Economic Research monograph)
Bibliography: p.
Includes index.
1. Taxation—United States—Mathematical models.
I. Ballard, Charles L.   II. Series.
HJ2381.G46   1985   336.2'00724   84-28096
ISBN 0-226-03632-4

National Bureau of Economic Research

Relation of the Directors to the
Work and Publications of the
National Bureau of Economic Research

1. The object of the National Bureau of Economic Research is to ascertain and to present to the public important economic facts and their interpretation in a scientic and impartial manner. The Board of Directors is charged with the responsibility of ensuring that the work of the National Bureau is carried on in strict conformity with this object.

2. The President of the National Bureau shall submit to the Board of Directors, or to its Executive Committee, for their formal adoption all specific proposals for research to be instituted.

3. No research report shall be published by the National Bureau until the President has sent each member of the Board a notice that a manuscript is recommended for publication and that in the President's opinion it is suitable for publication in accordance with the principles of the National Bureau. Such notification will include an abstract or summary of the manuscript's content and a response form for use by those Directors who desire a copy of the manuscript for review. Each manuscript shall contain a summary drawing attention to the nature and treatment of the problem studied, the character of the data and their utilization in the report, and the main conclusions reached.

4. For each manuscript so submitted, a special committee of the Directors (including Directors Emeriti) shall be appointed by majority agreement of the President and Vice Presidents (or by the Executive Committee in case of inability to decide on the part of the President and Vice Presidents), consisting of three Directors selected as nearly as may be one from each general division of the Board. The names of the special manuscript committee shall be stated to each Director when notice of the proposed publication is submitted to him. It shall be the duty of each member of the special manuscript committee to read the manuscript. If each member of the manuscript committee signifies his approval within thirty days of the transmittal of the manuscript, the report may be published. If at the end of that period any member of the manuscript committee withholds his approval, the President shall then notify each member of the Board, requesting approval or disapproval of publication, and thirty days additional shall be granted for this purpose. The manuscript shall then not be published unless at least a majority of the entire Board who shall have voted on the proposal within the time fixed for the receipt of votes shall have approved.

5. No manuscript may be published, though approved by each member of the special manuscript committee, until forty-five days have elapsed from the transmittal of the report in manuscript form. The interval is allowed for the receipt of any memorandum of dissent or reservation, together with a brief statement of his reasons, that any member may wish to express; and such memorandum of dissent or reservation shall be published with the manuscript if he so desires. Publication does not, however, imply that each member of the Board has read the manuscript, or that either members of the Board in general or the special committee have passed on its validity in every detail.

6. Publications of the National Bureau issued for informational purposes concerning the work of the Bureau and its staff, or issued to inform the public of activities of Bureau staff, and volumes issued as a result of various conferences involving the National Bureau shall contain a specific disclaimer noting that such publication has not passed through the normal review procedures required in this resolution. The Executive Committee of the Board is charged with review of all such publications from time to time to ensure that they do not take on the character of formal research reports of the National Bureau, requiring formal Board approval.

7. Unless otherwise determined by the Board or exempted by the terms of paragraph 6, a copy of this resolution shall be printed in each National Bureau publication.

(Resolution adopted October 25, 1926, as revised through September 30, 1974)

Contents

Preface

In economics, as in other fields, beliefs are reinforced or amended as successive researchers replicate or refute previous findings. For any particular contribution, the reader's confidence in the results depends fundamentally on his ability to reproduce them, regardless of whether he chooses to do so. When a large simulation model is summarized for the constrained space of a journal article, however, the reader may learn no more than the general approach of the model. The summary may be viewed as cryptic, and the model may be viewed as a black box. Confidence is accordingly limited. These considerations may have led Donald McCloskey to ask:

> What is legitimate simulation? Between A. C. Harberger's modest little triangles of distortion and Jeffrey Williamson's immense multi-equation models of the American or Japanese economies since 1870 is a broad range. Economists have no vocabulary for criticizing any part of the range. They can deliver summary grunts of belief or disbelief but find it difficult to articulate their reasons in a disciplined way. (1983, p. 502)

The purpose of this book is to provide all of the equations, data, and procedures that would be required to replicate the findings of one such simulation model. This numerical general equilibrium model of the United States tax system has been used in a number of previous journal articles to evaluate a number of tax issues and proposed tax reforms, but its detail has not yet been made generally available. We hope that this detail on particular procedures, equations, and data will be useful to other researchers pursuing similar objectives, and we hope that its availability will increase confidence in these previously published results. This considerable modeling detail is preceded by a general discussion of tax issues and methodology, and it is followed by updated results on the issues addressed in several of the previous papers.

Since its beginning in 1976, work on various aspects of this model has been supported by the Treasury Department's Office of Tax Analysis, by several grants from the National Science Foundation, and by the National Bureau of Economic Research. We are very grateful for this financial assistance, as we are for data, suggestions, and other contributions of a great many other researchers. Individuals at the Commerce Department's National Income Division were particularly helpful. The model originated with work for the Treasury Department, and it is still being operated there, so it is sometimes known as the Treasury general equilibrium model. It is also known as GEMTAP, for general-equilibrium-model taxation analysis package.

Some of the papers using this model have been coauthored by Charles Becker, Antonio Borges, Shantayanan Devarajan, Roger H. Gordon, Lawrence H. Goulder, Yolanda K. Henderson, Timothy J. Kehoe, A. Thomas King, Andrew B. Lyon, and Richard A. Musgrave. Additional research assistance has been provided by Thomas Kronmiller, Radwan Shaban, and Janet Stotsky. All of these individuals have made substantial contributions toward this book.

In addition to many seminar participants and anonymous referees, we are grateful for suggestions made by Alan J. Auerbach, J. Gregory Ballentine, Peter Baltaxe, Alan Blinder, George Borts, Miachel Boskin, David F. Bradford, Peter Diamond, Larry Dildine, Daniel Feenberg, Martin Feldstein, Harvey Galper, Mart Gertler, Malcolm Gillis, Ronald E. Grieson, Robert E. Hall, Arnold C. Harberger, Glenn Harrison, Robert H. Haveman, Charles R. Hulten, Dale W. Jorgenson, Michael Kaufman, Wouter Keller, Jon Kesselman, Nicholas Kiefer, Mark Killingsworth, Larry Kimbell, Mervyn A. King, Laurence Kotlikoff, Arthur B. Laffer, Charles McLure, Peter Mieszkowski, Hudson Milner, Franco Modigliani, John R. Piggot, Sherman Robinson, Harvey S. Rosen, Herbert Scarf, Jaime Serra-Puche, Joel Slemrod, Nicholas H. Stern, Wayne Thirsk, and Norman B. Ture.

Successive versions of this manuscript were typed by Althea Chaballa and Patrick Higgins. The long hours and outstanding work that they gave to this project have made our tasks much easier.

1   Introduction

Many questions of economic policy can be analyzed within a partial equilibrium framework. When the policy changes being considered are relatively small, it may be appropriate to neglect the general equilibrium interactions among many different markets. However, when large policy changes are considered, partial equilibrium analysis becomes painfully inadequate. In recognition of this fact, a vast increase has occurred in the past twenty years in the number of economists who use general equilibrium models.

The work on applied general equilibrium models can be divided into two traditions. The first tradition owes a great deal to Arnold Harberger and Harry Johnson. Most of Johnson's work (e.g., Johnson and Krauss 1970) deals with international trade issues. Harberger's work has helped to increase the popularity of general equilibrium models among public finance economists. We shall discuss the Harberger model in greater detail in chapter 2. Because these models are difficult to manipulate, they are usually operated at a rather high level of abstraction, with only two sectors or countries, two factors, and two goods. The models can yield strong results, but they do so at the cost of abstracting from much of the complexity of the real-world economy.

The second tradition in general equilibrium analysis uses computational techniques, recently developed, that enable us to investigate economies with many more sectors, goods, and factors. Within the last decade especially, the literature based on this type of general equilibrium analysis has grown phenomenally. In this book we describe our model of the United States economy and tax system, which is a part of this second tradition of general equilibrium analysis.

Here are a few of the salient features of our model:

—We model the economy with twelve consumer groups that differ in endowments and preferences.

—We divide the production side of the economy into nineteen producer sectors that differ in production technology. This is a reasonably high level of disaggregation.

—In addition to consumers and producers, we model the activities of the government and the foreign sector.

—We operationalize the model using actual data for 1973 from the National Income and Product Accounts and other sources.

—We specify the growth of the economy's endowments over time, so that we can analyze intertemporal efficiency issues as well as intersectoral ones. This is crucially important to our analysis of the consumption tax, and it also plays an important role in our analysis of other tax policy issues.

—We model the tax system in great detail. We include not only personal income taxes and corporate income taxes, but also property taxes, payroll taxes, sales and excise taxes, and a variety of smaller taxes. Consequently, our model is capable of analyzing a large number of tax policy questions within a second-best framework.

A brief outline of this volume follows: In chapter 2, which discusses general equilibrium analysis with taxes, we begin with a discussion of general equilibrium without taxes, and then consider the ways in which the model is changed in order to include a variety of taxes. We outline the fundamentals of the computational algorithm, and we describe the calculation of *equal-revenue-yield equilibria*. In almost every case when we compare two simulations, we require that the same revenues be collected in both simulations. Otherwise, our results would be a mixture of the effects of changes in the configuration of taxes with changes in the overall size of government. Revenue yield equality can be preserved in a number of different ways, and we shall see that different methods can lead to different results.

In chapters 3 through 7 we discuss our model in detail. Chapter 3 describes our assumptions about the behavior of consumers, producers, the government, and the foreign sector. In each case we specify the functional form of the relevant production function or utility function. Without specific functional forms we would not be able to make precise numerical calculations.

Chapters 4 and 5 deal with the basic benchmark data for 1973. In chapter 4 we cover the production side of the model, including data on factor use by industry, factor taxes by industry, and intermediate production. Chapter 5 covers the data on household income and expenditure, government expenditure, imports, and exports.

The data described in chapters 4 and 5 come from many sources and must be adjusted in several ways before they satisfy the conditions of a general equilibrium. For example, consumer expenditure must equal consumer income, and the value of the factor endowments of consumers and government must equal the factor payments made by industry. We describe these consistency adjustments in chapter 6.

Even with a consistent data set, we still do not have enough information to perform general equilibrium calculations. We must first choose parameters for the utility and production functions. The parameterization is also covered in chapter 6. It is important to recognize that the various parameters cannot all be chosen independently. If an arbitrary set of parameter values were imposed upon the model, and if we then were to solve for a set of equilibrium prices and quantities, we would not generally be able to replicate the benchmark data set. We first choose a few important parameters and impose them on the model. Then we use the model equilibrium conditions and the assumptions of cost minimization and utility maximization to generate all of the remaining parameters. This procedure insures that the complete set of parameters will replicate the benchmark data set exactly. Finally, in chapter 6 we describe our choices of the saving elasticity, labor supply elasticity, foreign trade elasticities, elasticities of substitution in production, and other key parameters.

We deal with the dynamic features of our model in chapter 7. The dynamic features deserve special emphasis because they represent a major departure from earlier applied general equilibrium analyses. Our analyses begin with 1973 and project the economy into the future by computing a sequence of equilibria. We assume that the economy was on a balanced growth path in 1973. This implies that without an alteration of government policies, all relative prices will remain constant over time. Factor endowments grow over time as a result of exogenous growth of the labor endowment and endogenous saving decisions by consumers. We choose the growth rate of labor so that in a *base-case sequence* of equilibria with no change in tax policy, labor and capital will grow at the same rate. Therefore, the base-case sequence replicates the balanced growth path on which the 1973 equilibrium was assumed to be.

In order to analyze a proposed change in tax policy, we alter some of the tax rates and rerun the model. (We do not change the behavioral parameters between a base-case sequence and a *revised-case sequence*; otherwise, we would be unable to isolate the effects of the tax change.) For the purpose of policy analysis, the next step is to compare the base-case sequence with the revised-case sequence. Chapters 8 through 11 contain many such comparisons.

In chapter 8 we consider a variety of proposals for integrating the personal income tax and the corporate income tax. In this regard, an important feature of our work is that we have a detailed model of the aspects of the personal income tax that affect the allocation of capital among industries. We consider proposals for full integration, as well as partial integration plans such as a dividend deduction in the corporate income tax. This chapter represents an updating and extension of work in Fullerton, King, Shoven, and Whalley (1980, 1981).

In chapter 9 we analyze proposals for the adoption of a consumption tax. Again we consider a variety of plans, including plans that only move us part of the way toward a consumption tax. For comparison we also analyze the effects of adopting a more pure income tax, which would involve removing the existing preferences for saving in the individual income tax. This chapter updates work in Fullerton, Shoven, and Whalley (1983).

Chapter 10 includes an analysis of Laffer curves. In this chapter we determine the combinations of tax rates and behavioral parameters that could lead to a decrease in tax revenue collections, even though tax rates are increased. Here we update work published in Fullerton (1982).

Chapter 11 includes descriptions of alternative models of the behavior of the foreign sector. In our basic model, we assume that foreign commodity trade can be characterized by constant elasticity import supply and export demand functions. We also assume that there are no international capital flows. In chapter 11 we put forth three alternative models of the foreign sector. In the first of these, we model some imports as being imperfectly substitutable with domestic production. The other two alternative models allow for an international capital rental market and for international purchases of capital, respectively. We then analyze a number of tax policy changes using each of these models. We take another look at corporate tax integration and at the consumption tax. We also model a value-added tax and evaluate its effects under each of the models of the foreign sector. This chapter represents an extension of Goulder, Shoven, and Whalley (1983).

The simulations we report in chapters 8 through 11 should not be viewed as precise predictions. We believe that our model is good for providing insights about the general direction in which tax policy ought to move, rather than providing an exact guide to policy. With this qualification in mind, we now give a brief summary of some of our results.

We find that integration of the corporate and personal income taxes could generate substantial welfare gains for the economy. The welfare gain from full integration, accompanied by indexation of capital gains taxes, is about $695 billion in 1973 dollars if the lost revenues are replaced with lump-sum taxes. However, the gains are sensitive to the form of the replacement tax. When revenues are recouped with equiproportional increases in the marginal tax rates faced by consumers, the gains are only about $311 billion. These dollar figures represent 1.39 percent and 0.62 percent of the total present value of welfare in the base case. Full integration yields greater gains than the partial-integration plans. All of the plans lead to changes in the industrial allocation of capital and in its relative prices. These changes can be substantial, especially in the case of full integration.

The integration plans improve economic efficiency in two ways. First, they increase the efficiency with which capital is allocated among industrial sectors. Second, by reducing the overall tax burden on capital, they increase intertemporal efficiency. In chapter 9 we focus more closely on the intertemporal aspects of the model by considering proposals to move toward a consumption tax. These proposals involve substantial increases in the proportion of savings that is sheltered from tax, and our model indicates that they could lead to large welfare gains. Increasing this proportion to the level that would shelter all savings would lead to welfare gains of between $537 billion and $616 billion, depending on the way in which revenues are replaced. When we combine the consumption tax with corporate tax integration, the gains can be as large as $1,304 billion. This is 2.61 percent of the total present value of national welfare. We find that our results for the consumption tax are somewhat sensitive to the assumption about the elasticity of saving with respect to the rate of return. Also in chapter 9 we investigate the length of the "long run." We find that it usually takes around thirty years from the time of the policy change before the economy begins to settle close to its new steady state.

In chapter 10 we consider Laffer curves. While we accept the possibility that extremely high tax rates may lead to decreases in tax revenue, we find no reason to believe that the United States is now at such a point. At current tax rates, the labor supply elasticity would have to be about 3.0 in order to put the economy onto the "prohibitive range" of the Laffer curve. This far exceeds any econometric estimate of the labor supply elasticity. Alternatively, if we assume that the labor supply elasticity is 0.15, tax rates would have to approach 70 percent before we would observe perverse revenue effects.

In chapter 11 we reexamine the consumption tax and corporate tax integration under a variety of different formulations of the foreign sector. Our results do not change much when we consider an imperfectly substitutable import. However, the results are fairly sensitive to the modeling of international capital flows. In this chapter we also consider different types of value-added tax (VAT). We show that the VAT would have the same effects, regardless of whether it is levied on the origin basis or the destination basis. However, a VAT of the consumption type (which resembles a consumption tax in many ways) would be much more beneficial than a VAT of the income type. In general, VATs of the consumption type lead to gains of $94 billion to $498 billion, or between 0.19 percent and 0.98 percent of the total present value of welfare. Income-type VATs generally are less beneficial, according to our calculations.

2   General Equilibrium Analysis of Tax Policies

In this chapter we describe the general equilibrium approach to the analysis of the impact of taxes which underlies our later evaluation of U.S. tax policies. We begin with a discussion of the pathbreaking work of Arnold Harberger (1959, 1962, 1966, 1974). Harberger's analyses represent a great advance over partial equilibrium models, but they have their own shortcomings. In particular, the Harberger model quickly becomes intractable in dealing with more than two sectors or two factors. Also, the model is not suited for considering large policy changes. We use a model that overcomes these shortcomings. After dealing with the Harberger model in section 2.1, we lay the foundations for our own model. In section 2.2 the essential elements of general equilibrium models are presented. Then we discuss the incorporation of taxes into the model in section 2.3. Section 2.4 covers computational techniques. Section 2.5 follows with a discussion of computations in which the size of government is held constant, even though the configuration of taxes is changed. Finally, we discuss a method by which the number of prices that must be computed can be reduced greatly. The details of our model of the United States and the data follow in chapters 3 through 7.

2.1 Harberger's General Equilibrium Tax Analyses

In the general equilibrium tax literature, Harberger's analyses of the incidence and efficiency effects of taxes have been a major stimulus to subsequent work. The Harberger approach enabled general equilibrium effects to be quantified for the first time. Although our work in this book goes further than that of Harberger in many ways, our dependence on Harberger's work will be obvious to anyone familiar with the literature. The 1962 Harberger general equilibrium tax model uses standard neo-

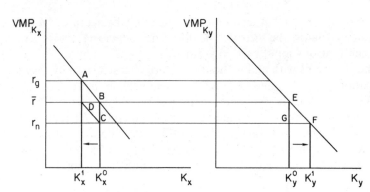

Fig. 2.1   The intersectoral allocation of capital in the Harberger general equilibrium model.

classical assumptions. It is assumed that the aggregate supplies of capital and labor are fixed, that factors are perfectly mobile among industries, and that perfect competition exists in factor and product markets. Production takes place under constant returns to scale. There are two sectors, each of which produces a single, homogeneous output. Harberger assumes a closed economy (i.e., there is no foreign trade). The model considers the effects of a distorting tax on capital in one of the sectors.[1]

The model is represented by a series of differential equations. For discrete changes, the analysis is only a local approximation. Using estimates of elasticities of substitution in production and consumption that are based on econometric literature, Harberger generates estimates of the incidence of particular taxes. Perhaps the most famous finding from this model is that the corporate tax is borne by all capital owners, regardless of whether their capital is used in incorporated enterprises.

Harberger also develops a procedure for estimating the welfare cost of a distortionary factor tax. In the case of capital tax distortions, he considers the economy to be represented ty two sectors, "heavily taxed" and "lightly taxed." These are represented as sectors X and Y in figure 2.1. Each sector uses capital in production, and the marginal revenue product schedules are assumed to be linear. The economy has a fixed capital endowment. In the absence of any taxes, market forces will ensure that capital is allocated between the two sectors such that the rate of return, $\bar{r}$, is equal. If, instead, a tax operates on capital income in sector X, the gross

---

1. A number of these assumptions have been relaxed in subsequent work. McLure has extended the model to cover interregional incidence (1969), and has introduced immobile factors (1971). Thirsk (1972) has extended the analysis to the case of three goods, and Mieszkowski (1972) has considered the case of three factors. Anderson and Ballentine (1976) have extended the analysis to incorporate the case of monopoly. Finally, Vandendorpe and Friedlaender (1976) extend the Harberger formulation to encompass an initial situation with a number of distortionary taxes.

rate of return, r_g, in that sector must be such that the net rate of return, r_n, is equalized across the sectors. The difference between r_g and r_n is the tax on each unit of capital used in sector X.

The situations with and without taxes are characterized by the capital allocations (K_x^1, K_y^1) and (K_x^0, K_y^0), respectively. In figure 2.1, the area $ABK_x^0K_x^1$ represents the value of the lost output in sector X when K_x decreases from K_x^0 to K_x^1 as the tax is imposed. $EFK_y^1K_y^0$ represents the value of the increased output of sector Y. Full employment guarantees that $K_x^0 - K_x^1 = K_y^1 - K_y^0$. The area $ABCD$ $(= ABK_x^0K_x^1 - EFK_y^1K_y^0)$ represents the welfare cost of the tax, L, and is given by:

$$(2.1) \qquad L = \tfrac{1}{2}(r_g - r_n)\, \Delta\, K_x = \tfrac{1}{2}\, T\, \Delta\, K_x,$$

where t is the tax rate on capital in sector X. The tax rate can be determined from readily available data. Harberger calculates $\Delta\, K_x$ by solving his two-sector general equilibrium model for this variable.

In his 1964 paper, Harberger applies a similar form of local analysis in an examination of the welfare costs of several key distortions in the tax system. In this paper, he presents the generalized triangle formula for the welfare cost of a distorting tax, upon which so much intuition for the size of the distorting costs of taxes has subsequently been based.

This intuition is most easily seen in the simple case of an output tax on a single product where the supply function is perfectly elastic. This is shown in figure 2.2 where DD' is the compensated demand function.

The tax is assumed to be paid by suppliers of the product, so that the supply curve in figure 2.2 shifts by the amount of the tax, and the quantity bought in the presence of the tax falls from q_0 to q_1. At q_1, the gross-of-tax price represents the demand-side evaluation of the welfare gain from an extra unit of production. The net-of-tax price represents the social opportunity cost of extra production. As long as the demand price exceeds the net-of-tax supply price, a gain is thus possible from extra production, and the shaded triangle in figure 2.2 is the welfare cost of the distorting tax.

Defining the difference between the gross-of-tax and net-of-tax prices as Δp, and $q_0 - q_1$ as Δq, the area of this triangle is the deadweight loss, L:

$$(2.2) \qquad L = \tfrac{1}{2}\, \Delta q\, \Delta p.$$

If units for q are chosen such that $p = 1$ in the no-tax equilibrium, then $\Delta p = t$, where t is the ad valorem tax rate. Defining the demand elasticity as ϵ gives $\Delta q = \epsilon \Delta p \cdot q/p$. Evaluated at q_0 where $p = 1$ and $\Delta p = t$, we have $\Delta q = \epsilon t q_0$. Thus,

$$(2.3) \qquad L = \tfrac{1}{2}\, t^2\, \epsilon\, q_0.$$

The deadweight loss increases with the square of the tax rate, and linearly with elasticities.

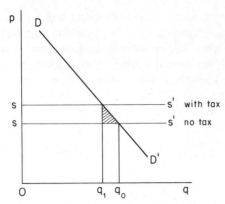

Fig. 2.2 The excess burden of an output tax in partial equilibrium.

To evaluate the overall efficiency of this tax as a source of revenue, it is sometimes useful to look at the deadweight loss per dollar of revenue R. Since $R = tq_0$ initially (where $p = 1$), we can rewrite the deadweight loss formula as $L = \frac{1}{2}\, t\epsilon R$. The deadweight loss per dollar of revenue is $L/R = \frac{1}{2}\, t\epsilon$. Thus the deadweight loss per dollar of revenue is linear in t and ϵ.

For comparison purposes, however, we may want to know the additional excess burden associated with a marginal dollar of revenue from each tax instrument. The numerator of this ratio is

$$(2.4) \qquad dL/dt = \epsilon t q_0.$$

The denominator, dR/dt, is q_0. Therefore, the marginal excess burden is

$$(2.5) \qquad \frac{\text{Marginal Loss}}{\text{Marginal Revenue}} = \frac{\epsilon t q_0}{q_0} = \epsilon t.$$

As noted by Browning (1976), Stuart (1984), and Ballard, Shoven, and Whalley (1982), the marginal cost of an extra dollar raised from an existing distorting tax exceeds the average welfare cost of all revenue raised by the tax. In this simple model, marginal deadweight loss is twice as great as average deadweight loss.

2.2 General Equilibrium Models

General equilibrium models have four essential ingredients—the endowments of consumers, their demand functions, the production technology, and the conditions for equilibrium.

In general, consumers may possess endowments of any or all of the commodities in the economy. The nonnegative economy-wide endowments are given by the vector W; $W_i \geq 0$, $i = 1, 2, \ldots, N$, where N is the number of commodities. In our model, consumers only possess endowments of capital and labor. Market demand functions are specified for each commodity. Demands are nonnegative and depend in a continuous manner on all prices. The market demand functions are denoted by $D_i(P), i = 1, \ldots, N$, where the vector P represents the N market prices. The demands are homogeneous of degree zero in all prices, i.e., if all prices were to double, the quantities demanded would not change. Because of the homogeneity property, an arbitrary normalization of prices can be chosen; a common treatment is to consider nonnegative prices that sum to unity, i.e., prices that lie on the unit price simplex.

$$\left(P_i \geq 0; \ \sum_{i=1}^{N} P_i = 1\right).$$

Commodity demands are also assumed to obey Walras's law, which states that the value of market demands equals the value of endowments at *any* set of prices, regardless of whether they are equilibrium prices. Market demand functions are typically represented as the sum of the individual household demand functions, each of which may or may not be derived from utility maximization subject to a budget constraint. In our model, each representative consumer group has commodity demands derived from constrained utility maximization.

On the production side of a general equilibrium model, technology is usually described by a set of constant returns to scale activities, or by production functions that exhibit nonincreasing returns to scale. The advantage of the activity analysis approach is that the conditions for equilibrium are especially simple when production is modeled in this way. On the other hand, production functions are more convenient to use in applied work. Production functions are easy to parameterize, since most of the relevant econometric literature involves the estimation of production functions.

In this chapter we describe both activity analysis production and continuous production functions. In subsequent chapters we will only use production functions. With the activity analysis approach, each of the constant returns to scale activities which is available to the economy is represented as a vector of coefficients. Each coefficient, a_{ik}, represents the input or output of good i when activity k is operated at unit intensity. We adopt the convention that the a_{ik} are negative for inputs and positive for outputs. If there are K activities, the coefficients can be arranged in an $(N \times K)$ matrix, which we shall call A. The first N columns of this matrix are usually disposal activities, which allow for costless disposal of each commodity. Joint products are possible, i.e., an activity may have more than one output. However, activities are restricted to satisfy the boundedness condition that at any nonnegative set of activity levels x, $Ax + W$ is bounded. The interpretation of this condition is that it excludes infinite production of any of the commodities.

In the case of a continuous production function with constant return to scale, any set of prices leads to unique cost-minimizing input proportions. We can think of a continuous production function as an infinite set of activities.

Equilibrium in the activity analysis model is characterized by a non-negative vector of prices and activity levels (P^*, x^*), where the $*$ denotes the equilibrium level. At (P^*, x^*), demands equal supplies for all commodities:

$$(2.6) \qquad D_i(P^*) = \sum_{k=1}^{K} a_{ik} x_k^* + W_i \qquad \text{for } i = 1, \ldots, N.$$

Also, no activity makes positive profits, with those in use breaking even:

$$(2.7) \qquad \sum_{i=1}^{N} P_i^* a_{ik} \leqq 0 \ (= 0 \text{ if } x_k^* > 0) \qquad \text{for } k = 1, \ldots, K.$$

A simplified numerical example of a model representative of those actually used in this book may help in understanding the general equilibrium structure (see table 2.1). For expositional purposes, we consider a model with two final goods (manufacturing and nonmanufacturing) and two factors of production (capital and labor). We consider two classes of consumers. Consumers have initial endowments of factors but have no initial endowments of goods. The "rich" consumer group owns capital, while the "poor" group owns labor. Production of each good takes place

Table 2.1   **Specification of Production Parameters, Demand Parameters, and Endowments for a Simple General Equilibrium Economy**

Production Parameters			
	Φ_i	δ_i	σ_i
Manufacturing	1.5	.6	2.0
Nonmanufacturing	2.0	.7	.5

Demand Parameters			
	α_{MFG}	α_{NonMFG}	σ
Rich consumers	0.5	0.5	1.5
Poor consumers	0.3	0.7	0.75

Endowments		
	K	L
Rich households	25	0
Poor households	0	60

according to a constant elasticity of substitution (CES) production function, and each consumer class has demands derived from maximizing a CES utility function subject to its budget constraint.

The production functions are given by

$$(2.8) \quad Q_i = \Phi_i \left(\delta_i^{\frac{1}{\sigma_i}} L_i^{\frac{\sigma_i - 1}{\sigma_i}} + (1 - \delta_i)^{\frac{1}{\sigma_i}} K_i^{\frac{\sigma_i - 1}{\sigma_i}} \right)^{\frac{\sigma_i}{\sigma_i - 1}} \quad i = 1, 2, \ldots$$

where Q_i denotes output of the ith industry, Φ_i is the scale or units parameter, δ_i is the distribution parameter, K_i and L_i are the factor inputs, and σ_i is the elasticity of factor substitution.

The CES utility functions are given by

$$(2.9) \quad U_j = \left(\alpha_j^{\frac{1}{\sigma_j}} D_{1j}^{\frac{\sigma_j - 1}{\sigma_j}} + (1 - \alpha_j)^{\frac{1}{\sigma_j}} D_{2j}^{\frac{\sigma_j - 1}{\sigma_j}} \right)^{\frac{\sigma_j}{\sigma_j - 1}},$$

where D_{ij} is the quantity of good i demanded by consumer j, α_j are share parameters, and σ_j is the substitution elasticity. If we maximize equation (2.9), subject to the constraint that the consumer cannot spend more than his income, $(P_1 D_1 + P_2 D_2 \leq P_L W_L + P_K W_K)$, we get the demand functions:

$$(2.10) \quad D_{ij} = \frac{\alpha_j I}{P_i^{\sigma_j} (\alpha_j P_1^{1 - \sigma_j} + (1 - \alpha_j) P_2^{1 - \sigma_j})} \quad i = 1, 2, \ldots$$

where I is income and P_i are market prices.

Once we have specified the parameters of these production and utility functions, plus the individual endowments, we have a complete general equilibrium model such as the one in table 2.1. Market-clearing conditions require that supply equals demand for each good and factor, with no excess profits. This model is much less complicated than the general equilibrium model to which most of this book is devoted. Nevertheless, the two models bear distinct formal similarities. Each can be solved with any of several computational algorithms. In computing the equilibrium prices for the system of table 2.1, we use an algorithm that searches across the unit simplex. However, in reporting our results, we find it more convenient to adopt the normalization that the price of labor is unity. (We continue to use this normalization in later chapters.) The approximate solution for this illustrative model is shown in table 2.2. The solution shows that, at these prices, the total demand for each output exactly matches the amount produced. It follows that producer revenues equal consumer expenditures. It also is true, to a high degree of approximation, that the labor and capital endowments are fully employed and that consumer factor incomes equal producer factor costs. The cost per

Table 2.2   Equilibrium Solution for Illustrative Simple General Equilibrium Model (specified in table 2.1)

Equilibrium Prices	
Manufacturing output	1.399
Nonmanufacturing output	1.093
Capital	1.373
Labor	1.000

Production				
	Quantity	Revenue	Capital	Capital Cost
Manufacturing	24.942	34.894	6.212	8.529
Nonmanufacturing	54.379	59.436	18.789	25.797
TOTAL		94.330	25.001	34.326

	Labor	Labor Cost	Total Cost	Cost per Unit Output
Manufacturing	26.364	26.364	34.893	1.399
Nonmanufacturing	33.634	33.634	59.431	1.093
TOTAL	59.998	59.998	94.324	

Demands			
	Manufacturing	Nonmanufacturing	Expenditure
Rich households	11.514	16.674	34.333
Poor households	13.428	37.705	59.997
TOTAL	24.942	54.379	94.330

	Labor Income	Capital Income	Total Income
Rich households	0	34.325	34.325
Poor households	60	0	60.000
TOTAL	60	34.325	94.325

unit of output in each sector matches the price, meaning that economic profits are zero. The expenditure of each household exhausts its income. Thus the solution closely approximates all of the properties of an equilibrium for this economy. The degree of approximation can be improved by increasing the amount of computation time allowed for the solution algorithm.

Our general equilibrium analysis of the U.S. tax system follows closely the approach of the example shown above. We construct a numerical general equilibrium model for policy analysis, assuming that the data and analysis are representative of conditions in the U.S. economy. Tax distortions are introduced and equilibria are computed under different policy regimes. Finally, since utility functions are explicitly specified, changes in consumer welfare can easily be computed.

This set of exercises would not be particularly instructive if the equilibrium were not unique for any particular tax policy. There is no theoretical argument that guarantees uniqueness in models of this type. Fortunately, uniqueness has been demonstrated for the model used here in a paper by Kehoe and Whalley (1982).

2.3 Incorporating Taxes in a General Equilibrium Model

We can incorporate a system of taxes and government expenditures into our general equilibrium model. The taxes may apply to the purchases of goods and services by consumers, the use of factors and intermediate inputs by producers, and the final outputs of the various production sectors. The tax rates may differ for each good, consumer, and producer. The government uses the tax proceeds to finance transfer payments to consumers and to purchase final goods and services. In our model, in equilibrium, the government budget must be balanced, i.e., any government income remaining after transfers to persons must be spent on commodity purchases.[2]

The methods for incorporating taxes into a formal general equilibrium model are presented in Shoven and Whalley (1973). In order to get the flavor of that analysis, consider the very simple case in which the only taxes are consumer purchase taxes and the government makes no exhaustive expenditures, i.e., all revenues are returned to consumers as transfer payments. Each of the J consumers is assigned a vector of nonnegative ad valorem tax rates, $e_j = (e_{1j}, \ldots, e_{Nj})$, which must be paid on expenditures on each of the N commodities. The total tax revenue, R, is used to distribute among consumers according to a proportional distribution scheme;

$$R_j = r_j R; \ r_j \geq 0, \ \sum_j r_j = 1.$$

This scheme for tax revenue distribution leads to a fundamental problem that did not exist in a model with no government. The problem is one of simultaneity. Consumers cannot determine their demands until they know their incomes, and they do not know their incomes until they know the amount of their transfer revenues. At the same time, the transfer payments cannot be determined until the total revenue is known, and revenue will not be known until consumers make their purchases.

---

2. The government could run deficits or surpluses if the model included a government bond market. The model described in this book does not include bonds. For an attempt to integrate a bond market into a general equilibrium model, see Feltenstein 1984.

This problem of simultaneity can be solved if we model consumers and producers as reacting to revenue as well as prices. That is, demand functions depend on (P,R), where (P,R) denotes the vector $(P_1, \ldots, P_N, R)$. The market demand functions $D_i(P,R)$ are (as before) assumed to be nonnegative, continuous functions. However, they are now assumed to be homogeneous of degree zero in the vector (P,R), which means that a doubling of all prices and tax revenues will double both incomes and consumer prices, so that physical quantities demanded are unchanged. Whereas we previously normalized prices so that they fell on the unit simplex in prices, $(\Sigma_{i=1}^{N} P_i = 1)$, we now use an augmented simplex in prices and revenue $(\Sigma_{i=1}^{N} P_i + R = 1)$.

We still assume that the demand functions satisfy Walras's law. Now, however, Walras's law states that the value of market demands, gross of expenditure taxes, is equal to total consumer incomes:

$$(2.11) \qquad \sum_{j=1}^{J} \sum_{i=1}^{N} P_i D_{ij}(P,R)(1 + e_{ij}) = \sum_{j=1}^{J} \left(\sum_{i=1}^{N} P_i W_{ij} + R_j \right),$$

where D_{ij} is the quantity of good i consumed by consumer j, and e_{ij} is the ad valorem rate of expenditure tax on good i faced by consumer j. Equation (2.11) will hold at any vector (P,R). In addition to vectors of expenditure tax rates, each of the J consumers may be assigned a nonnegative income tax rate τ_j which is charged on taxable income.[3] We can also model taxes which are levied on the production side of the economy. In the model with activity analysis production, vectors of ad valorem tax rates T^i can be assigned to each of the productive activities, where $T^i = (t_{1k}, \ldots, t_{Nk})$. We adopt the convention that t_{ik} are nonnegative for outputs and nonpositive for inputs, such that the taxes paid will be nonnegative. The producer who operates activity k at unit intensity will incur a tax liability of $\Sigma_{i=1}^{N} \alpha_{ij} t_{ij} P_i$. As before, competitive equilibria can be examined, but now these equilibria reflect the presence of taxation. Market prices have to be defined with care when taxation is introduced into the economy. The prices included in the vector (P,R) are those equalized across all the traders on any market. Thus, prices P_i are sellers' prices for inputs (prices net-of-producer input taxes) and wholesale prices for outputs (prices net-of-consumer purchase taxes, but gross of any producer output taxes). An equilibrium in the presence of taxation is thus a vector $((P^*,R^*),(x^*))$ such that:

$$(2.12) \qquad \sum_{i=1}^{N} P_i^* + R^* = 1; \; P_i^*, R^* \geq 0; \; P_i^* > 0 \text{ for at least one } i.$$

---

3. Characteristics of income taxation systems, such as an annually exempt amount of income or deductions for expenditures on particular commodities, can be incorporated into the model, although these are ignored here to simplify the notation.

Once again, the * denotes the equilibrium level. In equilibrium, demands equal supplies for all commodities:

$$(2.13) \qquad D_i(P^*, R^*) = W_i + \sum_{k=1}^{K} a_{ik} x_k^* \qquad (i = 1, \ldots, N).$$

In equilibrium, no activity yields any producer the possibility of positive profit after payment of producer taxes, with those activities in use just breaking even:

$$(2.14) \qquad \sum_{i=1}^{N} P_i^* a_{ik}(1 - t_{ik}) \leq 0 \qquad (= 0 \text{ if } x_k^* > 0) \ (k = 1, \ldots, K).$$

In equilibrium the budget will be balanced, so that

$$(2.15) \qquad R^* = \sum_{i=1}^{N} \sum_{k=1}^{K} a_{ik} t_{ik} P_i^* x_K^* + \sum_{i=1}^{N} \sum_{j=1}^{J} e_{ij} P_i^* D_{ij}(P^*, R^*)$$

$$+ \sum_{j=1}^{J} \tau_j \left(\sum_{i=1}^{n} P_i^* W_j + R_j^* \right).$$

The three terms on the right hand side of equation (2.15) are the revenue from producer output taxes, consumer purchase taxes, and income taxes.

This approach to incorporating taxes in a general equilibrium model can also be followed in a model with continuous production functions. Production taxes would then apply to the capital and labor inputs, as well as to outputs, consumer purchases, and incomes. The simultaneity involving tax revenues in the evaluation of market functions remains, and it necessitates characterizing the equilibrium in terms of prices and revenues, as shown. Our model of the U.S. economy and tax system uses this production function approach.

2.4 Computing General Equilibria with Taxes

Our general equilibrium model is sufficiently complicated that equilibrium prices cannot be determined analytically. Instead, we use a grid search algorithm developed by Orin Merrill (1972). Merrill's algorithm is based on an algorithm developed by Herbert Scarf (1967, 1973). Since the focus of this book is on the tax model of the United States and its policy applications, we devote only a short section to computational method here. For descriptions of several such algorithms, the interested reader is referred to Scarf (1973, 1981, 1984).

The algorithms of Scarf and Merrill are examples of methods that are guaranteed to find fixed points of certain mappings. The algorithms can be used to solve many types of computational problems, including many noneconomic ones. For the models discussed here, we are able to formulate the problem in such a way that fixed points and economic equilibria are one and the same.

An intuitive grasp of Scarf's algorithm can be obtained by considering a simple case of a mapping that meets the conditions necessary for the Brouwer (1910) fixed-point theorem. The theorem states that, if S is a nonnull, closed, bounded, convex set mapped into itself by the continuous mapping $X \rightarrow F(X)$, then there exists a fixed point, i.e., a point $\hat{X} \epsilon S$ for which $F(\hat{X}) = \hat{X}$.

Suppose that S is taken to be the unit interval $(0,1)$, and the continuous mapping is the function $F(X)$, whose values all lie on the same unit interval. A fixed point in this case is given by the intersection of the correspondence $(X, F(X))$ and 45° line, as drawn in figure 2.3.

It is easy to find the fixed point $\hat{X}$ in figure 2.3, since the problem is so simple. This rapidly becomes more difficult as the dimension of the problem increases. Scarf's algorithm exploits a property of graph theory to provide an ingenious way of always finding a fixed point, $\hat{X}$, irrespective of the dimensionality involved.

The intuition underlying this method can be illustrated with the same diagram as in figure 2.3, redrawn with the unit interval on the X axis subdivided into a number of line segments of equal length (see figure 2.4). Each end point of these line segments has associated with it a label that is either 0 or 1. The label is calculated using the following rule: if $F(X) \geq X$ the label is 0, otherwise the label is 1.

By construction, the end points of the unit interval have the labels 0 and 1. Since all other points have either a label 1 or 0, there must exist a line segment that has both labels. For this line segment, $F(X) \geq X$ at one end point, and $F(X) < X$ at the other. Thus, since the function is

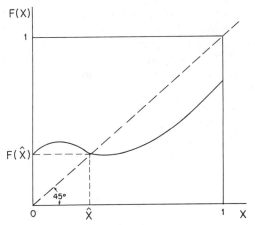

Fig. 2.3   A fixed point of a continuous mapping.

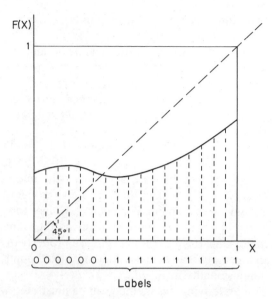

Fig. 2.4   Using labels to approximate a fixed point.

continuous, a fixed point where $F(\hat{X}) = \hat{X}$ must exist within this line segment. If the number of these line segments becomes large, the approximation to a fixed point represented by the completely labeled line segment will be more accurate. In the limit, where a dense grid of points on the line segment is approached, the calculation of the fixed point will be exact.

Scarf's algorithm appeals to this idea in higher dimensional space. In the case of an economic problem in which three prices are to be determined, we would deal with the unit simplex shown in figure 2.5.

A major accomplishment in general equilibrium economics was the proof of the existence of an equilibrium (see Arrow and Debreu 1954; Debreu 1959). This was achieved by finding a mapping that met the conditions of Brouwer's theorem and whose fixed point could be interpreted as an economic equilibrium. The simplest such mapping is for a model of pure exchange. Let $g_i(P) = D_i(P) - W_i$ be the excess demand for commodity i. These excess demand functions are continuous since the demand functions are continuous, and note that Walras's law states that $\sum_{i=1}^{N} P_i g_i(P) = 0$. Consider the following mapping of prices in the simplex into image prices P':

$$(2.16) \qquad P_i' = \frac{P_i + \text{Max}\,(0, g_i(P))}{1 + \sum_{i=1}^{N} \text{Max}\,(0, g_i(P))} \qquad \text{for } i = 1, \ldots, N.$$

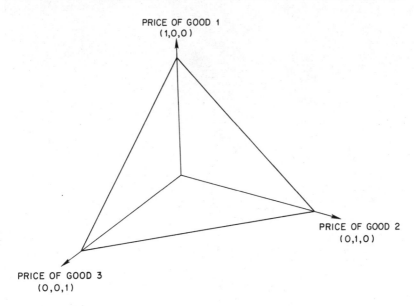

PRICE OF GOOD 1
(1,0,0)

PRICE OF GOOD 2
(0,1,0)

PRICE OF GOOD 3
(0,0,1)

Fig. 2.5   The unit simplex.

Note that

$$(2.17) \qquad \sum_{i=1}^{N} P_i' = \frac{1 + \sum\limits_{i=1}^{N} \text{Max}\,(0,\,g_i(P))}{1 + \sum\limits_{i=1}^{N} \text{Max}\,(0,\,g_i(P))} = 1,$$

and that $P_i' \geq 0$ for all i. Thus P' is on the unit simplex and a continuous function of P. Therefore, the conditions of Brouwer's theorem apply, and a fixed point of this mapping must exist. At this fixed point where $P_i' = P_i$, all $g_i \leq 0$, which is the condition for equilibrium in a pure exchange model.

This existence proof made it possible to contemplate the problem of computing an economic equilibrium. Unfortunately, however, the Brouwer mapping demonstration of existence does not readily suggest a computational procedure. The computational methods use labels as demonstrated above and an ingenious numerical analysis technique of Lemke and Howson (1964). For the three-dimensional pure exchange problem of figure 2.5, one could examine a large number of candidate equilibrium price vectors on the simplex. The label for any point could be the number associated with the commodity with the largest excess demand. Along each side of the simplex, where one commodity price is zero, the label would be that commodity number. We might expect that the simplex would be labeled in a manner somewhat like figure 2.6.

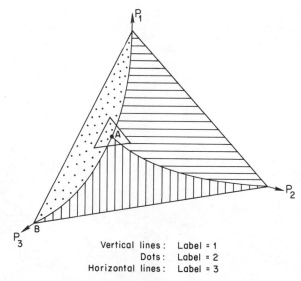

Fig. 2.6   Economic equilibrium in the three-good case.

In figure 2.6, equilibrium will be at point A. At any one time, Scarf's algorithm examines N price vectors that are close together in a sense that he defines precisely. The algorithm can be shown to converge to a set of N candidate vectors that are very close together, each of which has a different label. If each price vector is labeled with the number of the commodity with the largest excess demand and if each vector has a different label, then each of these excess demands must be nearly zero. This is true because Walras's law states that at any specific price vector, the price-weighted sum of the excess demands is zero:

$$(2.18) \qquad \sum_{i=1}^{N} P_i g_i(P) = 0.$$

The excess demands are continuous, and if within a very small region of the price simplex each commodity has the largest excess demand, then the excess demands must all be close to zero. Thus, this labeling technique results in the computation of a fixed point that represents an economic equilibrium.

For a general equilibrium model with taxes, the necessary labels are described in Shoven and Whalley (1973). This involves using the traditional price simplex used in most general equilibrium models, but augmented by one additional dimension for tax revenue. The labeling procedure outlined by Shoven and Whalley is for a general equilibrium model with production, with taxes on both producers and consumers. Their labeling rule guarantees that a subsimplex that is completely labeled provides the required approximation to a general equilibrium with taxes. The problem with Scarf's algorithm is that it uses a relatively large amount of computational time. It starts at a corner of the simplex and therefore usually evaluates the excess demands at many points before approaching an approximate equilibrium. Even if we have a good guess about where the equilibrium might be, we cannot use that information. Also, since the algorithm uses a fixed grid of candidate price vectors, it is not possible to improve the accuracy of the solution once we find an approximate equilibrium. Consequently, there is a stringent trade-off between accuracy and computational time. For the calculations used in this book, we use Merrill's algorithm, because it overcomes these problems while still guaranteeing convergence. Other algorithms of this type which allow for fast computations are those of Kuhn and MacKinnon (1975), Eaves (1972), and van der Laan and Talman (1979).

2.5 Equal Yield Equilibria

In this section we describe an important extension to the general equilibrium approach to tax policy. Through the use of an equal-tax-yield equilibrium concept, we are able to undertake "differential" analysis in the tradition of Musgrave (1959). Such analysis allows an existing tax to be replaced by an alternative tax system that raises equivalent revenue. This change in procedure allows us to maintain the size of government when the effects of an existing tax are evaluated. This is important, since a changing size of government can contaminate model findings. Because we are interested here in the effects of changes in the structure rather than the level of taxes, we want to be able to interpret our results without worrying about changes in the pattern of total demands that are caused by changes in the amount of government spending.

The exact meaning of equal revenue yield is somewhat unclear because, in general, the adoption of a new tax regime will lead to different equilibrium prices. It is not satisfactory merely to give the government the same number of dollars as it had before the tax change, since the goods that government buys with those dollars will have changed in price. Shoven and Whalley (1977) discuss a variety of price indexes that might be used to correct for these price changes, so as to preserve equal "real" revenue.

In the present model we do not use price indexes as such. Instead, we give the government a utility function, and then use the corresponding expenditure function to calculate the revenue required for the government to achieve constant utility at any set of prices. The expenditure function expresses the amount of money necessary to attain a given level of utility at a given set of prices. When we calculate a *base-case equilib-*

rium, we calculate the government's utility. In equilibrium calculations for changes in tax regime, we give the government enough revenue so that it reaches the same level of utility. This is the exact sense in which we preserve "real" government revenue.

Most of the simulations reported in this book involve reductions in revenues. This is the case for corporate tax integration and for the adoption of a consumption tax. In these cases, equal yield calculations involve increasing taxes somewhere else in the economy.

In general, a number of replacement tax schemes could be used. However, it is simplest to consider only those schemes where the replacement tax can be expressed in terms of a single scalar. In using our model, we employ four such replacement schemes.

1. *Lump-Sum Taxes.* In this case, the reduction in revenues caused by a tax change is recovered by lump-sum taxes paid by each consumer group. The weights for the division of these taxes among the household groups are fixed, but the size of the lump-sum taxes in aggregate is determined endogenously.

2. *Additive Changes to Marginal Income Tax Rates.* Here revenues are recovered by adding the same number of percentage points to all household marginal income tax rates.

3. *Multiplicative Changes to Marginal Income Tax Rates.* In this case, revenues are recovered by multiplying the marginal tax rates of all households by the same scalar. (Thus the rates of the higher-bracket taxpayers are increased by higher absolute amounts.)

4. *Multiplicative Changes to Consumer Sales Tax Rates.* In this case, we raise the required revenue by multiplying the consumer sales tax rates facing all consumers by the same scalar.

Distributional effects clearly depend upon this choice of tax replacement. We also consider a few cases in which additional revenues are created by the tax change. Examples are the adoption of a value-added tax or reductions in deductions for saving. In these instances we use yield-preserving subsidies instead of taxes. Once again, we use subsidies of the lump-sum, additive, and multiplicative types.

We should note that there is no guarantee that equal yield equilibria will always exist. Obviously, we could not replace the entire revenue system of the United States with a tax on popcorn. We typically consider broadly based replacement taxes, in order to minimize the possibility of being unable to calculate an equal yield equilibrium.

2.6 Computations in the Space of Factor Prices

Even though we use Merrill's algorithm for our equilibrium computations, we are still concerned with reducing computational costs in every way possible. The amount of time required to compute an equilibrium at any level of accuracy increases rapidly with the number of dimensions. Until now, we have described general equilibrium tax models as if a separate price must be computed for every commodity in the model. A convenient procedure to use in computation is to reduce the number of prices by expressing some of the commodity prices as functions of other prices. In our model we separate commodities into goods and factors, and calculate goods prices from factor prices. Since we use a fixed-coefficient input-output matrix with no joint products, we are able to use the Samuelson (1951) nonsubstitution theorem to calculate goods prices directly from factor prices. This enables us to compute an equilibrium in the space of factor prices rather than the space of all commodity prices,

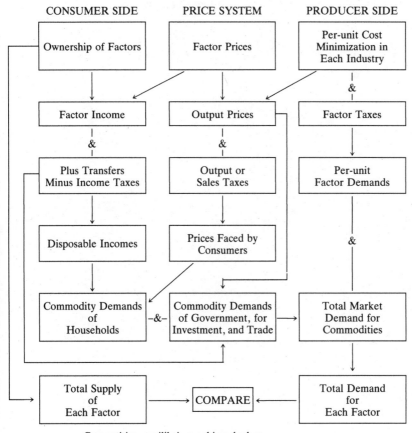

Competitive equilibrium achieved when:
  1. Demands equal supplies for all goods and factors
  2. Zero profits (net of taxes) prevail in all industries

Fig. 2.7   Flow diagram of factor space calculations in general equilibrium tax model.

reducing greatly the cost of computation. In our model we calculate equilibria in three dimensions—the factor prices, capital and labor—and an additional dimension for government revenues.

In figure 2.7 we present a stylized version of the way in which our factor space computations work. The starting point is factor prices. Using factor prices and the conditions for cost minimization by producers, we can evalutate the cost-covering prices of goods. This directly imposes the zero profit condition for each industry. When consumers know their incomes and the prices of goods, they can calculate their demands for goods. If producers meet demands, this gives derived demands for factors, which results in a system of two-factor excess demand correspondences (capital and labor), and a government budget imbalance. An equilibrium is attained when all three correspondences equal zero.

3   The Single Period Submodel

3.1   Overview of Structure of the Model

In this chapter we describe the basic structure of the model that we use to calculate each equilibrium. We begin with an overview of the entire model, and then we present each feature in greater detail. The appendix to this chapter provides a glossary of notation, including each symbol in order of appearance in the text, the definition of that symbol, the equation where it is first used, and the data or source of its derivation. The model's structure is summarized diagrammatically in figure 3.1. We begin our discussion with an overview of the production side of the model, which is represented on the left-hand side of the diagram.

The model includes nineteen profit-maximizing producer good industries, which are listed in table 3.1. Each industry uses labor and capital in a constant elasticity of substitution (CES) value-added function. We choose substitution elasticities for each industry from the econometric literature. Values typically range from 0.6 to 1.0, as described in chapter 6. The *Survey of Current Business* (*SCB*) and unpublished data from the National Income Division of the Bureau of Economic Analysis are used to obtain each industry's payments for labor and capital in the 1973 benchmark equilibrium. Like Harberger (1966), we determine the quantities of primary inputs (labor and capital) by using the convention that a unit of each primary factor is that amount which earns one dollar net of taxes in the benchmark year. For intermediate inputs of other commodities, we derive a fixed-coefficient input-output matrix from Bureau of Economic Analysis tables.

As indicated in figure 3.1, final demands for each producer good include direct demands by government, demands for export, and demand for investment. Producer goods for consumption, however, are only

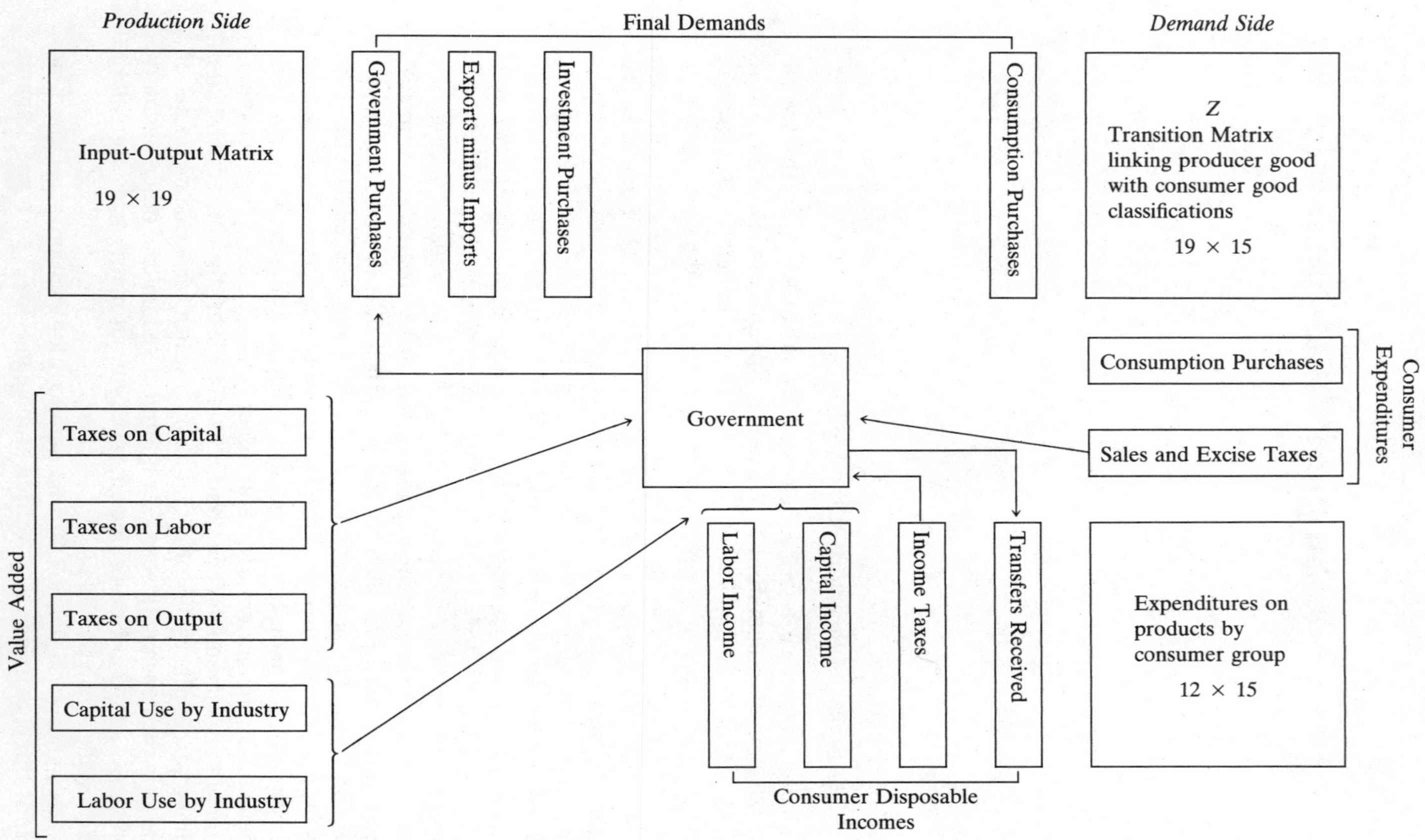

Consumer Expenditures

Demand Side

Z
Transition Matrix
linking producer good
with consumer good
classifications

19 × 15

Consumption Purchases

Sales and Excise Taxes

Expenditures on
products by
consumer group

12 × 15

Consumption Purchases

Transfers Received

Income Taxes

Capital Income

Labor Income

Consumer Disposable
Incomes

Government

Final Demands

Investment Purchases

Exports minus Imports

Government Purchases

Production Side

Input-Output Matrix

19 × 19

Taxes on Capital

Taxes on Labor

Taxes on Output

Capital Use by Industry

Labor Use by Industry

Value Added

Figure 2.1   Basic structure of the single-period submodel.

demanded indirectly. We use a fixed-coefficient Z matrix of transition between the nineteen producer goods and the fifteen consumer goods. The Z matrix is shown in figure 3.1, and the fifteen consumer goods are listed in table 3.1. This transition is necessary because the Commerce Department data include industries such as mining, machinery, and trade, while the Labor Department's Survey of Consumer Expenditures provides data on purchases of goods like furniture, appliances, and recreation.

Table 3.1   **Classification of Industries, Consumer Expenditures, and Consumer Groups**

Producer Goods (Industries)	Consumer Goods (Expenditure Categories)
1. Agriculture, forestry, and fisheries	1. Food
	2. Alcoholic beverages
2. Mining	3. Tobacco
3. Crude petroleum and gas	4. Utilities
4. Contract construction	5. Housing
5. Food and tobacco	6. Furnishings
6. Textiles, apparel, and leather	7. Appliances
	8. Clothing and jewelry
7. Paper and printing	9. Transportation
8. Petroleum refining	10. Motor vehicles, tires, and auto repair
9. Chemicals, rubber, and plastics	11. Services
10. Lumber, furniture, stone, clay, and glass	12. Financial services
	13. Reading, recreation, and miscellaneous
11. Metals, machinery, instruments, and miscellaneous manufacturing	14. Nondurable, nonfood household items
	15. Gasoline and other fuels
12. Transportation equipment and ordnance	
13. Motor vehicles	
14. Transportation, communications, and utilities	
15. Trade	
16. Finance and insurance	
17. Real estate	
18. Services	
19. Government enterprises	

Household Consumer Groups
(classified by gross money income in 1973 dollars)

1.	0–2,999	5.	6,000–6,999	9.	12,000–14,999
2.	3,000–3,999	6.	7,000–7,999	10.	15,000–19,999
3.	4,000–4,999	7.	8,000–9,999	11.	20,000–24,999
4.	5,000–5,999	8.	10,000–11,999	12.	25,000 +

Table 3.1 also shows the 1973 income levels that define the twelve household classes. Industry and government payments to buy labor and capital services are matched by total household receipts from the supply of each factor. The Treasury Department's Merged Tax File provides information on labor and capital income for each of the twelve consumer classes. The Merged Tax File also provides data on tax payments and an estimate of the average marginal income tax rate for each group. These marginal tax rates range from 1 percent for the first income classes to 40 percent for the highest income class. As discussed later in this chapter, we model the graduated income tax system as a series of linear schedules, one for each group. Then, as discussed in chapter 5, we estimate that 30 percent of savings flow through tax-free vehicles such as pensions, Individual Retirement Accounts, and Keogh plans. This fact is reflected in the model by exempting a fixed 30 percent of savings from personal income taxation.

Table 3.2 provides a brief description of the treatment of taxes in the model. The corporation income tax, state corporate franchise tax, and local property taxes are modeled as ad valorem taxes on each industry's use of capital. The Social Security payroll tax and workmen's compensation tax are modeled as ad valorem taxes on industry use of labor. Various federal excise taxes and indirect business taxes are modeled as output taxes for each of the nineteen industries. State and local sales taxes apply to each of the consumer goods.

Another important feature of our model is the *personal factor* tax. This construct is described more thoroughly later, but it is designed to capture the features of the personal income tax that discriminate among industries. For each industry we calculate the fraction of capital income that is fully taxable at the personal level. This fraction is determined using data on dividends, capital gains, interest, and rent. The personal factor tax acts as a withholding tax at the industry level. We model personal taxes on capital as if they were collected at the industry level at the overall average marginal personal income tax rate. At the consumer level, rebates are given to groups with lower rates, while additional taxes are collected from those with higher than average marginal tax rates. The model thus captures the favorable treatment of industries with a high proportion of retained earnings, industries that receive large amounts of noncorporate investment tax credits, and the housing industry.

Consumer demands are based on budget-constrained maximization of a nested CES/Cobb-Douglas utility function. In the first stage of the maximization process, consumers save some income for future consumption. They allocate the rest to a subutility function defined over present consumption and leisure. The elasticity of substitution between future and present consumption is based on estimates of the elasticity of saving with respect to the net-of-tax rate of return. These estimates, and our choice among them, are discussed in section 6.4.3. In our standard case we use Michael Boskin's (1978) estimate of 0.4 for the uncompensated saving elasticity, but we also perform sensitivity analyses using different values. Consumers make their saving decisions under the (myopic) expectation that all present prices, including the rental price of capital, will prevail in all future periods. In the second stage of the consumer's maximization problem, consumers allocate income between current consumption goods and leisure. The elasticity of substitution between leisure and consumer goods is based on estimates of the elasticity of labor supply with respect to the net-of-tax wage. These are discussed in sèction 6.4.2. In our standard case we use an estimate of 0.15 for the uncompensated labor supply elasticity, but again we perform sensitivity analyses. Expenditures on individual consumption goods are based on a Cobb-Douglas subutility function.

Consumer decisions regarding factor supplies are made jointly with consumption decisions. Demands for leisure and for saving depend on the prices of both factors and goods. The model simultaneously considers the uses of income and the sources of income in determining the utility of any group.

Saving is converted immediately into investment demand for producer goods. The distribution of investments among producer goods is based on national accounting data for fixed private investment and inventories. We model the foreign trade sector with constant elasticity export supply and import demand functions. This treatment closes the model, maintains the trade balance, and makes it easy for us to calculate trade quantities, once prices are known.

We complete the static model by specifying the government sector. The government uses revenues from the various taxes for transfer payments and for purchases of labor, capital, and producer goods. The government budget is always in balance. Lump-sum transfers to each consumer group are based on unpublished Treasury Department data for Social Security receipts, welfare, government retirement, food stamps, and similar programs. We assume that the government demands factors and commodities according to fixed expenditure shares.

3.2 Treatment of Taxes

In table 3.2 we give a brief summary of the ways in which we model the components of the United States tax system. These treatments fall squarely within the Harberger tradition, but they also reflect our best summary judgments regarding the incentive effects of each tax. Controversies exist, however, with respect to the appropriate treatment of

Table 3.2   United States Taxes and Their Treatment in the Model

Tax	Treatment
1. Corporate taxes (including state and local) and corporate franchise taxes	Ad valorem tax on use of capital services by industry
2. Property taxes	Ad valorem tax on use of capital services by industry
3. Social Security taxes, unemployment insurance, and workmen's compensation	Ad valorem tax on use of labor services by industry
4. Motor vehicles tax	Ad valorem tax on use of motor vehicles by producers
5. Retail sales taxes	Ad valorem tax on purchases of producer goods
6. Excise taxes	Ad valorem tax on output of producer goods
7. Other indirect business taxes and nontax payments to government	Ad valorem tax on output of producer goods
8. Personal income taxes (including state and local)	Linear function for each consumer; 30 percent of savings currently tax sheltered

many parts of the tax system. In this book we do not test the sensitivity of our results to most of these treatments, but we mention some of the alternative treatments that economists have proposed.

We treat corporate taxes as ad valorem taxes on the use of capital services, with different rates across industries. For each industry we calculate an average effective tax rate by looking at the ratio of observed taxes to a measure of observed capital income. In the standard model we assume that the rate on marginal investment is equal to this average rate in each industry. Joseph Stiglitz (1973) has emphasized that interest payments are deductible from the corporate tax, so there would be no corporate tax on the normal income earned by a debt-financed investment. Stiglitz then argues that if corporations use debt finance at the margin, the corporate tax will be nondistortionary. Whereas our simulations in chapter 8 imply that the corporate tax leads to serious welfare losses, this would not be the case if all investments were debt financed at the margin. Since we do not model the choice among different financial assets, we do not deal explicitly with the different tax treatments of debt and equity.[1]

1. Tax rates equal the ratio of taxes to capital income in each industry, so they reflect lower corporate taxes in debt-intensive industries. Since these tax rates apply to marginal uses of capital in the model, we implicitly assume that marginal investments are financed by the average proportions of debt and equity.

A second issue concerning the corporate tax arises from our assumption that marginal and average capital tax rates are equal. A cost-of-capital approach can be used to calculate tax distortions at the margin, as done by Fullerton and Gordon (1983). This procedure leads to tax rate estimates that are different from those used in most of this book. The choice between the marginal cost of capital approach and the average effective tax rate approach is a difficult one. The advantage of the former is that it is more consistent with the microeconomic theory, while a disadvantage is that it cannot capture the extreme complexity of the tax code.

Finally, as emphasized by Fullerton and Gordon (1983), an explicit treatment of risky investments can greatly alter the standard results. If the real risk-free return to corporate investment is only a small part of total corporate income, then most of the tax applies to a risk premium. Since government would take an equal share of risk and the premium, these taxes would not distort investment behavior at the margin. Only the tax on the real risk-free return would be distorting. In contrast to Fullerton and Gordon, Bulow and Summers (1984) argue that the corporate tax does not share risk proportionately. The appropriate treatment of risk is therefore not clear. For further discussion, see Slemrod (1982, 1983).

We also treat property taxes as ad valorem taxes on the use of capital services. Charles Tiebout (1956) shows that, under a set of special assumptions about the provision of local public goods, local property taxes may be thought of as benefit-related charges. Therefore, these taxes could also be modeled as nondistortionary. We doubt, however, that the restrictive assumptions necessary for the Tiebout model are matched very closely in the actual economy.[2]

Some would model the property tax as an excise tax rather than as a tax on capital income. Mieszkowski (1972) reconciles these two views by pointing out that a common tax rate in all jurisdictions would operate as a factor tax while deviations from this common rate would have excise tax effects. Our model captures the fact that property tax rates on capital income differ by industry, so our general equilibrium results include excise tax effects on the prices of industry outputs. (Since we model the government as a single jurisdiction, we do not measure the effects of the differences in property taxes among different local governments.)

We treat Social Security payroll taxes as ad valorem taxes on the use of labor services by industry, and we treat Social Security benefits as lump-sum transfers. It could be argued that the Social Security system is a contributor-financed insurance scheme that has no distorting effects by

---

2. Fullerton and Gordon (1983) also investigate results in a model with nondistorting property taxes.

industry. Our treatment abstracts from these controversies.[3] Also, we do not capture the effect of Social Security on saving through the substitution of Social Security wealth for private sector capital accumulation, or the effect of Social Security on retirement decisions. For a discussion of these issues, see Feldstein (1974c).

We also treat unemployment compensation taxes as an ad valorem tax on the use of labor services, and unemployment benefits as lump-sum transfer receipts. Once again the relationship between benefits and contributions is inexact. Most states have minimum and maximum tax rates, such that firms with high or low rates of unemployment do not have actuarially fair tax rates.

We model sales and excise taxes as consumer purchase taxes on the fifteen goods. For most of the consumer goods, this treatment is probably not controversial. However, taxes on alcohol and tobacco could be viewed as Pigovian externality-correcting taxes. Gasoline taxes are used to support highway construction, and thus might be modeled as if they were related to benefits.

We model income taxes as linear functions of income for each of the twelve consumer groups. Each group has a negative intercept and a single positive marginal tax rate. Thus, although we capture the fact that the tax system is progressive, we do not capture the fact that each consumer faces a graduated rate schedule. We also do not account for the high implicit marginal tax rates faced by recipients of transfers who might be able to work (see Aaron 1973).

Clearly, our model of the tax system is not the only model that one could adopt. We have tried to adopt a simple treatment for each tax, while at the same time recognizing the diverse controversies that exist in the literature.

3.3   Value Added and Intermediate Production

We assume that there are two primary factors of production—capital and labor—each of which is homogeneous, mobile among sectors,[4] and internationally immobile.[5] Capital, K, is owned by the twelve consumer

3. Blinder, Gordon, and Wise (1980) find that the Social Security system provides a net benefit for older workers. See Burkhauser and Turner 1981 for a reply. While the degree of net tax or benefit may depend greatly on age and other personal characteristics, our model differentiates labor by industry of employment. To our knowledge, no study has measured net incentive effects by industry.

4. In an extension of this model, Fullerton (1983) considers cases in which only new capital investments are mobile across sectors. The interindustry adjustments resulting from tax changes thus occur more slowly, and the welfare changes from tax reforms are typically slightly smaller than in the model with instantaneous capital mobility.

5. This assumption is conventional in general equilibrium tax models, but it is very important for the results they produce. If we were to consider the extreme alternative case of a small, open, price-taking economy facing a perfectly elastic foreign supply of capital,

groups and by government. We denote endowments by $K_j (j = 1, \ldots,$ 12) and K_g. Capital can be used in any of the nineteen producer industries or in the general government sector. These uses of capital are denoted by the i subscript in $K_i (i = 1, \ldots, 20)$. Only consumers have endowments E_j $(j = 1, \ldots, 12)$ of labor, but due to consumption of leisure, their actual supplies are L_j $(j = 1, \ldots, 12)$. This factor can be used in any of the twenty sectors as labor $L_i (i = 1, \ldots, 20)$ or can be retained by consumers for leisure, $\ell_j (j = 1, \ldots, 12)$. For each consumer, then, we have $E_j = L_j + \ell_j$. In total, we have

$$(3.1) \qquad E = \sum_{j=1}^{12} E_j = \sum_{i=1}^{20} L_i + \sum_{j=1}^{12} \ell_j = L + \ell.$$

We define each of these factors in service units per period. When a unit of capital services is rented out for one period, the owner receives a price, P_K, which is net of factor taxes and net of depreciation. In addition to the rental prices, P_L and P_K, which are paid to factor owners, producers are required to pay ad valorem taxes at rates t_{Li} and t_{Ki}. These taxes differ by sector. The ith factor user thus faces gross-of-tax factor costs of P_{Li}^* and P_{Ki}^*, which equal $P_L(1 + t_{Li})$ and $P_K(1 + t_{Ki})$, respectively.

Capital and labor appear in a constant elasticity of substitution (CES) value-added function of the form

$$(3.2) \qquad VA = \phi \left[\delta L^{\frac{\sigma-1}{\sigma}} + (1-\delta)K^{\frac{\sigma-1}{\sigma}} \right]^{\frac{\sigma}{\sigma-1}} \quad \text{for each industry,}$$

where ϕ and δ are production parameters, and σ is the elasticity of substitution.[6] For expositional simplicity, we have suppressed the i subscripts of all variables and parameters in these expressions.

The model uses a 19×19 fixed coefficient input-output matrix, denoted by A, with columns giving the intermediate input requirements per unit of output. The industry outputs are represented as $Q_i (i = 1, \ldots, 19)$. In the standard version of the single period submodel we do not allow for substitution between intermediate inputs and value-added.

A single output is produced by each industry, under constant returns to scale. Producer behavior is characterized by cost minimization for each unit of output. Minimization of factor costs $(P_L^* L + P_K^* K)$ subject to the constraint that $VA = 1$ in equation (3.2) yields the factor demand requirements per unit of value-added. For each industry, these are:

---

results could be changed significantly. In this case, capital would not bear the burden of capital taxes. We return to these issues in chapter 11.

6. Chapter 6 specifies σ for the nineteen industries. In cases where $\sigma = 1$, equation (3.2) reduces to a Cobb-Douglas production function. Also, we define capital costs as net of depreciation. In the Cobb-Douglas case, the constant fraction of value added used for expenditures on capital excludes depreciation expenditures.

$$(3.3) \qquad R_L = \phi^{-1} \left[(1 - \delta) \left(\frac{\delta P_K^*}{(1 - \delta)P_L^*} \right)^{1-\sigma} + \delta \right]^{\frac{\sigma}{1-\sigma}},$$

$$(3.4) \qquad R_K = \phi^{-1} \left[\delta \left(\frac{(1 - \delta)P_L^*}{\delta P_K^*} \right)^{1-\sigma} + (1 - \delta) \right]^{\frac{\sigma}{1-\sigma}}.$$

Given the parameters δ, ϕ, and σ for each industry, we use the net-of-tax factor prices together with tax rates to calculate each producer's gross-of-tax price for each factor. Thus the tax system distorts factor input decisions.

Consumer goods, X_m ($m = 1, \ldots, 15$), are produced from producer goods, Q_i ($i = 1, \ldots, 19$), through the fixed-coefficient Z matrix shown in the upper right of figure 3.1. Each coefficient, z_{im}, gives the amount of producer goods i needed to produce one unit of consumer good m. For example, a unit of "alcoholic beverages" will include parts of the outputs of three industries: food and tobacco; transportation, communications, and utilities; and trade.

We can impose different ad valorem tax rates on each industry's intermediate purchases from each other industry. State and local motor vehicle registration fees, for example, are modeled as a tax on intermediate use of the motor vehicle industry's output, t_{MVi} ($i = 1, \ldots, 19$). Each industry also pays an output tax at rate t_{Qi} on its own output, regardless of where the output is used.

Because of perfect competition, producers make zero profits after making payments for factors, factor taxes, intermediate inputs, motor vehicle input taxes, and output taxes. The zero-profit prices of the nineteen producer outputs are P_i ($i = 1, \ldots, 19$). Zero-profit conditions also apply to production of consumer goods. Cost-covering consumer good prices are given by:[7]

$$(3.5) \qquad P_m = \sum_{i=1}^{19} z_{im} P_i \qquad m = 1, \ldots, 15.$$

The expenditure matrix is shown in the lower right of figure 3.1. When consumers purchase the consumer goods, X_m, they must pay additional ad valorem taxes. We model sales taxes on the purchase of each good at rates t_m ($m = 1, \ldots, 15$). Gross-of-tax prices paid by consumers are $P_m^* = P_m(1 + t_m)$.

---

7. An unfortunate effect of using this Z matrix is that differential price effects are dampened. Each of the fifteen consumer goods is a weighted average of the nineteen producer goods, with weights given by each column of the Z matrix. The implicit capital/labor ratios in the construction of each consumer good must therefore vary less than the capital/labor ratios of producer goods. When factor prices vary, consumer good prices will

3.4   Household Saving, Labor Supply, and Commodity Demands

The submodel described in this chapter refers only to a single period. In chapter 7 we will consider a sequence of equilibrium periods by incorporating the effects of current savings on the future capital stock and household income. Within a single period, however, individuals make savings decisions based on expectations about the resulting increment to future consumption. We assume that expectations are myopic in the sense that individuals expect all current prices, including the return to capital, to remain constant through all future periods. With this assumption, we can calculate the savings of individuals based only on current prices.[8]

Saving decisions are based on the maximization of a nested utility function, where the outer nest is defined over present consumption and the expected future consumption stream made possible from saving. Bequests are excluded, as is any explicit life-cycle structure. Consider the general case of a consumer who faces the decision of choosing between consumption today (H) and consumption in future periods $(C_1, C_2, \ldots)$.

The consumer choice problem can be represented as the maximization of

$$(3.6) \qquad U = U(H, C_F),$$

subject to a budget constraint. Here, H is a composite of present consumption goods and leisure, and C_F is a composite of the future consumption stream $(C_1, C_2, \ldots)$. We describe specific functional forms below. Implicit in these forms is a rate-of-time preference between H and C_F. In the calculations below, we assume C_F to be the annual consumption of a perpetual annuity made possible through the current period's saving.

In a more complete model of life-cycle behavior, households would calculate, in each period, the discounted present value of resources over their remaining lifetimes. In this model, by contrast, households in each period only concern themselves with the allocation of current income between consumption and saving. While a full lifetime model is beyond the scope of this book, this important contrast should be emphasized.[9]

The structure of our nested CES/Cobb-Douglas utility functions is outlined in figure 3.2. Each consumer starts with a budget, I, which

---

vary less than producer prices; consumer purchases will vary less than they would if consumers bought producer goods directly. However, the weights differ enough to capture substantial effects.

8.   Ballard and Goulder (1982) have investigated the effect of giving consumers foresight into the movements of relative prices over time. When a capital-deepening tax change is introduced, consumers will save less if they have foresight, because they see that the return to capital will decrease over time. The results of our simulations change somewhat, depending upon the expectational structure, but the magnitude of the change is not great.

9.   See Summers 1981 and Auerbach, Kotlikoff, and Skinner 1983 for numerical life-cycle models incorporating tax effects.

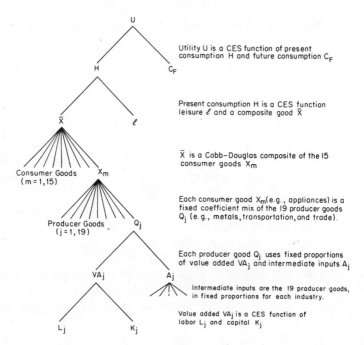

Fig. 3.2   The structure of consumption and production in the model.

equals the rental value of his capital and labor endowments (whether sold or retained as leisure), plus transfers, minus taxes. We refer to I as expanded income to differentiate it from observed money income. Because of the nested CES form, we can divide consumer decisions into stages. In the first stage, the consumer divides this income between present consumption, H (costing P_H as described later), and future consumption, C_F. Next, the consumer decides how to divide present consumption, H, into consumption of leisure time, ℓ (costing P_ℓ), and a composite consumption commodity, $\bar{X}$ (costing $\bar{P}$). When we subtract the values of savings and leisure from I, we have the earned income available for present goods consumption. Since the composite good $\bar{X}$ has a composite price $\bar{P}$, expenditure on consumption goods is $\bar{P}\bar{X}$. In the final utility nest shown in figure 3.2, individuals divide these expenditures among the fifteen consumer goods, X_m ($m = 1, \ldots, 15$), according to a Cobb-Douglas function. Consumers face gross-of-tax prices, P_m^* ($m = 1, \ldots, 15$), on these consumer goods. (Figure 3.2 goes on to show how each consumer good is a combination of nineteen producer goods, and how each producer good is a combination of primary factors and intermediate inputs.)

We assume that consumers use their saving to purchase a saving good, S. The implicit assumption is that consumer groups own real capital and rent it directly to the ultimate users in industry and the government. When individuals save, they must add to their stocks of real capital. The model therefore assumes that the household sector buys investment goods with their saving. This saving-investment commodity, S, is actually a composite of the nineteen industry outputs. The nineteen outputs go into the composite in fixed proportions. The proportions are given by the observed 1973 total investment purchases from each industry.[10]

Capital services, K, are measured in units of asset rental per time period (like machine-hours, except that our capital asset is homogeneous). Since we define a unit of K as that which earns P_K in the benchmark period, *net* of taxes and depreciation, the net saving of consumers corresponds to the net investment purchases of the nineteen outputs.

This treatment excludes variations in the composition of investment that might occur in response to variations in tax rates. For example, corporate tax reductions might imply a reallocation of capital from real estate to incorporated industries. The fixed-coefficient composition of S would not, however, reflect the decreased investment purchases from the construction industry, or the increased purchases of machinery. Of course, the model does capture the reallocation of K itself.

The savings commodity can be interpreted as a composite of newly produced capital goods, since saving is invested immediately. The price of saving, P_S, can also be interpreted as the composite price of investment goods. The capital goods purchased with savings will yield a flow of capital services in the future. This flow can, in turn, be sold for future consumption. Each unit of S is assumed to yield γ units of capital services in each future period, and each of these capital service units is expected to earn P_K per period. (Because $P_K = 1$ in the benchmark year, γ is the initial real after-tax rate of return.) The capital income in each future year finances planned future consumption, which is expected to cost $\bar{P}$. Therefore, $P_K \gamma S = \bar{P} C_F$. If we multiply both sides of this equality by P_S and rearrange, we have

(3.7) $$P_S S = \frac{P_S \bar{P}}{P_K \gamma} C_F, \text{ for each consumer}.$$

This equation states that the value of saving matches the discounted present value of expected future consumption. The parameter γ denotes the physical service flow per unit of capital goods purchased. We specify γ exogenously. A given value of savings, $P_S S$, earns a return of $P_K \gamma S$ in every future period. Therefore, the endogenous after-tax rate of return is

---

10. Firms decide how much capital to use in the current period, but they do not make explicit intertemporal investment decisions in our model. The intertemporal decisions of consumers determine future capital stocks.

$P_K \gamma / P_S$, which we denote by r. Since the price of consumption goods, $\bar{P}$, is not expected to change, r is also the expected real rate of return.

The consumer's budget constraint is given by

(3.8) $$I = P_H H + P_S S,$$

where I is current expanded income after taxes and transfers, $P_S S$ is the value of saving, and P_H is the price of composite present consumption H. If we use equation (3.7), we can write the consumer's maximization problem as

(3.9)   Max $U[H, C_F]$, subject to $I = P_H H + \dfrac{P_S \bar{P}}{P_K \gamma} C_F$.

Each consumer group has its own parameters and values in the CES form of this utility function, but we suppress indexes for expositional simplicity. The consumer utility function is:

(3.10) $$U = \left[\alpha^{\frac{1}{\sigma_2}} H^{\frac{\sigma_2 - 1}{\sigma_2}} + (1 - \alpha)^{\frac{1}{\sigma_2}} C_F^{\frac{\sigma_2 - 1}{\sigma_2}} \right]^{\frac{\sigma_2}{\sigma_2 - 1}},$$

where α is a weighting parameter and σ_2 is the elasticity of substitution between H and C_F. Constrained maximization of this utility function yields:

(3.11) $$H = \frac{\alpha I}{P_H^{\sigma_2} \Delta_2}$$

and

(3.12) $$C_F = \frac{(1 - \alpha) I}{\left(\dfrac{P_S \bar{P}}{P_K \gamma} \right)^{\sigma_2} \Delta_2}, \quad \text{where}$$

(3.13) $$\Delta_2 = \alpha (P_H)^{1 - \sigma_2} + (1 - \alpha) \left(\frac{P_S \bar{P}}{P_K \gamma} \right)^{\sigma_1 - \sigma_2}.$$

We discuss P_H below. Using equation (3.7) from above, we translate the demand for C_F into the demand for saving:

(3.14) $$S = \frac{(1 - \alpha) I}{P_S^{\sigma_2} \left[\dfrac{\bar{P}}{P_K \gamma} \right]^{(\sigma_2 - 1)} \Delta_2}.$$

After saving $P_S S$, consumers have $I - P_S S$ to spend on consumption of H. In the second stage, they maximize

(3.15) $H = \left[(1 - \beta)^{1/\sigma_1} \bar{X}^{(\sigma_1 - 1)/\sigma_1} + \beta^{1/\sigma_1} \ell^{(\sigma_1 - 1)/\sigma_1}\right]^{\sigma_1/(\sigma_1 - 1)},$

subject to

(3.16) $I - P_S S = \bar{P} \bar{X} + P_\ell \ell,$

where β is a weighting parameter, and σ_1 is the elasticity of substitution between $\bar{X}$ and ℓ. The price of leisure, P_ℓ, is taken to be the after-tax return to labor of each group. Since a unit of labor earns P_L after factor taxes, $P_\ell = P_L(1 - \tau_j)$, where τ_j is the jth consumer's personal marginal tax rate. Constrained maximization of the subutility function, H, provides the demand functions:

(3.17) $$\bar{X} = \frac{(1 - \beta)(I - P_S S)}{\bar{P}^{\sigma_1} \Delta_1},$$

and

(3.18) $$\ell = \frac{\beta(I - P_S S)}{P_\ell^{\sigma_1} \Delta_1}, \text{ where}$$

(3.19) $$\Delta_1 = (1 - \beta)\bar{P}^{(1-\sigma_1)} + \beta P_\ell^{(1-\sigma_1)}.$$

We will discuss $\bar{P}$ below.

After spending $P_\ell \ell$ on leisure, consumers have $I - P_S S - P_\ell \ell$ to spend on the consumption components of $\bar{X}$. In the third stage, they maximize a Cobb-Douglas form for the subutility function

(3.20) $$\bar{X} = \prod_{m=1}^{15} X_m^{\lambda_m},$$

subject to

(3.21) $$I - P_S S - P_\ell \ell = \sum_{m=1}^{15} X_m \cdot P_m^*.$$

The λ_m weighting parameters are the Cobb-Douglas expenditure shares. Constrained maximization of the subutility function, $\bar{X}$, provides the demand functions

(3.22) $$X_m = \frac{\lambda_m(I - P_S S - P_\ell \ell)}{P_m^*}, \qquad m = 1, \ldots, 15.$$

An important property of the nested Cobb-Douglas and CES utility functions is that we can derive the indirect utility functions and expenditure functions easily. In the Cobb-Douglas case just described, for example, we form the indirect utility function by substituting the demand functions (3.22) into the direct utility function (3.20). If we use I_X to denote $I - P_S S - P_\ell \ell$, then

$$(3.23) \qquad \bar{X} = \prod_{m=1}^{15} \left(\frac{\lambda_m I_X}{P_m^*} \right)^{\lambda_m}.$$

The Cobb-Douglas function is defined such that the sum of the fifteen coefficients, λ_m, is unity. Thus we have

$$(3.23') \qquad \bar{X} = I_X \prod_{m=1}^{15} \left(\frac{\lambda_m}{P_m^*} \right)^{\lambda_m}.$$

The indirect utility function in this case expresses subutility, $\bar{X}$, as a function of income, prices, and preference parameters. From here, it is easy to solve for the expenditure function, which is the income solution of the indirect utility function.

$$(3.24) \qquad I_X = \bar{X} \cdot \prod_{m=1}^{15} \left(\frac{P_m^*}{\lambda_m} \right)^{\lambda_m}.$$

The expenditure function gives the income necessary to reach a given level of utility under a given configuration of prices.

Note that we can rewrite equation (3.21) as

$$(3.25) \qquad I_X = \bar{X}\bar{P}.$$

Combining equations (3.24) and (3.25), we see that

$$(3.26) \qquad \bar{P} = \prod_{i=1}^{15} \left(\frac{P_m^*}{\lambda_m} \right)^{\lambda_m}.$$

We have used the expenditure function to create a composite price index, $\bar{P}$, from the individual prices, P_m^*. An especially convenient property of this kind of price index for both the Cobb-Douglas and CES functions is that the composite price can be calculated without knowing the actual quantities, X_m. This property simplifies our calculations considerably.

We use similar procedures to derive the expenditure functions for the CES nests of the utility functions. The function H is a composite of $\bar{X}$ and ℓ, and the composite price is

$$(3.27) \qquad P_H = \left[(1 - \beta)\bar{P}^{(1-\sigma_1)} + \beta P_\ell^{(1-\sigma_1)} \right]^{\frac{1}{1-\sigma_1}}.$$

If we use I_H to denote $I - P_S S$, the income available for expenditure on H, we have the expenditure function,

$$(3.28) \qquad I_H = P_H H.$$

As with the Cobb-Douglas nest, the quantity of a composite good times the composite price equals the expenditure on the good.

The function U is a composite of H and C_F, and its composite price is

$$(3.29) \qquad P_U = \left[\alpha P_H^{(1-\sigma_2)} + (1-\alpha) \left[\frac{P_S \bar{P}}{P_K \gamma} \right]^{(1-\sigma_2)} \right]^{\frac{1}{1-\sigma_2}}.$$

The overall indirect utility function is $U = I/P_U$, and the overall expenditure function is $I = P_U \cdot U$.

3.5 Household Income and Taxes

The U.S. personal income tax (PIT) has graduated marginal rates that differ among income groups. It also includes special features that discriminate by industry. Some industries, for example, are more heavily incorporated than others, with a higher proportion of capital income in the form of retained earnings. These industries are more lightly taxed at the personal level than are other industries in which capital income is more heavily comprised of dividends and interest. The housing industry is favored by the PIT, because the imputed net rents of owner-occupied homes are not taxed. This model incorporates both the increasing marginal income tax rates by income class and the industrial discrimination of the PIT.

In order to describe the discriminatory aspects of the personal and corporate tax systems in more detail, we first calculate each industry's capital income net of corporate income tax, corporate franchise tax, and property tax. We denote these figures by CAP_i ($i = 1, \ldots, 19$). The government's payments for privately owned capital are represented by CAP_{20}. The sum of this capital income is received by the twelve consumer classes in the model. Therefore,

$$(3.30) \qquad \sum_{i=1}^{20} CAP_i = \sum_{j=1}^{12} CAP_j,$$

where CAP_j is the capital income received by the jth consumer class.

Each of the twelve consumer classes has a marginal tax rate on all capital and labor income, denoted by τ_j ($j = 1, \ldots, 12$). We can then calculate τ, which is the weighted average of the marginal tax rates on capital income.

$$(3.31) \qquad \tau = \frac{\sum\limits_{j=1}^{12} CAP_j \tau_j}{\sum\limits_{j=1}^{12} CAP_j}.$$

For each of the nineteen industries and government, we define a fraction, f_i, which is the proportion of that sector's capital income subjected to full personal income taxation. This fraction will differ across industries for a number of reasons, including the variance in dividend/retention policies and differences in the degree to which unincorporated capital qualifies for the investment tax credit.

In order to capture these intersectoral differences in the taxation of capital income at the personal level, we employ a construct that we call the personal factor tax, PFT_i ($i = 1, \ldots, 20$). Total capital tax in each industry is the sum of corporate taxes, property taxes, and the personal factor tax. For each sector, the total personal factor taxes paid are given as

$$(3.32) \qquad PFT_i = f_i\, CAP_i \tau, \qquad i = 1, \ldots, 20,$$

where the personal factor tax rate on CAP_i is $f_i \tau$.

It is then possible to define net capital income, $NCAP_i$, as capital income net of the corporate taxes, property taxes, and the personal factor tax on capital income in that industry:

$$(3.33) \qquad NCAP_i = CAP_i - PFT_i = CAP_i(1 - f_i \tau).$$

The average fraction of CAP_i that is fully taxable by the personal income tax is

$$(3.34) \qquad \bar{f} = \frac{\sum\limits_{i=1}^{20} CAP_i f_i}{\sum\limits_{i=1}^{20} CAP_i}.$$

If we define CAP and $NCAP$ as the sums of CAP_i and $NCAP_i$ over twenty sectors, then the last two equations imply:

$$(3.35) \qquad NCAP = CAP(1 - \bar{f}\tau).$$

This expression provides an average conversion from capital income net of corporate and property taxes to capital income net of all taxes.

Although consumers in fact receive CAP_j ($j = 1, \ldots, 12$) and pay their own personal income taxes, we model the PIT on capital income as if it were paid at the industry level. Since tax at rate τ has been paid on an average $\bar{f}$ of capital income CAP_j, however, there must be a correction for differences among the marginal rates at the personal level. The personal factor tax at the industry level can be viewed as a withholding tax. For consumer j, with capital income of CAP_j, the amount of tax paid at the industry level is $\tau \bar{f} CAP_j$. Consumer j should actually pay a tax of

$\tau_j \bar{f} CAP_j$, however, so consumers for whom τ_j exceeds τ must pay additional taxes at the personal level (in addition to the personal factor tax at the industry level). Those for whom τ_j falls below τ get rebates. Thus the correction at the personal level is

$$(3.36) \qquad \Gamma_j = (\tau_j - \tau)CAP_j \bar{f}.$$

Since τ is the capital-weighted average of the marginal tax rates, the sum of these corrections at the personal level is zero. Since $NCAP_j = CAP_j$ $(1 - \bar{f}\tau)$, personal tax correction can also be described as

$$(3.37) \qquad \Gamma_j = (\tau_j - \tau)NCAP_j \frac{\bar{f}}{1 - \bar{f}\tau}.$$

This rearrangement is necessary because our endogenously determined rental price P_K is defined as the amount earned by each unit of capital, net of *all* taxes. Net capital income $P_K K_j$ is used for $NCAP_j$ in equation (3.37) for our model calculations.

Many transfer payments are not subject to the income tax. In our model we assume that all transfers are tax-exempt. Labor income is fully taxable. Therefore we have the following formula for income taxes paid by group j:

$$(3.38) \qquad T_j^I = B_j + \tau_j P_L L_j + (\tau_j - \tau)P_K K_j \frac{\bar{f}}{1 - \bar{f}\tau}.$$

The intercept of each linear tax function, B_j, is negative to reflect the fact that marginal tax rates exceed average tax rates. While marginal changes in income are taxed at the appropriate marginal rate for each group, this marginal rate does not change as income changes. Expanded income, I_j, equals transfers plus labor and capital income, plus the value of leisure, minus income taxes. Since $E_j = L_j + \ell_j$, we have

$$(3.39) \qquad I_j = T_j^R - B_j + E_j P_L (1 - \tau_j) + P_K K_j \left[1 - (\tau_j - \tau) \frac{\bar{f}}{1 - \bar{f}\tau} \right],$$

where T_j^R are the lump-sum transfers. Transfer payments are held constant in real terms by a price index on each consumer group's consumption purchases. If the value of leisure, $P_\ell \ell_j$, were subtracted from this expression, we could rearrange it using equation (3.38) to obtain a more usual definition of income:

$$(3.40) \qquad I_j - P_\ell \ell_j = T_j^R + P_L L_j + P_K K_j - T_j^I.$$

The price of leisure, P_ℓ, is equal to $P_L(1 - \tau_j)$.

3.6   Government Receipts and Expenditures

We divide government activities into two broad categories. Some publicly supplied goods and services are offered free of charge. We refer to these as general government activities. Other goods and services are subject to user charges, even though the charges may not cover costs (e.g., postal services and some utilities). We refer to these as government enterprise or industry 19. This industry is modeled like the eighteen private industries, and its particular data is described in chapter 4. Consequently, we will not describe it in detail here. The remainder of this section covers the modeling of general government activities.

Expenditures by government other than those for public enterprises are an element of final demand. We model the government as if it were a single consumer, with a Cobb-Douglas utility function defined over all nineteen producer goods, capital, and labor.[11] These government expenditures do not enter the utility functions of consumers as public goods. When tax rates are changed for a simulation, the equal yield feature ensures that enough tax revenue is obtained from an alternative source so that government expenditures at the new equilibrium prices leave the government with the utility level it had in the old equilibrium. Consequently, we only need to be concerned with changes in consumer utility when we want to calculate the total welfare change from some policy.

The government obtains income by collecting taxes and by renting out its endowment of capital services. It makes redistributive transfer payments to consumers in a lump-sum fashion; we use data for Social Security, food stamps, Aid to Families with Dependent Children, and similar programs to determine the amounts of these transfers. These transfers are held constant in real terms, using a Laspeyres price index for each consumer group. The government uses the remaining revenues to buy producer goods at the prices P_i ($i = 1, \ldots, 19$), to buy labor at the gross-of-tax price $P_L (1 + t_L^G)$, and to buy capital at the gross-of-tax price $P_K (1 + t_K^G)$.

The tax rate paid for labor is based on Social Security and railroad retirement taxes paid by the government and its employees. When the government pays these taxes on its use of labor, it pays the taxes to itself. Consequently, the income effects cancel out. However, the price effects measure correctly the opportunity cost to government of hiring additional labor.

The tax rate on capital used by government, t_K^G, is more problematic. Governments in the United States do not typically pay corporate income taxes or property taxes. If we were to model t_K^G as only the personal tax on

---

11. This formulation allows government to purchase quantities that depend at least somewhat on output prices, but in any case it does not greatly affect the results of the model that pertain to structural tax reform.

that capital income, the government's tax rate on K would be substantially less than the private sector's tax rate. The benchmark equilibrium would imply a misallocation of capital in favor of government use. Any reduction in the capital taxes faced by the private sector would imply reallocation flows from the government sector to the private sector. Since the gross-of-tax capital price in the private sector reflects the marginal product of capital, this capital flow from the public to the private sector would imply (possibly large) welfare gains.

We do not want to contaminate our calculations of the welfare effects of distorting taxes in this way. Therefore, in our model the entire government sector faces a price for capital that is equal to $P_K(1 + \Phi)$, where Φ is the weighted average tax rate on capital used in industry. Then, if the industry tax rates were to change, the government's price would change accordingly. The new price of capital faced by the government would be $P_K \cdot 1$ plus the new weighted average industry tax rate. For example, if industry tax rates were reduced through corporate tax integration, the price of capital used in government would not change relative to the price faced by producers. Thus capital would not flow from the government to the private sector.[12]

3.7 External Sector

We treat the foreign trade activity of the United States in a simple manner, so as to close the model.[13] In our standard model we do not differentiate between commodities on the basis of origin, i.e., U.S.-produced cars and imported cars are considered to be identical.

Foreign trade introduces a difference between the demands of consuming groups in the United States (broadly defined to include business investment and government purchases) and the demands for products faced by U.S. domestic industries. We can represent this distinction by introducing a vector of imports and a vector of exports, using the producer good classification of the model. These vectors account for differences between the demands of U.S. groups and the demands facing U.S. industries.

12. If the government acts to maximize social welfare, it would recognize that each unit of capital taken out of the private sector reduces general welfare by the gross-of-tax price paid by the private purchasers of capital. When government uses another unit of capital, it gives up not only P_K but also the tax revenue that a private producer would pay if that unit of capital were to be used in the private sector. If the government realizes this and acts to maximize social welfare, it would charge itself a shadow price equal to $P_K(1 + \Phi)$.

13. For modeling and results of several alternative trade and international capital flow specifications in this context, see chapter 11. The treatment of foreign trade in this chapter is based on Whalley and Yeung 1948. Alternatives include the use of the Armington assumption (that imports differ from domestically produced goods) and the possibility of imbalanced commodity through international capital flows. The capital flows might be in capital goods or in capital services.

The demand for U.S. exports by foreigners has a negative price elasticity, while the supply of imports to the United States has a positive price elasticity. The relative prices of traded goods are determined endogenously in the model. Trade balance is assured, since the export demand and import supply functions satisfy budget balance.

For each of the nineteen producer goods, we specify foreign export demand and import supply functions. These functions incorporate parameters that determine constant price elasticities of import supply and export demand:

(3.41)
$$M_i = M_i^0 (P_{Mi}^w)^\mu, \qquad \begin{matrix} 0 < \mu < \infty \\ i = 1, \ldots, 19; \end{matrix}$$

$$E_i = E_i^0 (P_{Ei}^w)^\nu, \qquad \begin{matrix} -\infty < \nu < 0 \\ i = 1, \ldots, 19; \end{matrix}$$

where M_i and E_i are import demand and export supply, M_i^0 and E_i^0 are constants, P_{Mi}^w is the world price of imports, and P_{Ei}^w is the world price of U.S. exports. These equations imply that the ith commodity can be both imported and exported. This phenomenon of *crosshauling* is evident from the trade statistics, even with highly disaggregated data, and it underlies much of the recent literature on intraindustry trade (see Grubel and Lloyd 1975). There are many reasons for this phenomenon. One explanation asserts that foreign commodities are qualitatively different from domestic goods. For example, U.S. and foreign cars are close but not perfect substitutes. This assumption, first discussed by Armington (1969), is considered explicitly in chapter 11. Crosshauling can also be explained by reference to geography and transportation costs. For example, it may be perfectly sensible for the United States to export Alaskan oil to Japan and at the same time import the identical product through ports on the East Coast and the Gulf of Mexico, given the cost of delivering Alaskan oil to the eastern United States.

In order to close the system and solve the general equilibrium model, we add the trade balance constraint:

(3.42)
$$\sum_{i=1}^{19} P_{Mi}^w M_i = \sum_{i=1}^{19} P_{Ei}^w E_i.$$

If we substitute for M_i and E_i from equation (3.41) into equation (3.42), we have

(3.43)
$$\sum_{i=1}^{19} P_{Mi}^w M_i^0 (P_{Mi}^w)^\mu = \sum_{i=1}^{19} P_{Ei}^w E_i (P_{Ei}^w)^\nu.$$

We define the relationship between U.S. and world prices through an exchange rate term, e, as $P_{Ei}^{US} = eP_{Ei}^w$ and $P_{Mi}^{US} = eP_{Mi}^w$. The model is, of course, a real trade model and has no financial exchange rate variables, but the use of this construct enables us to write foreign import supply and export demand functions as functions of U.S. prices rather than of world prices. U.S. prices are determined endogenously in the model. If we substitute these U.S. prices into (3.43), we have:

(3.44) $$e = \left(\frac{\omega_2}{\omega_1}\right)^{\frac{\mu}{\nu - \mu}}, \text{ where}$$

(3.45) $$\omega_1 = \sum_{i=1}^{19} (P_{Mi}^{US})^{\mu + 1} M_i^0,$$

$$\omega_2 = \sum_{i=1}^{19} (P_{Ei}^{US})^{\nu + 1} E_i^0.$$

Finally, substituting these results into equation (3.41), gives

(3.46) $$M_i = M_i^0 (P_{Mi}^{US})^{\mu} \left(\frac{\omega_2}{\omega_1}\right)^{\frac{\mu}{\mu - \nu}},$$

$$E_i = E_i^0 (P_{Ei}^{US}) \left(\frac{\omega_2}{\omega_1}\right)^{\frac{\nu}{\mu - \nu}}.$$

Note that ω_1 and ω_2 are themselves functions of U.S. import and export prices. Equations (3.46) can be thought of as foreign import supply and export demand functions, written as functions of U.S. prices, and incorporating zero trade balance. Thus, while equations (3.41) specify import and export behavior, the μ and ν parameters are not supply and demand elasticities that incorporate trade balance conditions. To derive expressions for an import supply elasticity and export demand elasticity that do satisfy trade balance, consider a simplified two commodity case in which each country exports one item and imports the other. Let us say that the foreigner demands our exports of good 1. Then, suppressing the *US* superscript and substituting equations (3.45) into the export equation (3.46) we have:

(3.47) $$E_1 = E_1^0 (P_{E_1})^{\nu} \left(\frac{(P_{E_1})^{\nu + 1} E_1^0}{(P_{M_2})^{\mu + 1} M_2^0}\right).$$

It is simple to differentiate with respect to P_{E_1} and get the own-price elasticity of export demand:

(3.48) $$\epsilon_E^{FD} = \frac{\nu(\mu + 1)}{\mu - \nu}.$$

Similarly, we can find the own-price elasticity of import supply as:

(3.49) $$\epsilon_M^{FS} = \frac{-\mu(1 + \nu)}{(\mu - \nu)}.$$

We would like to restrict μ and ν so that the export demand curve slopes downward and the import supply curve slopes upward. These conditions will be met if $\mu \geq 0$ and $\nu \leq -1$.

In the two-good case, equations (3.48) and (3.49) can be used to set values for μ and ν that are consistent with econometric estimates of ϵ_E^{FD} and ϵ_M^{FS}. We follow the same procedure in our model with nineteen commodities (see chapter 6).

Appendix

Glossary of Notation

These variables are defined in approximately the order they appear in the text of chapter 3. (Some do not appear in equations until considerably after they are defined and used in the text.)

Table 3.A.1

Symbol	Definition	Equation Number of First Appearance	Data Source or Derivation
Section 3.3			
K_j	Capital endowment, in service units, of the jth consumer		Basic data, from Treasury Department Merged Data File
K_G	Capital endowment, in service, of general government		Basic data, imputed from capital stocks in Kendrick 1976
E_j	Labor endowment, in service units of the jth consumer	(3.1)	Basic model uses 1.75 of observed labor supply
ℓ_j	Leisure demand, in service units, of the jth consumer	(3.1)	Basic model starts with .75 of observed labor supply
L_j	Labor supply, in service units, of the jth consumer	(3.1)	Basic data, from Treasury Department Merged Tax File
VA_i	Value added in i^{th} industry	(3.2)	From basic data
Q_i	Output of the ith industry		From basic data on value added and intermediate use

Table 3.A.1 (continued)

Symbol	Definition	Equation Number of First Appearance	Data Source or Derivation
ϕ	CES production normalization parameter, for each industry	(3.2)	From calibration, chapter 6
δ	CES factor weighting parameter for each industry	(3.2)	From calibration, chapter 6
K_i	Capital use, in service units, of the ith industry	(3.2)	From Commerce Department data, and procedures of chapter 5
L_i	Labor use, in service units, of the ith industry	(3.1)	From Commerce Department data, and procedures of chapter 5
σ	CES elasticity of substitution between K and L for each industry	(3.2)	Econometric estimates, surveyed in Caddy 1976
P_K	Price of capital, in net rents per unit each period		Units convention in the benchmark, endogenous in any simulation
P_L	Price of labor, in net rents per unit each period		Units convention in the benchmark, endogenous in any simulation
t_{Ki}	ad valorem tax rate on capital for the ith industry		From Commerce Department data, and procedures of chapter 5
t_{Li}	ad valorem tax rate on labor for the ith industry		From Commerce Department data, and procedures of chapter 5
P_{Ki}^*	Gross-of-tax cost of capital to the ith industry	(3.3)	From P_K and t_{Ki}
P_{Li}^*	Gross-of-tax cost of labor to the ith industry	(3.3)	From P_L and t_{Li}
R_L	Requirement of labor per unit of output, for each industry	(3.3)	From equation (3.3)
R_K	Requirement of capital per unit of output, for each industry	(3.4)	From equation (3.4)
A	19 × 19 fixed-coefficient input-output matrix		From Commerce Department Bureau of Economic Analysis
a_{ik}	Element of the A input-output matrix		From Commerce Department Bureau of Economic Analysis
t_{MVi}	Tax on intermediate use of motor vehicles of the ith industry		From Commerce Department data, and procedures of chapter 5
t_{Qi}	ad valorem rate of tax on the output of the ith industry		From Commerce Department data, and procedures of chapter 5
P_i	Price of the output of the ith industry	(3.5)	Units convention in the benchmark, endogenous in any simulation

Table 3.A.1 (continued)

Symbol	Definition	Equation Number of First Appearance	Data Source or Derivation
X_m	Quantity of the mth consumer good		From Commerce and Consumer Expenditure Survey data
Z	19×15 fixed-coefficient matrix converting industry outputs to consumer goods		February 1974 *Survey of Current Business*
z_{im}	Element of the coefficient Z matrix	(3.5)	February 1974 *Survey of Current Business*
P_m	Price of the mth consumer good	(3.5)	From equation (3.5)
t_m	ad valorem sales tax rate on the mth consumer good, for each consumer		From Commerce Clearing House's *State Tax Handbook*
P_m^*	cum-tax prices paid for the mth consumer good, for each consumer	(3.21)	From P_m and t_m
Section 3.4			
H	Composite of present consumption, consumer goods, and leisure, for each consumer	(3.6)	From equation (3.15)
C_F	Composite of future consumption, $C_1, \ldots, C_T$, for each consumer	(3.6)	From definition as the annual consumption made possible by one unit of saving
U	Utility of each consumer	(3.6)	Defined in equation (3.10)
I	Expanded income of each consumer, from endowments and transfers after taxes	(3.8)	Defined in equation (3.39). Data from Treasury Department Merged Tax File, and procedures of chapter 5
P_H	The price of composite consumption H, for each consumer	(3.8)	Defined in equation (3.27)
P_ℓ	Price of leisure, ℓ, for each consumer	(3.16)	Defined as net-of-tax wage
$\bar{X}$	Composite of consumer goods, X_m, for each consumer	(3.15)	Defined in equation (3.20)
$\bar{P}$	Price of the composite $\bar{X}$	(3.7)	Defined in equation (3.26)
S	"Quantity" of savings-investment good, for each consumer	(3.7)	Basic data adjusted from Consumer Expenditure Survey
P_S	Price of the savings good, a composite of the 19 output prices, as they are used for investment	(3.7)	Units convention in benchmark, endogenous in any simulation
γ	The fixed constant that converts savings-investment into capital service units	(3.7)	Chosen as the real rate of return to capital in the benchmark

Table 3.A.1 (continued)

Symbol	Definition	Equation Number of First Appearance	Data Source or Derivation
α	CES utility-weighting parameter for H and C_F, for each consumer	(3.10)	From calibration, chapter 6
σ_2	CES utility elasticity of substitution between H and C_F, for each consumer	(3.10)	From η saving elasticity and calibration, chapter 6
Δ_2	Notational shorthand for part of H and C_F demands for each consumer	(3.11)	Defined in equation (3.13)
β	CES utility-weighting parameter for $\bar{X}$ and ℓ, for each consumer	(3.15)	From calibration, chapter 6
σ_1	CES utility elasticity of substitution between $\bar{X}$ and ℓ, for each consumer	(3.15)	From labor supply elasticity and calibration, chapter 6
τ_j	The marginal personal income tax rate of the jth consumer	(3.31)	From Treasury Department Merged Tax File
Δ_1	Notational shorthand for part of $\bar{X}$ and ℓ demands, for each consumer	(3.17)	Defined in equation (3.19)
λ_m	Cobb-Douglas utility-weighting parameter on the mth consumer good, for each consumer	(3.20)	From Consumer Expenditure Survey and calibration, chapter 6
I_X	Income after leisure and savings	(3.23)	Defined in equation (3.25)
I_H	Income after savings	(3.28)	Defined in equation (3.28)
P_U	Price index for composite utility units	(3.29)	Defined in equation (3.29)
Section 3.5			
CAP_i	Capital payments from the ith industry, net of corporate and property taxes	(3.30)	Commerce Department and procedures of chapter 5
CAP_j	Capital income of the jth consumer, net of corporate and property taxes	(3.30)	Treasury Department Tax File data, procedures of chapter 5
CAP	Sum of 20 CAP_i or of 12 CAP_j	(3.35)	See above, CAP_i or CAP_j
τ	Capital-weighted average of the 12 consumers' marginal tax rates	(3.31)	Defined in equation (3.31)
f_i	The proportion of the ith sector's CAP_i that is subject to the personal income tax	(3.32)	Defined in equation (4.1)
PFT_i	Personal factor tax in the ith sector	(3.32)	Defined in equation (3.32)
$\bar{f}$	The capital-weighted average of the 20 sectors' f_i parameters	(3.34)	Defined in equation (3.34)
$NCAP_i$	Capital payments from the ith industry, net of all taxes	(3.33)	Defined in equation (3.33); equals $K_i P_K$ in simulations

Table 3.A.1 (continued)

Symbol	Definition	Equation Number of First Appearance	Data Source or Derivation
$NCAP_j$	Capital income of the jth consumer, net of all taxes	(3.36)	Treasury Department Merged Tax File; equals $K_j P_K$ in simulations
$NCAP$	Sum of 20 $NCAP_i$ or of 12 $NCAP_j$	(3.35)	See above; defined in equation (3.35)
Γ_j	Personal factor tax of the jth consumer	(3.36)	Defined in equations (3.36) and (3.37)
T_j^I	Personal income tax of the jth consumer	(3.38)	Treasury Department Merged Tax File data, as defined in equation (3.38)
B_J	Negative intercept in the linear personal tax function of the jth consumer	(3.38)	Treasury Department Merged Tax File and calibration, chapter 6
T_j^R	Lump-sum government transfers to the jth consumer group	(3.39)	Treasury Department Merged Tax File data
t_L^G	ad valorem tax rate on the labor purchased by government		From Commerce Department data on Social Security and railroad retirement taxes paid by government
t_K^G	ad valorem tax rate on the capital purchased by government		Set to Φ as discussed in section 3.6
Φ	Weighted average industry tax rate		From t_{Ki}, weighted by K_i, for $i = 1, \ldots, 19$
Section 3.7			
M_i	Quantity of imports of the ith producer good	(3.41)	Benchmark data from OECD trade statistics
M_i^O	Constant in import supply	(3.41)	Based on benchmark imports
P_{Mi}^w	World price of imports of ith producer good	(3.41)	Not used in actual calculations
P_{Mi}^{US}	Domestic price of imports of ith producer good	(3.45)	Equal to P_i which is from the units convention in the benchmark, endogenous in simulations
μ	Price elasticity of import supply	(3.41)	From Stern, Francis, and Schumacher 1977
E_i	Quantity of exports of the ith producer good	(3.41)	Benchmark data from OECD trade statistics
E_i^O	Constant in export demand	(3.41)	Based on benchmark exports
P_{Ei}^w	World price of exports of the ith producer good	(3.41)	Not used in actual calculations
P_{Ei}^{US}	Domestic price of exports of the ith producer good	(3.45)	Equal to P_i which is from the units convention in the benchmark, endogenous in simulations

Table 3.A.1 (continued)

Symbol	Definition	Equation Number of First Appearance	Data Source or Derivation
e	Exchange rate between domestic and foreign prices	(3.44)	Solved out in equation (3.44)
ν	Price elasticity of export demand	(3.41)	From chapter 6
ω_1	Notational shorthand functions of import and export prices	(3.44)	Defined in equation (3.45)
ω_2	Notational shorthand functions of import and export prices	(3.44)	Defined in equation (3.45)
ϵ_E^{FD}	Foreign price elasticity of demand for U.S. exports	(3.50)	Defined in equation (3.50)
ϵ_M^{FS}	Foreign price elasticity of supply for U.S. imports	(3.51)	Defined in equation (3.51)

4   Data on Intermediate Production and Value Added

4.1   Introduction

In both this and the following chapter we describe our 1973 benchmark data set. We describe in some detail the raw data and the many adjustments in order to assist anyone who wishes to reconstruct or modify any part of the data set. In this chapter we deal with data on the use of factors by industry, taxes by industry, input-output transactions, and government enterprises. Chapter 5 is concerned with data on household incomes and expenditures, general government expenditures, and foreign trade.

Value added consists of net payments to the factors of production plus factor taxes. We use the National Income and Product Accounts (NIPA) to obtain figures for capital income, labor income, and tax by industry in 1973. We listed the nineteen industries used for our production data in table 3.1. These nineteen industries are a direct aggregation of the fifty-nine industries given in detailed tables of the *Survey of Current Business* (*SCB*) or of the eighty industries given in Bureau of Economic Analysis (BEA) input-output tables. These, in turn, are based on the Standard Industrial Classification (SIC). Appendix A of this chapter shows how we aggregate the eighty BEA industries.[1] This disaggregation provides us with richer detail than many of the tables published in the *SCB*, which only report information for twelve industries. For this reason much of our data comes from unpublished worksheets of the Commerce Department's National Income Division (NID).[2] Even with this greater degree of disaggregation of the production sector of the economy, we are

1. The relationship between our classification and the SIC can be seen in a table in U.S. Department of Commerce, BEA 1975, p. 10.
2. The staff at NID were extremely helpful in providing us with detailed worksheets. We also received excellent suggestions for additional sources and alternative adjustments procedures.

left with fairly aggregated groups. We have tried to maintain separate classifications for industries that are quantitatively important and taxed differently.

While chapter 6 describes overall adjustments to the data that are necessary to meet general equilibrium consistency requirements, this chapter describes many adjustments that were made to the raw data for definitional consistency. However, two discrepancies cannot be corrected here. First of all, the National Income Division collects some data on an establishment basis and other data on a company basis. For our purposes, the best measure is income generated in the production of each good, but data are not available on this basis.[3] The second problem is that the accounts use a "national" definition of economic activity, where we would prefer a "domestic" definition.[4]

4.2 Labor Income and Labor Taxes by Industry

The gross-of-factor-tax return to labor is the sum of employee compensation and the estimated return to the labor of self-employed individuals. The NIPA definition of employee compensation includes wages and salaries and supplements to wages and salaries.[5] These supplements include employer contributions for social insurance (ECSI) and other labor income (OLI). Employer contributions include those for Old Age, Survivors, Disability, and Hospital Insurance (OASDHI or Social Security), unemployment insurance, public workmen's compensation, and railroad retirement. Other labor income includes private workmen's compensation, pensions, group health and life insurance, and supplemental unemployment benefits.

The return to the labor of self-employed persons is an unknown fraction of the total return to the entrepreneur who invests his time and capital jointly. NID provides us with data for the total return to unincorporated enterprises by industry. However, we must still estimate the portion of this return that accrues to labor. In order to estimate this return, we assume that partners or proprietors in an industry earn the

3. "The establishment basis is used for the industrial classifications of wages and salaries, supplements to wages and salaries, income of unincorporated enterprises and inventory valuation adjustment, and interest paid by noncorporate enterprises. However, the company basis is used for corporate profits, the corporate inventory valuation adjustment, and interest paid and received by corporations" U.S. Department of Commerce, OBE 1954, p. 67.

4. The national definition measures "the income and product attributable to factors of production supplied by residents of the country rather than the income and product of factors physically located in the country" ibid., p. 32.

5. Wages and salaries include all monetary remuneration of employees, including the compensation of corporate officers, commissions, tips, bonuses, and receipts in kind that represent income to the recipients. These are on an accrual, not disbursement basis. Definitions of this kind can be found in U.S. Department of Commerce, BEA 1976a, pp. 34–38.

same return as other workers in that industry. We derive the average compensation of employees in each industry from two tables in the July 1976 *SCB* (U.S. Department of Commerce, BEA 1976b). Next we divide employee compensation by the full-time equivalent number of employees (providing average annual labor income for each industry). Then, using NID data on the numbers of proprietors and partners, with a correction for hours worked, we estimate the imputed return to the labor of self-employed individuals.[6]

For several industries—construction, utilities, real estate, and manufacturing—the estimated labor component exceeds the total unincorporated income. This problem is less serious in manufacturing, because unincorporated enterprises only produce a small proportion of manufactured goods. However, large segments of construction, utilities, and real estate are unincorporated. These three industries are land intensive and probably have a high rate of accrued capital gains. These gains would not show up in the figures for unincorporated income. Rather than assign a large return to labor and a negative return to capital in these industries, we simply assign the total unincorporated return to labor.

The sum of the imputed return to labor in the unincorporated sector, and wages and salaries in the corporate sector, yields gross-of-tax labor income for our nineteen industries. These appear in column (1) of table 4.1.

We define taxes on labor income to include employer contributions for social insurance (ECSI), employee contributions for OASDHI, plus contributions for OASDHI by self-employed individuals. We include all taxes on labor income that discriminate among industries. OASDHI has a fixed rate up to a maximum per employee, so that high-income employees pay a smaller tax per dollar of labor income than employees whose incomes fall below the maximum. Thus industries with higher-than-average compensation of employees tend to pay a lower effective rate on OASDHI. Unemployment insurance also discriminates by industry, since the tax is greater for those firms with a higher incidence of unemployment.

We treat contributions for public workmen's compensation (part of ECSI) as a tax, although we treat contributions for private workmen's compensation (part of OLI) as ordinary income. This distinction is somewhat arbitrary, since both are mandatory insurance payments. We make the distinction because the contributions for workmen's compensation go

---

6. If this imputed return to labor is subtracted from total unincorporated income, the residual is an estimate of the return to capital. Alternatively, using an asset basis, if we can measure the capital stock of both the corporate and noncorporate sectors in each industry, we can attribute to noncorporate capital the same net-of-tax rate of return as that of corporate capital. Subtracting this estimate of return to capital from the total unincorporated income yields a residual return to labor estimate. In practice, the latter (asset basis) method is more difficult, with capital stock by industry and by sector generally unavailable.

to government. NID supplies us with breakdowns of ECSI items by industry. Since the Social Security program involves matching contributions, we use the employer share to estimate the employee share.[7] The total for contributions by self-employed individuals is given in the July 1976 *SCB*. However, NID does not divide this total by industry. We allocate the total among industries by the proportion of self-employed labor income in each industry.

The total tax on labor for each industry is shown in column (2) of table 4.1. We subtract this from gross-of-tax labor income to get labor income net-of-tax, which is column (3).

Using columns (2) and (3) of table 4.1, we calculate the effective tax rates on labor by industry, which are shown in column (4). The rates differ by industry, but they are close to the overall weighted average of 10.1 percent. This dispersion is not great for two reasons. First, our procedure for estimating self-employed contributions to OASDHI by industry actually assumes the same rate of tax in all industries. However, these contributions represent only $2.5 billion out of $63 billion of labor taxes. Second, when we combine detailed industries into less-detailed ones, we tend to reduce the dispersion of tax rates. The rate of .0702 for agriculture, for example, reflects the fact that many agricultural workers are not covered by insurance programs. The rate of .0903 on services is due to a low level of coverage and some high salaries àbove the ceiling for OASDHI.

4.3   Capital Income and Capital Taxes by Industry

The return to capital, net-of-factor taxes, includes corporate profits after tax, the return to unincorporated capital, net interest paid, and net rents paid. We would like to include real accrued capital gains in our measure of capital income in each industry, but the data are not available. (Moreover, constancy of relative prices is consistent with our parameterization of an equilibrium economy with no excess profits.)[8] Now we will discuss the various components of capital income.

4.3.1   Corporate Profits after Tax

The July 1976 *SCB* gives corporate profits after deducting property taxes and indirect business taxes. *SCB* table 6.21 shows corporate profits *after* the corporate income tax. This corresponds to a net-of-tax definition. This series includes profits after the capital consumption allowance

---

7. This step is justified empirically, since 1973 employer contributions to OASDHI total $30,549 million, while employee contributions total $30,388 million. (See U.S. Department of Commerce, BEA 1976b, table 3.11.)

8. Since we include corporate profits after tax, we account for any capital gains on shares that might result from real retained earnings.

Table 4.1   **Labor Income, Tax, and Effective Rates by Industry in the U.S. for 1973**

	Labor Income Gross of Tax (1)	Tax on Labor (2)	Labor Income Net of Tax (3)	Effective Tax Rate (2) ÷ (3) (4)
All industries	708,037	64,997	643,040	.1011
Agriculture, forestry, fisheries	17,398	1,141	16,257	.0702
Mining	5,182	464	4,718	.0983
Crude petroleum and gas	3,723	308	3,415	.0902
Contract construction	56,216	5,308	50,908	.1043
Food and tobacco	18,823	1,859	16,964	.1096
Textiles, apparel, and leather	19,715	2,268	17,447	.1300
Paper and printing	20,944	1,948	18,996	.1025
Petroleum refining	3,073	239	2,834	.0843
Chemicals, rubber, and plastics	21,344	1,957	19,387	.1009
Lumber, furniture, stone, clay, glass	19,349	1,930	17,419	.1108
Metals, machinery, instruments, and miscellaneous manufacturing	97,163	9,167	87.996	.1042
Transport equipment and ordnance	15,131	1,393	13,738	.1014
Motor vehicles	16,422	1,358	15,064	.0901
Transportation, communications, utilities	65,274	6,188	59,086	.1047
Trade	143,984	13,745	130,239	.1055
Finance and insurance	36,000	3,161	32,839	.0963
Real estate	8,609	827	7,782	.1063
Services	122,964	10,179	112,785	.0903
Government enterprises	16,723	1,557	15,166	.1027

Note: All figures are in millions of dollars. Component detail is available upon request.

(tax depreciation) but before the capital consumption adjustment (correction to economic depreciation) or the inventory valuation adustment (IVA). The capital consumption adjustment will be treated separately later. We obtained the IVA from NID of Commerce.[9] Column (1) of table 4.2 shows profits after correction for the IVA.[10] The total is $45,633 million.[11]

9. The negative $301 million IVA for mining and crude petroleum is divided between the two by their proportions of value added in 1973. The negative $178 million for "other" corporate industries is allocated entirely to services, since this is the largest component, with a majority of inventories.

10. The relationship between these NIPA corporate profits and the IRS definition can be seen in U.S. Department of Commerce, BEA 1976b, table 8.5. The NIPA starts with IRS numbers and adds depletion, bad-debt adjustment, and other dividends, and the cost of issuing securities, in order to reach a measure related to current production.

11. Federal Reserve Board (FRB) earnings are included in corporate income figures, and FRB payments to the Treasury are counted as part of the corporate income tax. This

Table 4.2 Capital Income Components by Industry in the U.S. for 1973 (millions of dollars)

	Corporate Profits after Tax with IVA (1)	Capital Consumption Adjustment (2)	Return to Noncorporate Capital (3)	Net Rents Paid (4)	Net Interest Paid (5)	Total Capital Income (6)
All industries	45,633	8,221	33,541	21,237	65,530	181,973
Agriculture, forestry, fisheries	523	—[d]	22,865	4,067	3,323	30,778
Mining	840[b]	—	37	80	179	1,136
Crude petroleum and gas	2,446[b]	—	561	304	59	3,370
Contract construction	500	—	0	75	448	1,023
Food and tobacco	335	572	0	64	846	1,817
Textiles, apparel, and leather	428[a]	138	0	49	471	1,086
Paper and printing	2,376	−96	0	242	199	2,721
Petroleum refining	3,583	3,578	0	640	481	8,282
Chemicals, rubber, and plastics	3,172	132	0	71	535	3,910
Lumber, furniture, stone, clay, glass	3,115[b]	512	0	181	421	4,229
Metals, machinery, instruments, and miscellaneous manufacturing	5,527	2,144	0	427	2,303	10,401
Transport equipment and ordnance	−91[a]	61	0	22	176	168
Motor vehicles	2,785	1,180	0	30	852	4,847
Transportation, communications, utilities	4,292	—	0	357	8,606	13,255
Trade	7,198	—	367	898	1,258	9,721
Finance and insurance	6,843[c]	—	809	188	0	7,840
Real estate	88[a]	—[d]	0	13,013	43,731	56,832
Services	1,673	—	8,902	529	1,642	12,746
Government enterprises	—	—	—	—	—	7,811[e]

[a] Averaged over 1971–73.   [c] Includes FRB earnings.   [e] Imputed.
[b] Includes depletion.   [d] CCA already included.

4.3.2   Capital Consumption Adjustment

Neither published nor unpublished sources at the Commerce Department give sufficiently disaggregated industry data on the capital consumption adjustment or on "economic" depreciation. In the aggregate, the Commerce Department uses straight-line depreciation for consistent accounting and a replacement cost basis to measure economic depreciation. Then they subtract from the capital consumption allowance (as measured by the Internal Revenue Service) to get the capital consumption adjustment. We took capital consumption adjustment figures for manufacturing industries from Coen (1980) and aggregated them to our industrial classification. These figures are shown in column (2) of table 4.2, along with nonmanufacturing data taken from the Commerce Department.

4.3.3   Return to Unincorporated Capital

The procedure used to calculate these numbers has been described in the earlier section on labor income. We impute a return to the labor of proprietors and partners, and subtract this from the total to yield a residual capital return. If the imputed labor share is too large, we assign capital a share of zero. The results are shown in column (3) of table 4.2.

4.3.4   Net Rents Paid

Rents paid by an industry are payments for "borrowed" capital, property, buildings, and machinery. The Internal Revenue Service (IRS) and the NIPA treat these payments as a cost deduction for the renting firm and as income for the owners of the rented property. Since we seek to measure all payments to capital used in each industry, we treat rents paid as capital income in the paying industry. For each industry we would like to add to capital income all payments for rental property and subtract rental earnings. This would be equivalent to adding net rents paid. The NIPA has no industry distribution for rents paid, and the IRS *Statistics of Income (SOI)* show only gross rents paid by industry. However, the NID does provide the total of net rental income, which is equal to the total net rents paid. This total and its components are shown in table 4.3.

We treat net rents from farm realty as a return to capital used in industry 1 (agriculture, forestry, and fisheries). The NIPA measure of imputed net rent from owner-occupied and other dwellings sum to $12,917 million. This figure is added to the capital income of our real estate industry.

---

operation is not covered by the corporate income tax system and should be excluded from calculations on that tax. FRB earnings do make up part of capital income in our finance and insurance industry, however, and their payments to the Treasury can best be modeled as part of a tax on capital income in that industry, but not part of the corporate tax.

Table 4.3   **Net Rental Income Components, 1973**

Source	Amount
1. Net rents from farm realty	3,879
2. Imputed net rent from owner-occupied dwellings	10,334
3. Net rents from other dwellings[a]	2,583
4. Royalty earnings	1,498
5. Net rents from business and government[b]	3,124
5a. Nonfarm business 2,884	
5b. Nonprofit organizations 59	
5c. U.S. government 160	
5d. Foreign governments 21	
6. Total net rental income from the private sector[c]	21,237

Note: All figures are in millions of dollars. Items 1 through 5 were obtained from NID and include the capital consumption adjustment for an economic measure of depreciation.
[a]The sum of items 2 and 3 is net rents from housing, equal to $12,917 million, found in table 1.20 of the July 1976 *SCB*. These include farm housing.
[b]Items 5a through 5d are an approximate breakdown of item 5. See text for procedure.
[c]The sum of items 1 through 4, 5a and 5b.

Similarly, copyrights, patents, and royalties paid for natural resources should be counted as capital income in the industry where these capital assets are used and paid for. This item 4 in table 4.3 totals $1,498 million, but we are not supplied with industry division. The *SOI* show only royalties received. We therefore resort to a procedure used by Rosenberg (1969, p. 152), and allocate 12.5 percent to printing and publishing, 12.5 percent to electrical machinery (phonograph records), and 75 percent to natural resources. We approximate the use of natural resources by industry from the depletion deductions taken for tax purposes in 1973 (U.S. Department of the Treasury, IRS 1977a and 1977b). We assign deductions proportionally by depletion to six industries: petroleum and natural gas, other mining, petroleum refining, lumber, primary metals, and utilities.[12]

Finally, NID supplies us with net rents from business and government. These total $3,124 million, as shown in table 4.3. Net rents paid by each group are unavailable, so we use the proportion of gross rent paid to divide the total net rent paid.[13]

Nonprofit organizations are part of the services industry. We attribute the estimated net rents of these institutions directly to the services industry. The $2,884 million estimated net rental payments of business were

12. Rosenberg (1969) distributes 75 percent among three oil- and gas-using industries, despite the existence of "royalty" payments for lumber and other mining.
13. Gross nonresidential rent paid by business and government was $45,235 million. The portions paid by nonfarm business, nonprofit organizations, the U.S. government, and foreign governments were also provided by NID. We used these data to calculate items 5a to 5d in table 4.3.

allocated among industries by the proportion of gross rent paid by industry, furnished in the corporate and business *SOI*. This procedure generally follows Rosenberg (1969), and the results are shown in column (4) of table 4.2.

The NIPA imply that all of these rents originate in the real estate industry. The NIPA real estate industry includes housing services, other real property, and intermediation services. We redistribute the second component, but are still left with a somewhat curious definition of the real estate industry: housing services and intermediation in real property.

4.3.5 Net Interest Paid

The amount of an industry's capital return that is paid to bondholders will be reflected in that industry's net interest payments. We have used detailed worksheets by industry, provided by the NID. The worksheets show interest flows for 1973.

The dollar payments of interest by each industry are referred to as net monetary interest paid. Since all kinds of producers issue bonds to raise capital, these payments are positive for all industries except one. Finance and insurance (F&I) has a large negative value for net monetary interest paid, due to the peculiar structure of that industry. The F&I industry engages in financial intermediation, thus its interest receipts exceed the interest it pays on deposits. These net interest receipts are the form in which the F&I industry receives payment for services rendered. We argue above that net interest paid should be added to capital earned in each industry. If we add the (negative) net interest paid to the profits of the F&I industry, total capital is measured by a negative number. In 1973, net monetary interest paid by F&I was negative $61,181 million.

A consistent solution to this problem exists if we assume that F&I companies do not issue bonds to raise funds. That is, we assume that no interest payments are made for the capital used in the provision of intermediation services.[14] In fact, we can raise the F&I net-interest-paid figure to zero by *imputing* additional interest payments to other industry and to persons. Thus, we have two separate kinds of interest payments: monetary payments and imputed payments. This view of the world

---

14. Savings and loan associations in 1973 paid $12 billion in interest on deposits and $1 billion on borrowed money. Most of the latter went to the Federal Home Loan Bank Board, which means that the savings and loan associations paid for borrowed reserves at certain times. It is not obvious how to classify this kind of borrowing: it is borrowed capital used to provide financial services, but it is not for building plant or equipment as a factor of production. Commercial banks paid $20 billion interest on deposits, $4 billion on federal funds (borrowed reserves), $.5 billion on other borrowing, and $.25 billion interest on capital notes and bonds. Only the last category is clearly analogous to interest paid by other industries, but it is such a small portion of F&I net interest paid that it can be safely ignored. These two types of institutions had the only substantial payments on borrowed money.

attributes all property income of F&I straight through to the depositors who also make (imputed) service charge payments to F&I.[15]

The Commerce Department NID has made some of these imputations, but they only total $41,702 million. This falls $19,479 million short of the total for net monetary interest paid by F&I. There are several reasons for the difference. For instance NID does not make an imputation for finance companies and small-business investment companies. We have chosen to force the net interest paid by F&I (including both monetary and imputed interest) to be zero. To do this we impute an additional $19,479 million of interest paid by F&I.

These interest payment imputations should be allocated to other industries according to their use of financial services. As a proxy for the use of financial services, NID distributes the imputed interest receipts in proportion to cash held (including demand deposits) by each industry. These data come from the *SOI*. We use the same proportions to allocate all $61 million of imputed interest, including the $19 billion that are not imputed by NID. Based on these proportions, we allocate 79 percent of the total to persons and government. Out of the amount that we allocate to persons and government, some $15,388 million (or 79 percent of the $19,479 of extra imputed interest) is not counted by NID. The result is a GNP increase of $15,388 million. No one is better off, but our accounting shows larger consumer interest income, offset by larger (imputed) service charge payments to the finance and insurance industry. Net interest paid, both monetary and imputed, is shown in column (5) of table 4.2.

4.3.6 Special Treatment of Depletion Deductions

To obtain profits for tax purposes, natural resource firms in 1973 could deduct a percentage of revenues to reflect the depletion of their reserves. The combination of these depletion deductions and expensing of exploration costs is a case of double counting, because in competitive equilibrium, exploration costs are matched by the value of expected discoveries. We can avoid this double counting by adding depletion deductions to IRS income figures. Data in the *Statistics of Income* indicate that these deductions totaled $9,301 million for corporations and $429 million for unincorporated enterprises in 1973. The Commerce Department adds the noncorporate figure to its income statistics, but adds only $5,828 million of the corporate figure. The difference ($3,473 million, which equals 37 percent of corporate depletion deductions) is allocated as follows: We take corporate deductions for mining and lumber times .37 and add the result to incomes in those industries. We take the total of crude petroleum and petroleum-refining deductions times .37 and add this to

15. This treatment is consistent with competition and the absence of abnormal profits. If an F&I company is superior at discovering investments for its clients, it can make larger service charges.

income in crude petroleum alone. We do this because the income statistics for petroleum-refining corporations are on a company basis, so their deductions are for crude petroleum operations. These adjustments are reflected in column (1) of table 4.2.

4.3.7 Tax on Capital Income

In our model, the tax on capital income at the industry level has three components—the corporation income tax levied by the federal government, corporation franchise taxes levied by the state governments, and property taxes levied at the state and local levels. We use capital income as the tax base for all three taxes, even though the legal tax bases for the latter two taxes are capital stock and capital assets, respectively.

Information on the corporation income tax comes from table 6.20 of the July 1976 *SCB*. We list this information in column (1) of table 4.4. Information on corporate franchise taxes, from an unpublished worksheet from NID, is displayed in column (2) of table 4.4.

There are no good national statistics for the property tax by industry. The best data for 1973 are contained in a worksheet from NID. The NID data are collected from a wide variety of sources. For some industries data are gathered on yearly property tax payments from publications like *Agriculture Statistics*, *Life Insurance Fact Book*, and *Statistics of Common Carriers*. Property taxes in the manufacturing industries are estimated from a property tax survey in the 1958 *Census of Manufacturing*. In some cases NID took the estimated property tax rate for one of these industries and applied it to an *SOI* estimate of the assets of another industry for which no direct information on property taxes was available. In the remaining industries NID built up an estimate of property taxes for the entire nation by taking a weighted average of the property tax rates of the states.

We must make one adjustment to the NID property tax figures. In adjusting our figures on net rents paid, we move some income from the real estate industry to other industries where industrial real properties were used. The property tax figures from NID still include tax on those properties in the real estate industry, so we redistribute a part of the real estate industry's tax to other industries. Rather than assume the real estate industry tax rate on the income reassigned, we assume the rate of the industry where the property is used. First, we calculate a subtotal for capital income without net rents paid. Then, we calculate effective property tax rates in each industry and apply these rates to the net rent reassigned from NID's real estate industry. The property tax figures with this adjustment are given in column (3) of table 4.4.

Column (4) of table 4.4 shows the sum of the three capital taxes. Total net-of-tax capital income is shown in column (5) of table 4.4. The effective tax rates (column 4 divided by column 5) are shown in column (6),

Table 4.4   Capital Taxes by Industry in the U.S. for 1973 (millions of dollars)

	Corporate Income Tax (1)	Corporate Franchise Tax (2)	Adjusted Property Tax (3)	Total Tax on Capital (4)	Capital Income Net of Tax (5)	Effective Tax Rate (4 ÷ (5)) (6)
All industries	48,702	1,161	46,033	95,896	181,973	.5270
Agriculture, forestry, fisheries	309	10	2,420	2,739	30,778	.0890
Mining	237	8	273	518	1,136	.4560
Crude petroleum and gas	194	4	804	1,002	3,370	.2973
Contract construction	1,012	18	334	1,364	1,023	1.3333
Food and tobacco	2,585	45	617	3,247	1,817	1.7870
Textiles, apparel, and leather	1,221	23	264	1,508	1,086	1.3886
Paper and printing	2,125	31	479	2,635	2,721	.9684
Petroleum refining	1,282	92	256	1,630	8,282	.1968
Chemicals, rubber, and plastics	3,573	44	574	4,191	3,910	1.0719
Lumber, furniture, stone, clay, glass	1,647	28	422	2,097	4,229	.4959
Metals, machinery, instruments, and miscellaneous manufacturing	8,094	138	1,979	10,211	10,401	.9817
Transport equipment and ordnance	536	7	542	1,085	168	6.4583
Motor vehicles	2,974	19	276	3,269	4,847	.6744
Transportation, communications, utilities	4,007	319	5,313	9,639	13,255	.7272
Trade	7,513	125	3,252	10,890	9,721	1.1203
Finance and insurance	9,457[a]	178	968	10,603	7,840	1.3524
Real estate	700	47	25,354	26,101	56,832	.4593
Services	1,236	25	1,906	3,167	12,746	.2485
Government enterprises	0	0	0	0	7,811	.0000

[a]Includes 4,341 for FRB payments to the Treasury.

where .5270 is the average rate for all industries. Agriculture has the lowest effective tax rate and transportation equipment has the highest.[16]

We use capital income net of all taxes to reflect the use of capital in each industry, but we should note that measuring the industrial use of capital services by capital income is not the only method available. Several studies, including those by Kendrick (1976) and Jorgenson and Sullivan (1981) have collected data on capital *stock* by industry. In a perfect risk-free equilibrium with perfect measurement, both data sets would show the same distribution among industries. Capital would be allocated so that the ratio of net capital income to value of capital stock is the same in every industry. Without a perfect equilibrium measurement, however, we could still ignore the capital income figures derived here, use capital stocks, and attribute the same rate of return to all industries. Such alternatives have been investigated, but they do not make a major difference to the results of simulating alternative tax structures in the general equilibrium model.

4.4   Personal Factor Taxes

In section 3.3 we described the construct we use to model the features of the personal income tax (PIT) which discriminate by industry. Equation (3.31) shows how personal taxes are collected at an average personal marginal rate τ on a fraction f_i of the ith industry's payments for capital (CAP_i). This weighted average personal marginal tax rate is 27.8 percent. The personal factor tax (PFT), is thus equal to $CAP_i f_i \tau$. Corrections at the personal level ensure that individual groups pay their own marginal rate, τ_j, ($j = 1, \ldots, 12$) on an average fraction, $\overline{f}$, of capital income from industry.

To calculate the f_i, we use data on the various types of capital income by industry. These include corporate profits (dividends and retained earnings), net interest payments (monetary and imputed), net rent payments (including the imputed net rent from owner-occupied homes), and the return to capital used in noncorporate business. These types of capital income are treated differently by the personal income tax. In our model we calculate the proportion, g, of each type of capital income that is fully taxable by the personal income tax. An industry's f_i is the weighted average of these g proportions. The weights are the amounts of these capital income types in each industry. The formula for f_i is given as

$$(4.1) \quad f_i = \frac{\begin{aligned}DIV_i g_D + RE_i g_{RE} + INT_i g_I + MRENT_i g_{MR} + IRENT_i g_{IR} \\ + NCI_i g_{NC} - (NCITC_i/\tau) + \pi K_i g_{CG}/\gamma\end{aligned}}{DIV_i + RE_i + INT_i + MRENT_i + IRENT_i + NCI_i}$$

where the variables are defined in table 4.5 and discussed further below.

16. The next section describes how we add the personal taxation of capital income by industry to the effective tax rates of table 4.4.

The last term in the numerator of equation (4.1) is $\pi K_i g_{CG}/\gamma$. If π is the rate of inflation with no relative price changes, then nominal appreciation in the ith industry is equal to π times the capital assets used there.[17] We use 7 percent inflation for 1973, from the *Economic Report of the President* (Council of Economic Advisers 1973). In our model, K_i are measured in terms of capital service units, each of which earns a dollar per period in the benchmark. A real after-tax rate of return, $\gamma = .04$, is used to convert between capital stocks and capital service units, as described in section 3.4. Then K_i/γ is measured in capital assets, and $\pi K_i g_{CG}/\gamma$ is the taxable portion of nominal capital gains.

The denominator of (4.1) is equal to CAP_i, defined in section 3.3 as capital income net of corporate and property taxes. Our capital usage by industry, K_i, is net of personal factor taxes:

$$(4.2) \qquad K_i = CAP_i(1 - f_i \tau).$$

Thus the final term in the numerator, which involves K_i, implicitly includes a term in f_i. To solve for f_i by itself, define

$$(4.3) \qquad \begin{aligned} \Lambda_i &\equiv DIV_i g_D + RE_i g_{RE} + INT_i g_I + MRENT_i g_{MR} \\ &+ IRENT_i g_{IR} + NCI_i g_{NC} - (NCITC_i/\tau); \end{aligned}$$

then equation (4.1) can be rewritten as

$$(4.4) \qquad f_i = \frac{\Lambda_i + \pi CAP_i(1 - f_i \tau) g_{CG}/\gamma}{CAP_i}.$$

Solving for f_i, one obtains

$$(4.5) \qquad f_i = \frac{\Lambda_i}{CAP_i} + \frac{\pi g_{CG}}{\gamma}/(1 + \tau \pi_{CG}/\gamma).$$

Table 4.5 summarizes the parameter values we have chosen to implement these equations. In the case of dividends, the federal government lost an estimated $285 million of revenue due to the $100 dividend exclusion from the PIT in 1976 (U.S. Congress 1977). We divide this by τ to get an estimate of nontaxable dividends, equal to $1,024 million. Since total dividends paid were $24,631 million in that year, the proportion taxable was .9584. This figure is used for g_D.

We assume that retained earnings are reflected in appreciated values of

---

17. Relative price changes in 1973 might have provided real capital gains as a major component of capital income in land-intensive industries. However, the return to land is largely included in our return to capital already. Our capital income includes imputed returns to owner-occupied housing, and actual rents paid in all industries, and the profits of corporations that own the land they use. Only real appreciation of idle and vacant land would be excluded from our capital income figures.

corporate stock. Thus retained earnings are subject to some personal taxation through the capital gains tax. We use g_{RE} to denote the effective fraction of retained earnings that is fully taxed by the PIT. Martin Bailey (1969) has provided evidence that an average dollar of retained earnings leads to one dollar of capital gains, in present value terms over the long

Table 4.5   Variables in Equation (4.1) Used to Define f_i, the Proportions of Capital Income Taxable at the Personal Level

Symbol	Definition	Value or Source
DIV_i	Dividends paid by the ith industry	From table 6.22 of the July 1976 *SCB*
g_D	Portion of dividends taxable by personal income tax (PIT)	.9584, as discussed in text
RE_i	Retained earnings of the ith industry	Defined as corporate profits (corrected by the IVA, depletion, and capital consumption adjustments of section 4.3) minus DIV_i
g_{RE}	Portion of retained earnings taxable by PIT	.25, as discussed in text
INT_i	Net monetary and imputed interest paid by the ith industry	Column (5) of table 4.2, as discussed in section 4.3
g_I	Portion of interest taxable by PIT	1.0, since interest is fully taxable
$MRENT_i$	Net monetary rent paid by i^{th} industry	Column (4) of table 4.2 (except real estate), as discussed in section 4.3
g_{MR}	Portion of monetary rent taxable by PIT	1.0, since net rents are fully taxable
$IRENT_i$	Imputed rent earned in the ith industry	Zero for all but real estate, equal to \$10,334 million as shown in table 4.3
g_{IR}	Portion of imputed rent taxable by PIT	0.0, since no PIT on owner-occupied housing
NCI_i	Noncorporate capital income in the ith industry	Column (3) of table 4.2, as discussed in section 4.3
g_{NC}	Portion of noncorporate capital income taxable by PIT	1.0, since NCI is fully taxable
$NCITC_i$	Noncorporate investment tax credit in the ith industry	Described in text and shown in table 4.6
τ	Capital weighted average of personal marginal tax rates	.278, derivation in equation (3.31)
π	Inflation rate	.07, for 1973 from the *Economic Report of the President*
K_i	Use of capital service units in the ith industry	From 1973 capital income net of all tax
γ	Conversion from capital service units to capital assets units	.04, from the real after-tax rate of return as described in the text
g_{CG}	Portion of nominal capital gains taxable by PIT	Differs by industry, as described in text

run.[18] There are, however, tax rate and deferral advantages to this form of capital income. In 1973, gains deferred until death were not taxed at all. Bailey has shown that close to one-half of long-term capital gains is realized in a relatively short period, while the remainder is held for varying durations averaging perhaps thirty-five years or more. Weighing the advantages of deferral and these observations regarding holding periods leads us to the conclusion that a tax on $.25 of regular income would yield approximately the same personal income tax revenue as a tax on one dollar of retained earnings. Therefore, the g_{RE} for retained earnings is set at .25.

A value of 1.0 is assigned to the g parameters for interest, monetary rents, and noncorporate income, since these types of capital income are fully taxable by the personal income tax. Imputed net rents, which appear only in real estate, get a g_{IR} of zero because these are untaxed.

Since the noncorporate investment tax credit reduces the personal income tax (PIT) liability, we include in the numerator of equation (4.1) the amount of income that would result in the reduced tax liability. It is the amount $NCI - (NCITC/\tau)$ that, when multiplied by τ, yields tax collections of $NCI \cdot \tau - NCITC$. The statutory rate of investment tax credit for equipment was 7 percent in 1973. Estimates of the noncorporate investment tax credit (NCITC) here are intended to approximate the amounts that would have accrued by sector in 1973 if a 10 percent credit had been in effect and if there had been no limitations on the use of the credits. The Treasury Department's Office of Tax Analysis provided us with these estimates, and their procedures can be summarized as follows. The total 1973 NCITC estimate of $1,078 million is scaled up by 10/7. To allocate this total among the industries, it is assumed that the ratio of ITC to depreciation is the same for the corporate and noncorporate portions of each industry. Total noncorporate depreciation is taken from the IRS noncorporate *Statistics of Income*. Each industry's corporate depreciation is shown in the July 1976 *SCB*. Using the Treasury Department's corporate ITC estimates for each sector, the ratio of ITC to depreciation is applied to the total noncorporate depreciation. This gives an estimate of each industry's NCITC. This vector is scaled up slightly to the proper total of $1,540 million, shown in table 4.6, column (1).

The final parameter to discuss is g_{CG}. Because nominal capital gains receive the same deferral advantages as real capital gains, we set g_{CG} to .25 for all industries except housing and agriculture. For housing we note that, in value terms, 73 percent of residential structures are owner occupied.[19] We assume that owner-occupants effectively avoid the capital

---

18. For an alternative theoretical view, see Auerbach 1979b, Bradford 1980, and King 1977.

19. Unpublished national balance sheet from the Federal Reserve Board.

Table 4.6   **1973 Noncorporate Investment Tax Credit (in millions of 1973 dollars) and f_i Parameters for Each Industry**

Industry	Noncorporate ITC (1)	f_i Parameters (2)
Agriculture, forestry, fisheries	523.08	1.053
Mining	8.64	0.910
Crude petroleum and gas	18.52	1.281
Contract construction	78.94	0.891
Food and tobacco	4.36	1.353
Textiles, apparel, and leather	2.45	1.164
Paper and printing	15.90	0.899
Petroleum refining	0.00	0.655
Chemicals, rubber, and plastics	6.74	0.996
Lumber, furniture, stone, clay, glass	26.75	0.782
Metals, machinery, instruments, and miscellaneous manufacturing	13.28	0.971
Transport equipment and ordnance	0.73	2.500
Motor vehicles	0.00	0.963
Transportation, communications, utilities	443.76	1.296
Trade	133.54	0.921
Finance and insurance	13.91	0.768
Real estate	77.23	0.376
Services	172.26	1.182
Government enterprises	0.00	0.750
All industries	1,540.00	0.816

gains tax on their housing, whereas landlords pay taxes on 25 percent of their gains. The rate of inclusion on all of housing is thus only $(.27)(.25)$ = .0675. In the agricultural sector most farms are privately held and are seldom exchanged in a taxable manner. We have set g_{CG} in the agricultural sector to .10.

The resulting values for all benchmark f_i are shown in column (2) of table 4.6. Note that the f_i parameter is less than one for most industries. This reflects the low personal taxation of retained earnings and the noncorporate investment tax credit. The f_i for real estate is .376, reflecting the nontaxation of imputed net rents from owner-occupied homes. Some f_i are greater than one, however, because of the taxation of purely nominal capital gains.

The use of capital by government enterprises (industry 19) is assigned an f_i of .75. This reflects roughly the portion of interest payments that is taxable by the personal income tax. Approximately one-fourth of government's interest payments are on nontaxable state and local bonds.[20]

---

20. We assign an f_i of 1.0 to the use of private capital by general government. This simplification aids in our computations, but does not affect general government's capital tax rate, equal to the average industry tax rate (see section 3.5).

Finally, in table 4.7, we use the f_i parameters to derive the amount of personal factor tax in each industry, shown in column (3). When all capital taxes are subtracted from capital income, we have net income of column (4). The last column shows the effective tax rates that we use in the model—the ratios of all taxes to net capital income in each industry. Since the tax rate is defined as taxes relative to net income rather than to the more common use of gross income, the rates can exceed unity.

4.5 Input-Output Transactions Data

Our model requires data on interindustry transactions, that is, each industry's purchases from each other industry. We construct an interindustry transactions table from two separate tables of *The Detailed Input-Output Structure of the U.S. Economy, 1972*, published by the Bureau of Economic Analysis (U.S. Department of Commerce, BEA 1979). The first table is the "make" table, which gives the dollar values of the production of each commodity by each industry. The second is the "use" table, which gives the dollar values of the use of commodities by industries. Our goal is to transform these tables into a single table showing each industry's use of the outputs of the various industries.

To illustrate the procedure, let us consider the case with nineteen industries and eighty-five commodities. The make matrix, M, is thus 19×85 and the use matrix, U, is 85×19. The first step in arriving at a transactions table is to define a 19×85 matrix, $\bar{M}$, which is equal to M with the column sums normalized to unity. The (i, j) element of $\bar{M}$ is the proportion of the total production of commodity j that is produced by industry i. The transactions table, T, (19×19), is given as

$$(4.6) \qquad T_{i,j} = \sum_{k=1}^{19} \bar{M}_{ik} U_{kj} \text{ for } \begin{array}{l} i = 1, \ldots, 19 \\ j = 1, \ldots, 19 \end{array}$$

Figure 4.1 gives an example of the procedure for a hypothetical case of two industries and three commodities.

The resulting 1972 interindustry transactions table reports these transactions in millions of dollars at producer prices. The valuation at producer prices excludes distribution costs. The trade margin and transportation costs appear as inputs to each industry from the trade and transportation industries. It is important to note that only the trade margin is included as an input from the trade industry. The input-output tables do not trace the actual flows of commodities to and from the trade sector. If trade were shown as buying and reselling commodities, other industries would be shown as buying most of their inputs from the trade industry. Instead, commodities are shown as moving directly to the users, bypassing the trade sector.

Table 4.7   Capital Income and Taxes by Industry (in millions of 1973 dollars)

	Gross Income to Capital (1)^a	Corporate and Property Taxes (2)^b	Personal Factor Taxes (3)^c	Net Income to Capital (4)^d	Personal Factor Tax Rate (5)^e	Total Effective Tax Rate (6)^f
All industries	277,869	95,896	40,932	141,041	0.2902	0.9701
Agriculture, forestry, fisheries	33,517	2,739	9,016	21,762	0.4143	0.5402
Mining	1,654	518	288	848	0.3396	0.9505
Crude petroleum and gas	4,372	1,002	1,201	2,169	0.5522	1.0129
Contract construction	2,387	1,364	254	769	0.3303	2.1040
Food and tobacco	5,064	3,247	684	1,133	0.6037	3.4696
Textiles, apparel, and leather	2,594	1,508	352	734	0.4796	2.5341
Paper and printing	5,356	2,635	681	2,040	0.3338	1.6255
Petroleum refining	9,912	1,630	1,509	6,773	0.2228	0.4635
Chemicals, rubber, and plastics	8,101	4,191	1,084	2,826	0.3836	1.8666
Lumber, furniture, stone, clay, glass	6,326	2,097	921	3,308	0.2784	0.9123
Metals, machinery, instruments, and miscellaneous manufacturing	20,612	10,211	2,812	7,589	0.3705	1.7160
Transport equipment and ordnance	1,253	1,085	117	51	2.2941	23.5686
Motor vehicles	8,116	3,269	1,299	3,548	0.3661	1.2875
Transportation, communications, utilities	22,894	9,639	4,781	8,474	0.5642	1.7017
Trade	20,611	10,890	2,491	7,230	0.3445	1.8508
Finance and insurance	18,443	10,603	1,676	6,164	0.2719	1.9921
Real estate	82,933	26,101	5,945	50,887	0.1168	0.6298
Services	15,913	3,167	4,192	8,554	0.4901	0.8603
Government enterprises	7,811	0	1,630	6,181	0.2637	0.2637

^a Sum of columns (4) and (5) from table 4.4.
^b Column (4) of table 4.4.
^c $\tau_{fi} \cdot [(1) - (2)]$.
^d $(1) - (2) - (3)$.
^e $(3)/(4)$.
^f $((2) + (3)/(4))$.

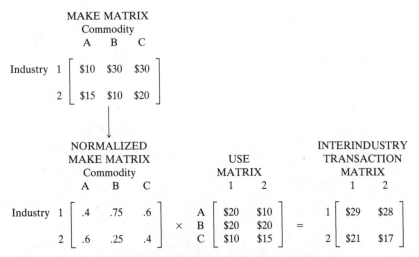

Figure 4.1   Example of construction of interindustry transactions table from make table and use table.

Table 4.8   United States Interindustry Transactions, 1972 (in millions of dollars at producers' prices)

	1	2	3	4	5	6	7	8	9
1.	26436.7	.5	.2	329.0	37436.9	1298.6	44.1	5.2	133.6
2.	166.1	1054.0	2.2	1394.1	55.5	27.9	203.5	129.1	945.5
3.	35.5	8.1	597.4	86.6	12.5	6.7	11.5	15007.6	93.9
4.	583.0	123.0	735.0	47.0	238.0	85.0	300.0	543.0	493.0
5.	5297.3	2.1	5.4	53.2	22976.1	517.4	192.2	48.7	611.3
6.	239.6	25.5	3.1	788.4	109.6	25829.1	387.9	13.3	1094.7
7.	281.4	93.8	63.0	1819.1	2378.6	483.8	10922.5	201.6	1613.2
8.	1341.3	222.6	70.8	3109.0	309.0	204.3	345.0	2308.3	1239.8
9.	3368.5	325.9	111.4	3629.9	1943.5	5663.5	1932.0	925.1	16671.7
10.	302.4	108.6	8.8	20545.1	4276.7	814.6	2160.5	205.9	1614.7
11.	929.8	1153.6	667.6	29355.0	4361.2	1194.9	1094.1	485.5	3193.9
12.	81.8	21.6	9.2	134.1	10.3	10.5	21.6	1.5	23.8
13.	62.6	62.7	6.3	192.7	32.8	14.4	34.5	3.0	46.9
14.	2138.6	572.0	378.1	5324.5	4429.3	1849.9	3046.1	2399.7	4873.7
15.	3036.0	358.9	91.2	12688.4	5083.5	2510.5	1666.7	295.5	2066.3
16.	1150.3	133.7	116.2	1072.5	600.5	348.1	382.6	205.7	538.0
17.	4730.8	666.7	2706.8	1013.0	575.9	644.8	1549.0	290.4	1487.1
18.	1436.0	390.8	462.8	7940.9	3869.2	1592.6	2629.9	643.5	5318.0
19.	172.0	93.0	53.7	319.2	389.9	258.7	636.7	175.5	485.8

The aggregated 19 × 19 matrix for 1972 appears in table 4.8.[21] The elements, (i, j), of this matrix are the amounts of the output of industry i that are used by industry j. Thus, if we look down the fifth column, we see that the food industry buys more from agriculture, forestry, and fisheries ($37,437 million) than from any other industry. Columns (8), (13), and (17) also provide intuitive stories: petroleum refining uses much crude petroleum, the motor vehicles industry is a heavy user of primary and fabricated metal and machinery, and real estate purchases a large amount from the construction industry. At this level of aggregation the elements along the diagonal of the matrix are quite large. If we were to use a more disaggregated industry classification, these diagonal elements would be relatively smaller.

Finally, this (19 × 19) transactions table is updated to 1973. Each column is multiplied by the ratio of 1973 value added to 1972 value added for that industry. These ratios are based on unpublished data from the Commerce Department's National Income Division. Since value added data are not available for the government enterprises industry, we use the weighted average ratio for the eighteen private industries. Table 4.9 contains all nineteen ratios. The only ratio far from the average is

21. The correspondence between the classification of the original matrix and our nineteen industries is in Appendix A of this chapter.

10	11	12	13	14	15	16	17	18	19
1809.0	93.6	13.3	5.3	202.2	127.4	9.8	730.7	2204.2	198.8
1165.3	4660.9	11.3	30.7	2316.7	2.3	.3	3.2	40.0	315.8
19.8	44.5	4.7	4.5	3879.5	58.9	7.7	16.8	56.9	16.9
306.0	1066.0	110.0	108.0	5013.0	863.0	298.0	10786.0	2631.0	2672.0
60.5	198.6	41.4	13.5	187.1	139.8	73.8	17.2	16450.7	56.2
888.3	921.2	292.2	1312.8	165.2	162.4	53.7	5.5	1487.8	69.5
3739.2	2447.6	262.4	290.8	1137.0	3320.6	2444.9	454.8	4388.3	251.4
575.9	1124.7	124.1	113.4	3879.7	1494.6	152.3	436.4	1375.3	304.9
2323.9	7060.0	524.2	2174.6	733.9	574.1	51.2	284.5	4430.0	321.4
11343.3	4853.0	1208.0	1394.8	92.5	477.3	9.2	3.8	1233.8	16.1
3352.6	81818.7	8636.5	16678.5	2175.6	590.1	237.2	114.4	7892.8	204.0
22.0	400.5	4092.2	125.7	1135.7	16.1	13.3	6.7	236.9	36.5
72.8	992.3	384.7	14461.5	341.8	73.3	8.6	4.9	5683.7	55.3
4276.3	10522.6	1058.0	1544.3	21578.3	9298.7	3075.8	1478.7	10611.3	2916.6
2249.7	8367.4	1043.1	3341.4	2309.2	2985.4	388.7	505.7	7259.9	182.4
500.2	1823.2	207.2	234.2	2636.6	3021.6	15580.9	3359.7	3446.3	268.0
707.6	2833.5	228.6	102.8	2655.9	8925.7	2468.2	11684.4	13999.9	450.1
1850.5	8948.8	1907.3	1672.1	8113.0	16240.7	7294.8	2856.3	22367.1	880.6
334.0	1095.8	134.8	169.1	2527.9	1750.6	1603.6	724.4	2317.3	323.5

Table 4.9   The Ratio of 1973 to 1972 Value Added in Each Industry

Industry	Ratio
1. Agriculture, forestry, fisheries	1.60012
2. Mining	1.27529
3. Crude petroleum and gas	1.09324
4. Contract construction	1.11718
5. Food and tobacco	1.01805
6. Textiles, apparel, and leather	1.06051
7. Paper and printing	1.12247
8. Petroleum refining	1.27558
9. Chemicals, rubber, and plastics	1.11344
10. Lumber, furniture, stone, clay, glass	1.15656
11. Metals, machinery, instruments, and miscellaneous manufacturing	1.14957
12. Transport equipment and ordnance	1.04596
13. Motor vehicles	1.13872
14. Transportation, communications, utilities	1.10443
15. Trade	1.11694
16. Finance and insurance	1.06860
17. Real estate	1.10290
18. Services	1.11783
19. Government enterprises	1.12368

agriculture, forestry, and fisheries. The large increase in value added in this industry is due largely to the sharp increase in grain prices that occurred at that time.

4.6 The Matrix of Transition between Producer Goods and Consumer Goods

The nineteen goods produced by our industry divisions do not correspond to the commodities purchased by consumers. For example, consumers make very few direct purchases of the outputs of the mining and crude petroleum industries. The same is true of the primary metals and machinery industries. Trade services and commodity transportation services are only purchased indirectly by consumers. The aggregate consumption vector for final demands of households, derived from table 2.6 of the July 1976 *SCB*, contains fifteen commodities rather than the nineteen industry outputs. The total is adjusted to exclude expenditures in the United States by foreigners. We also adjust the total to include the $15,388 million imputed service charge payments from consumers to the finance and insurance industry, which was discussed in section 4.3 above. After these adjustments, the total of $827,525 million in consumption expenditures on fifteen consumer goods corresponds directly to the $827,525 million consumption demand for nineteen producer goods. The latter vector represents the industry outputs that are used to form the fifteen consumer goods.

To accommodate these different classifications, we treat these producer goods as being converted into consumer goods by a fixed-coefficient Z matrix, estimated from table B in the February 1974 *SCB*. This table used 1967 input-output data and can easily be transcribed to an 86 $\times$ 84 matrix where the (i, m) element is the total amount of producer goods i used in consumer good m. The eighty-six industries used by the Bureau of Economic Analysis aggregate directly to our definition of nineteen industries. Their eighty-four consumption categories aggregate to our fifteen consumer goods according to information in Appendix B of this chapter.

We calculate the amounts of producer goods used by the saving commodity (commodity 16) by using data on business investment from the 1972 input-output table, scaled up to 1973 levels. We impose the requirement that the total saving of consumers should exactly equal the net investment of the business sector. After we add these amounts of producer goods used by the saving commodity, we have a 19 $\times$ 16 matrix. This matrix gives the amount of each industry's output used in producing each of the consumer goods. We divide each element of this matrix by its column total in order to obtain the Z matrix coefficients. These coefficients are presented in table 4.10. This table is fairly straightforward. The reader will not be surprised to see that most of food is produced by the food industry, most of housing by real estate, etc.

Each consumer good price is a weighted average of the producer good prices, where the weights are the elements of the appropriate column from the Z matrix. Demands for consumer goods are calculated using the sixteen prices and the consumer demand functions. When we feed the vector of total demands for consumer goods through the Z matrix, we get the consumption demands for the nineteen producer goods, as shown in figure 4.2.

4.7 Government Enterprises

Some publicly supplied goods and services are subject to a price, or user charge. In our model these goods and services are produced by the government enterprises industry (industry 19). We separate this industry from the other functions of government. In this section we present data for the government enterprises industry. The data cover labor use and taxes, capital use and taxes, and subsidies received.

Data on employee compensation for federal, state, and local government enterprises are available in unpublished, disaggregated tables that correspond to table 6.1 of the July 1976 *SCB*. We present these data in

Table 4.10   1973 Z Matrix Linking Producer and Consumer Good Classifications after Consistency Adjustments

Producer Good Classification	Consumer Good Classification							
	Food (1)	Alcoholic Beverages (2)	Tobacco (3)	Utilities (4)	Housing (5)	Furnishings (6)	Appliances (7)	Clothing and Jewelry (8)
1. Agriculture	0.054937	0.0	0.0	0.0	0.0	0.0	0.0	0.0
2. Mining	0.000021	0.0	0.0	0.0	0.0	0.0	0.0	0.0
3. Crude petroleum	0.0	0.0	0.0	0.0	0.0	0.0	0.0	0.0
4. Construction	0.0	0.0	0.0	0.0	0.0	0.0	0.0	0.0
5. Food and tobacco	0.571470	0.509381	0.591006	0.0	0.0	0.0	0.0	0.0
6. Textiles and apparel	0.0	0.0	0.0	0.0	0.0	0.184731	0.0	0.491791
7. Paper and printing	0.0	0.0	0.0	0.0	0.0	0.004101	0.0	0.001528
8. Petroleum refining	0.0	0.0	0.0	0.0	0.0	0.0	0.0	0.0
9. Chemicals	0.000241	0.0	0.0	0.0	0.0	0.005086	0.018693	0.010041
10. Lumber and furniture	0.0	0.0	0.0	0.0	0.0	0.236246	0.024396	0.0
11. Metal and machinery	0.0	0.0	0.0	0.0	0.0	0.080389	0.552817	0.038513
12. Transport equipment	0.0	0.0	0.0	0.0	0.0	0.000602	0.0	0.0
13. Motor vehicles	0.0	0.0	0.0	0.0	0.0	0.0	0.0	0.0
14. Transportation, communications	0.023043	0.013253	0.003813	0.984237	0.0	0.015258	0.016919	0.007251
15. Trade	0.350172	0.477365	0.405181	0.0	0.0	0.473477	0.387048	0.432833
16. Finance and insurance	0.000115	0.0	0.0	0.0	0.0	0.000109	0.000127	0.000146
17. Real estate	0.0	0.0	0.0	0.0	0.963323	0.0	0.0	0.0
18. Services	0.0	0.0	0.0	0.0	0.036677	0.0	0.0	0.017898
19. Government enterprises	0.0	0.0	0.0	0.015763	0.0	0.0	0.0	0.0

Consumer Good Classification

Producer Good Classification	Transportation (9)	Motor Vehicles (10)	Services (11)	Financial Services (12)	Reading, etc. (13)	Non-durable Nonfood (14)	Gasoline (15)	Savings (16)
1. Agriculture	0.0	0.0	0.0	0.0	0.049808	0.0	0.0	0.031513
2. Mining	0.0	0.0	0.0	0.0	0.0	0.000196	0.005499	0.013787
3. Crude petroleum	0.0	0.0	0.0	0.0	0.0	0.0	0.0	0.003978
4. Construction	0.0	0.0	0.0	0.0	0.0	0.0	0.0	0.459195
5. Food and tobacco	0.0	0.0	0.0	0.0	0.0	0.0	0.001545	-0.010129
6. Textiles and apparel	0.0	0.001242	0.0	0.0	0.006637	0.003132	0.0	-0.005661
7. Paper and printing	0.0	0.0	0.0	0.0	0.191114	0.101444	0.0	0.001125
8. Petroleum refining	0.0	0.0	0.0	0.0	0.0	0.0	0.463279	-0.000155
9. Chemicals	0.0	0.040905	0.0	0.0	0.001975	0.380230	0.001182	0.012216
10. Lumber and furniture	0.0	0.000055	0.001134	0.0	0.0	0.002594	0.001182	0.018404
11. Metal and machinery	0.0	0.050842	0.0	0.0	0.154909	0.073403	0.000091	0.274652
12. Transport equipment	0.0	0.007866	0.0	0.0	0.063302	0.0	0.0	0.003429
13. Motor vehicles	0.0	0.436738	0.0	0.0	0.0	0.0	0.0	0.047273
14. Transportation, communications	0.889504	0.015346	0.013243	0.0	0.059078	0.014387	0.040584	0.020776
15. Trade	0.0	0.223930	0.001275	0.0	0.322216	0.424615	0.486639	0.117918
16. Finance and insurance	0.0	0.000359	0.006236	1.000000	0.000110	0.0	0.0	0.000086
17. Real estate	0.0	0.0	0.005070	0.0	0.0	0.0	0.0	0.013863
18. Services	0.0	0.222716	0.953794	0.0	0.150850	0.0	0.0	-0.002270
19. Government enterprises	0.110496	0.0	0.019258	0.0	0.0	0.0	0.0	0.0

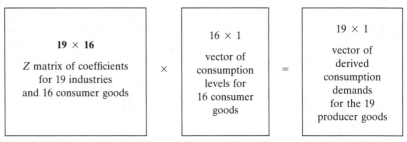

Fig. 4.2   Use of the *Z* matrix to create a vector of derived consumption demands for the producer goods.

table 4.11. Employer and employee contributions to retirement programs are given in table 3.11 of the July 1976 *SCB*. The total contribution for government employment is multiplied by the fraction of government labor in government enterprises, to produce an estimate of the labor tax attributable to this industry. The total tax is $1,557 million. When we subtract this figure from the gross-of-tax wage bill of $16,723 million, we get a net-of-tax labor bill of $15,166 million. The rate of tax on net-of-tax labor is .1027.

Capital estimates are considerably more difficult to produce. The *SCB* shows a profit-type return for government enterprises. This corresponds to their "surplus," which is often negative. Even if the aveiage surplus were positive, this would not be an appropriate measure of the return to capital in government enterprises. Our procedure is to impute the amount of capital, used by the government enterprises industry, on the basis of capital/labor ratios in those private activities that are most similar to the activities of the government enterprises.

Seven components of this industry are listed in table 4.12 along with the comparable private industries. Since employee compensation data were

Table 4.11   Government Enterprise Labor Use and Tax (in millions of 1973 dollars)

	Federal	State and Local	Total
1. Government enterprise labor	$10,484	$6,239	$16,723
2. Total government labor	$62,407	$103,378	$165,785
3. Proportion of labor government enterprises $(1 \div 2)$	0.1680	0.0604	0.1009
4. Employer retirement contributions	$3,217	$6,828	$10,045
5. Employee retirement contributions	$2,246	$3,765	$6,011
6. Total contributions $(3 + 4)$	$5,463	$10,593	$16,056
7. Estimated labor tax in government enterprises (6×3)	$918	$639	$1,557

Table 4.12   Government Enterprise Components and Capital Estimates

	Intermediate Inputs (1)	Proportions of Total Inputs (2)	Corresponding Private Industry (3)	K/L Ratio of Private Industry (4)	Weighted K/L (2 × 4) (5)
Federal Total	3,075	1.00	—	—	.4020
Post office	1,233	.40	services	.14	.0560
Electric utilities	236	.08	utilities	1.07	.0856
Commodity credit corp.	863	.28	finance & insurance	.57	.1596
Other	743	.24	overall	.42	.1008
State and Local Total	4,405	1.00	—	—	.5764
Passenger transit	334	.08	transportation	.10	.0080
Electric utilities	1,221	.28	utilities	1.07	.2996
Other	2,851	.64	overall	.42	.2688

not available in this detail, and since value added includes the mismeasured surplus, we used the sum of intermediate inputs as a measure of the relative size of these activities. The inputs shown in column (1) are from the 1967 detailed input-output table. We assume that the proportions in column (2) would still be appropriate in 1973. Column (4) contains the capital/labor ratio (gross-of-tax) for the private counterparts of these activities, obtained from industry data presented earlier in this chapter. When we use gross-of-tax ratios, we impute a higher capital/labor ratio for the government enterprises industry than might seem appropriate, because the government pays no tax on the capital it uses. However, we believe this is appropriate treatment, since it also implies the same ratio of the marginal product of capital to the marginal product of labor in both the public and private portions of each industry.

We use the relative sizes of the seven components to get weighted averages of these capital/labor ratios for federal and for state and local government enterprises. Multiplying the federal ratio of .4020 by the federal government enterprises' use of labor capital of $10,484 million yields a capital estimate of $4,125 million. The state and local labor ratio is .5764. Multiplying this by labor of $6,239 million yields a $3,596 million capital estimate. Their sum of $7,811 million is the final gross-of-tax and net-of-tax capital estimate for government enterprises.

Finally, we use an estimate of the subsidy to the government enterprises industry. Capital use is valued at $7,811 million, while the 1973 surplus of government enterprises (from tables 3.2 and 3.4 of the July *SCB*) totals only $1,601 million. The difference of $6,210 million is the implied subsidy on these operations. NID worksheets list a single indirect business tax of $78 million for this industry, so the final output tax attributed to it is − $6,132 million. When we divide this figure by the total demand for the output of the government enterprises industry ($22,564 million), we have a 27 percent rate of subsidy on the output of this industry. The effect of this negative output tax is to lower the output price faced by purchasers.

Purchases by government other than those for public enterprises are considered an element of final demand and are described in the next chapter.

4.8 Other Production Taxes

The NID has provided a worksheet with their estimates of the amount of each indirect business tax paid by each industry in 1973. Each of these taxes requires a model-equivalent treatment that matches as closely as possible the legal base, rates, and rules of the tax.

State and local sales taxes are represented by various rates of tax on consumption. We will discuss these taxes in chapter 5. The motor vehicles

Table 4.13   Production Taxes

	Gross Output[a] (1)	Output Taxes (2)	Rate of Output Tax (3)	Intermediate Use of Motor Vehicles (4)	Estimated Tax on Use of Motor Vehicles (5)
All industries	2,001,452.0	15,060	—	31,162.4	1,656.00
Agriculture, forestry, fisheries	113,923.6	68	.0006	42.4	2.25
Mining	14,641.1	73	.0050	25.3	1.34
Crude petroleum and gas	15,092.0	826	.0547	0.0	.00
Contract construction	136,826.1	334	.0024	10.3	.55
Food and tobacco	134,519.6	379	.0028	11.3	.60
Textiles, apparel, and leather	70,081.8	28	.0004	7.6	.40
Paper and printing	54,179.7	38	.0007	0.0	.00
Petroleum refining	37,570.1	4,202	.1118	7.6	.40
Chemicals, rubber, and plastics	80,409.2	926	.0115	115.1	6.12
Lumber, furniture, stone, clay, glass	61,893.9	24	.0004	66.8	3.55
Metals, machinery, instruments, and miscellaneous manufacturing	252,288.7	199	.0008	3,678.7	195.49
Transport equipment, and ordnance	30,810.5	81	.0026	824.0	43.79
Motor vehicles	64,530.0	629	.0097	20,239.0	1,075.53
Transportation, communications, and utilities	163,899.9	5,919	.0361	283.8	15.08
Trade	229,707.5	3,237	.0141	275.7	14.65
Finance and insurance	96,306.9	1,155	.0120	0.0	.00
Real estate	163,230.8	2,856	.0175	660.4	35.09
Services	258,976.7	218	.0008	4,861.9	258.37
Government enterprises	22,563.9	−6,132[b]	−.2718	52.5	2.79

[a]In millions of 1973 dollars, from the *I/O* table, after RAS method.
[b]As described in section 4.7, "Government Enterprises."

tax is treated as a tax on the use of one product by other producers, i.e., as a tax on intermediate inputs. We divide the total collection of $1,656 million among producers according to their use of motor vehicles. We use the updated 1973 input-output table to determine each industry's purchase of this input. These are shown in column (4) of table 4.13. The estimated motor vehicle tax paid is shown in column (5).

We include state public utility taxes as a tax on the output of the transportation, communications, and utilities industry. We model severance taxes as a tax on the outputs of two industries: mining, and petroleum and gas. We treat occupation and business taxes, other license fees, and other taxes as ad valorem taxes on the output of various industries. The same is true for nontax payments. This last category includes inspection fees, special assessments, fines, etc.

Federal excise taxes and customs duties are the only categories that require an adjustment from NID estimates. The NID attributes manufacturers' excise taxes to the appropriate industry, but some of retailers' excises and customs payments appear under retail and wholesale trade. We reallocate a portion of these latter taxes, since they are not taxes on the output of the trade industry. We perform this reallocation using table 3 of the 1974 *Annual Report of the Commissioner of Internal Revenue* (U.S. Department of the Treasury, IRS 1974).

The result of these procedures is shown in table 4.13, column (2), where the output tax is the sum of federal excises, public utility, severance, occupation, and business taxes, license fees, and nontax payments to government. The negative output tax on government enterprises represents the subsidy discussed in the last section. Column (1) of table 4.13 shows the gross value of output.[22] If we divide column (2) by column (1), we get the output tax rates in column (3).

22. These figures reflect our consistency procedures. We describe these consistency procedures in chapter 6. They ensure that gross output can be measured by the sum of inputs and production taxes in an industry, *or* by the sum of intermediate and final uses of the product.

Appendixes

Appendix A

Table 4.A.1   **Correspondences between Our Producer Goods and Bureau of Economic Analysis (BEA) Categories**

Classification of Rows		Corresponding Elements from Original Matrix	
Row Number of Aggregated Matrix	Industry	Code Number(s) from Original Matrix	Numerical Position of Row(s) in Original Matrix
1.	Agriculture, forestry, fisheries	1,2,3,4	/1,2,3,4
2.	Mining	5,6,7,9,10	/5,6,7,9,10
3.	Crude petroleum and gas	8	/8
4.	Contract construction	11,12	/11,12
5.	Food and tobacco	14,15	/14,15
6.	Textiles, apparel, and leather	16,17,18,19,33,34	/16,17,18,19,33,34
7.	Paper and printing	24,25,26	/24,25,26
8.	Petroleum refining	31	/31
9.	Chemicals, rubber, and plastics	27,28,29,30,32	/27,28,29,30,32
10.	Lumber, furniture, stone, clay, glass	20,21,22,23,35,36	/20,21,22,23,35,36
11.	Metals, machinery, instruments, and miscellaneous manufacturing	37,38,39,40,41, 42,43,44,45,46, 47,48,49,50,51, 52,53,54,55,56, 57,58,62,63,64, 82,83	/37,38,39,40,41, 42,43,44,45,46, 47,48,49,50,51, 52,53,54,55,56, 57,58,62,63,64, 82,83
12.	Transport equipment and ordnance	13,60,61	/13,60,61
13.	Motor vehicles	59	/59
14.	Transportation, communications, and utilities	65,66,67,68	/65,66,67,68

Table 4.A.1 (continued)

Classification of Rows		Corresponding Elements from Original Matrix	
Row Number of Aggregated Matrix	Industry	Code Number(s) from Original Matrix	Numerical Position of Row(s) in Original Matrix
15.	Trade	69	/69
16.	Finance and insurance	70	/70
17.	Real estate	71	/71
18.	Services	72,73,75,76,77,81	/72,73,74,75,76,81
19.	Government enterprises	78,79	/77,78
20.	Directly allocated imports	80A	/79
21.	Transferred imports	80B	/80
22.	Total intermediate inputs	I.	/88
23.	Special industries	84,85,86,87	/84,85,86,87

Classification of Columns		Corresponding Elements from Original Matrix	
Column Number of Aggregated Matrix	Industry	Code Number(s) from Original Matrix	Numerical Position of Column(s) in Original Matrix
1.	Agriculture, forestry, fisheries	1,2,3,4	/1,2,3,4
2.	Mining	5,6,7,9,10	/5,6,7,9,10
3.	Crude petroleum and gas	8	/8
4.	Contract construction	11,12	/11,12
5.	Food and tobacco	14,15	/14,15
6.	Textiles, apparel, and leather	16,17,18,19,33,34	/16,17,18,19,33,34
7.	Paper and printing	24,25,26	/24,25,26
8.	Petroleum refining	31	/31
9.	Chemicals, rubber, and plastics	27,28,29,30,32	/27,28,29,30,32
10.	Lumber, furniture, stone, clay, glass	20,21,22,23,35,36	/20,21,22,23,35,36
11.	Metals, machinery, instruments, and miscellaneous manufacturing	37,38,39,40,41, 42,43,44,45,46, 47,48,49,50,51, 52,53,54,55,56, 57,58,62,63,64, 82,83	/37,38,39,40,41, 42,43,44,45,46, 47,48,49,50,51, 52,53,54,55,56, 57,58,62,63,64, 81,82
12.	Transport equipment and ordnance	13,60,61	/13,60,61
13.	Motor vehicles	59	/59
14.	Transportation, communications, and utilities	65,66,67,68	/65,66,67,68
15.	Trade	69	/69
16.	Finance and insurance	70	/70
17.	Real estate	71	/71
18.	Services	72,73,75,76,77,81	/72,73,74,75,76,80
19.	Government enterprises	78,79	/77,78

Table 4.A.1 (continued)

Classification of Columns		Corresponding Elements from Original Matrix	
Column Number of Aggregated Matrix	Industry	Code Number(s) from Original Matrix	Numerical Position of Column(s) in Original Matrix
20. Imports		80	/79
21. Special industries		84,85,86,87	/83,84,85,86
22. Total intermediate output		88	/87
23. Personal consumption expenditures		91	/88
24. Gross private fixed capital formation		92	/89
25. Net inventory change		93	/90
26. Net exports		94	/91
27. Federal government purchases		97	/92
28. Federal government purchases, defense		9710	/93
29. Federal government purchases, nondefense		9720	/94
30. State and local government purchases		98	/95
31. State and local government purchases, education		9860	/96
32. State and local government purchases, other		9899	/97
33. Total final demand		9902	/98
34. Total output		9903	/99
35. Transfers out		9904	/100

Appendix B

Table 4.A.2   **Correspondences between Our Consumer Goods and Bureau of Economic Analysis (BEA) Categories (February 1974 *SCB*)**

Our Categories	Bureau of Economic Analysis Categories
Food	Food purchased for off-premises consumption
	Purchased meals and beverages
	Foor furnished to government and commercial employees
	Food produced and consumed on farms
Alcoholic beverages	(Subdivision of the food categories)
Tobacco	Tobacco products
Utilities	Electricity
	Gas
	Water and other sanitary services
	Telephone and telegraph
Housing	Owner-occupied nonfarm dwellings
	Tenant-occupied nonfarm dwellings
	Farmhouses
	Other housing

Table 4.A.2 (continued)

Our Categories	Bureau of Economic Analysis Categories
Furnishings	Furniture
	Other durable house furnishings
	Semidurable house furnishings
Appliances	Kitchen and other household appliances
	China, glassware, tableware
	Radio and TV receivers, musical instruments
Clothing and jewelry	Shoes and other footwear
	Women's and children's clothing
	Men's and boy's clothing
	Clothing issued to military personnel
	Jewelry and watches
	Other clothing, accessories, and jewelry
Transportation	Bridge, tunnel, ferry, and road tolls
	Street and electric railway and local bus
	Taxicabs
	Commuter railway
	Other railway
	Intercity bus
	Airline
	Other intercity transportation
Motor vehicles, tires, and auto repair	New and used cars
	Tires, tubes, accessories, and parts
	Automobile repair, greasing, washing, parking, storage, and rental
Services	Shoe cleaning and repair
	Cleaning and repair of garments
	Laundering
	Barbershops, beauty parlors
	Domestic service
	Other household operation
	Physicians
	Dentists
	Other professional service
	Legal service
	Funeral and burial expenses
	Other personal business
	Radio and TV repair
	Admissions to motion picture theaters
	Admissions to other theaters
	Admissions to spectator sports
	Clubs and fraternal organizations
	Commercial participant amusements
	Pari-mutuel net receipts
	Private higher education
	Private elementary and secondary schools
	Other private education and research
	Religious and welfare activities

Table 4.A.2 (continued)

Our Categories	Bureau of Economic Analysis Categories
Financial services	Health insurance
	Brokerage charges and investment counseling
	Bank service charges
	Services furnished without payment by financial intermediaries except insurance companies
	Expense of handling life insurance
	Automobile insurance premiums less claims paid
Recreation, reading, and miscellaneous	Books and maps
	Magazines, newspapers, and sheet music
	Nondurable toys and sports supplies
	Wheel goods, durable toys and sports equipment, boats, pleasure aircraft.
	Flowers, seeds, and potted plants
	Other recreation
	Foreign travel by U.S. residents
Nondurable, nonfood household items	Toilet articles and preparations
	Cleaning and polishing preparations, household supplies
	Stationery and writing supplies
	Drug preparations and sundries
	Ophthalmic products and orthopedic appliances
Gasoline and other fuel	Other fuel and ice
	Gasoline and oil

5 Data on Household Income and Expenditure, Investment, the Government, and Foreign Trade

5.1 Composition of Final Demands

Our model includes four major components of final demand for each of the nineteen goods. These vectors are private consumption, (C), business investment, (I), government purchases, (G), and total exports, (E). Intermediate input requirements are given by the product of the input-output coefficient matrix, (A), and the domestic gross output vector, (X). The gross supply of a good is simply the sum of domestic gross output, (X), and imports, (M). In equilibrium, total supply equals total demand for every commodity. For all commodities taken together, this relationship can be expressed as

$$(5.1) \qquad X + M = AX + C + I + G + E.$$

Rearrangement allows us to express gross output, X, as a function of other variables:

$$(5.2) \qquad X = (I^* - A)^{-1}(C + I + G + E - M),$$

where I^* is the identity matrix. For a given price vector, evaluation of the right-hand side of equation (5.2) provides the amount of domestic production necessary to satisfy demand.

Table 5.1 shows final demand data for each of the nineteen producer goods in the model. Column (1) provides consumption, (C), columns (2) and (3) together are used to obtain investment, (I), while columns (4), (5), and (6) represent government expenditure, (G), exports, (E), and imports, (M), respectively. Much of the rest of the chapter consists of a discussion of how we derive these data.

All agents finance their final demands with their disposable incomes. We assume that each agent obeys the relevant budget constraint. Private

Table 5.1   Components of Final Demand, Estimates by Industry for 1973 (in millions of dollars)

	Personal Consumption Expenditures (1)	Gross Private Fixed Capital Formation (2)	Net Inventory Change (3)	General Government Expenditures (4)	Exports (5)	Imports (6)
ALL INDUSTRIES	827,520.0	202,092.0	18,787	119,764	84,598.8	84,598.8
Agriculture, forestry, fisheries	10,194.9	0.0	3,248	−1,526	10,313.2	4,707.3
Mining	266.3	0.0	1,421	217	1,253.3	1,221.5
Crude petroleum and gas	0.0	0.0	410	0	103.1	5,190.6
Contract construction	0.0	115,132.0	−773	45,690	0.0	0.0
Food and tobacco	105,701.8	0.0	−1,044	1,522	6,831.7	5,690.4
Textiles, apparel, and leather	36,571.4	163.9	−652	669	3,475.3	5,741.5
Paper and printing	9,656.8	0.0	116	2,178	1,405.6	2,170.0
Petroleum refining	16,673.5	0.0	−16	1,501	556.7	3,139.8
Chemicals, rubber, and plastics	17,795.8	38.6	1,243	4,141	6,259.0	3,509.5
Lumber, furniture, stone, clay, and glass	8,154.0	2,508.2	849	927	1,700.9	2,760.9
Metals, machinery, instruments, and miscellaneous manufacturing	29,956.9	42,279.4	10,644	14,117	27,499.4	25,250.3
Transport equipment and ordnance	3,045.0	8,478.8	−3,189	16,103	4,653.3	1,084.2
Motor vehicles	21,643.9	16,154.6	−1,877	2,503	6,080.0	10,238.9
Transportation, communications, and utilities	57,192.2	3,493.1	682	9,961	8,662.3	11,584.3
Trade	191,084.4	10,040.2	7,959	2,121	0.0	0.0
Finance and insurance	57,997.9[a]	21.3	0	884	0.0	0.0
Real estate	122,201.5	3,419.9	0	1,783	0.0	0.0
Services	135,514.7	0.0	−234	16,154	5,805.0	2,309.6
Government enterprises	3,873.8	0.0	0	818	0.0	0.0

[a]Includes imputed service charge payments.

consumption is financed by household capital income, labor income, and transfer payments, less taxes and savings. The government finances transfer payments and commodity purchases with net government income. Business investments are financed by household savings. The foreign sector finances export demand by sales of imports to the United States. In this chapter we also present data on income and expenditures for each of these groups.

5.2   Disposition of Consumer Income

5.2.1   Expenditures on Commodities by Consumer Class

During 1972–74, the Bureau of Labor Statistics conducted a Consumer Expenditure Survey. This survey provides all of the household expenditure data for our model. The data are disaggregated by current gross income ranges for 1973, which are shown in table 3.1.

The survey consists of two separate components, each with its own sample of about 10,000 families each year. The first component is an interview panel survey for which each consumer unit was visited by an interviewer every three months over a fifteen-month period. The second component is a diary or record-keeping survey, completed by respondents for two consecutive one-week periods. The diary component was designed to gather information on small, frequently purchased items; the interview survey was designed to focus on larger items. Both surveys provide average expenditures for a household in each income class. In principle, these should be comparable. However, the diary survey provides average weekly expenditures for fiscal years. Therefore, it is necessary to multiply by fifty-two and take a price-indexed average of two fiscal years to get average yearly expenditures by income class for calendar year 1973. For the most part we use data from the interview survey. We supplement these data with information from the diary survey in a few cases.

The consumption data from the interview surveys are broken down into fifty-four categories. We use a detailed description of these categories in order to place them as accurately as possible into our classification of fifteen consumer goods. In the appendix to this chapter we show the correspondence between these categories. In that table we have indicated those categories for which the data come from the diary survey, rather than from the interview survey.[1]

1. In four instances we did not use the categories from the interview survey. First, none of the categories from the interview describes our nondurable household commodity very well, so we use different categories from the diary survey. Second, we chose not to use the personal care category from the interview survey. This category contains some appliances, some services, and some nondurable household items. Instead, we chose a more disaggre-

We adjust purchases of financial services to account for imputed interest and service charge payments. These adjustments have already been described in section 4.3. The $15,388 million of imputed interest income from the production data are spent on imputed service charge payments, and we use Consumer Expenditure Survey data on ownership of financial assets to allocate proportionately these expenditures among the twelve consumer groups.

In table 5.2 we show the average yearly per household expenditures of each consumer group on each of the fifteen commodities. Not surprisingly, per household expenditures tend to increase as we move to consumer groups with more income. However, this pattern does not hold monotonically for some goods, such as alcoholic beverages, tobacco, and transportation. While expenditures on housing increase with income, the share of income spent on housing actually decreases. The share of income spent on clothing and jewelry increases dramatically.

Before using these figures, we multiply by the total number of households in each of these groups in order to obtain total expenditure by each group for each product. We obtain the number of households in each group from the Treasury Department's Merged Tax File. These data are shown in table 5.3.

These expenditures on the fifteen consumer goods are converted into expenditures on nineteen producer goods using the Z matrix described in section 4.6 above. Column (1) of table 5.1 provides unadjusted data on personal consumption expenditures on our nineteen producer goods, from table 2.6 of the July 1976 *Survey of Current Business* (U.S. Department of Commerce, BEA 1976b). Chapter 6 describes how we adjust the data sources to match.

5.2.2 Consumer Expenditure Taxes

In this section our calculations of effective rates of tax on the fifteen consumer goods other than savings are explained. We have specific data for the taxes on alcoholic beverages, tobacco, and gasoline. For the other goods, we must make a series of imputations.

According to the July 1976 *SCB*, state and local liquor taxes yielded $2,013 million in 1973. The federal government collected $6,671 million in liquor taxes, bringing the total liquor tax to $8,684 million. State and local tobacco taxes amounted to $3,274.4 million, while federal tobacco taxes were $2,357 million, for a total of $5,631.4 million. Excise taxes on

---

gated classification from the diary survey. Third, we omitted the retirement pensions category, since this primarily represents savings. Finally, we did not use the cost of owned dwellings category. Instead, we use an estimated gross rent figure, which represents an owner's estimate of how much he would charge to rent the house to someone else. If it is accurate, this figure should reflect the homeowners' implicit expenditure on housing services.

Table 5.2   Matrix of 1973 Expenditures on Consumer Goods per Household (in dollars)

	Household Groups					
	(1)	(2)	(3)	(4)	(5)	(6)
1. Food	766.80	1,034.90	1,153.10	1,292.80	1,336.30	1,400.70
2. Alcoholic beverages	22.48	37.00	44.88	50.68	56.24	67.60
3. Tobacco	68.41	78.58	85.63	92.46	108.39	115.66
4. Utilities	271.60	340.40	388.10	407.40	448.20	442.80
5. Housing	1,094.23	1,323.34	1,353.06	1,439.94	1,480.34	1,540.81
6. Furnishings	72.97	112.32	131.92	131.56	157.80	183.19
7. Appliances	52.29	71.85	85.75	96.96	110.62	143.16
8. Clothing and jewelry	142.90	218.90	241.00	303.40	321.60	368.40
9. Transportation	47.14	65.83	68.63	69.41	59.29	79.75
10. Motor vehicles	288.80	419.80	470.10	502.60	768.90	804.90
11. Services	406.50	483.72	590.04	669.44	709.92	780.88
12. Financial services	191.19	289.06	404.61	400.24	471.25	497.38
13. Reading, recreation, and miscellaneous	102.30	150.90	147.50	200.60	204.80	255.50
14. Nondurable household items	135.46	165.10	188.24	219.96	235.56	243.62
15. Gas and other fuel	151.20	194.10	251.90	264.60	316.00	372.00

	Household Groups					
	(7)	(8)	(9)	(10)	(11)	(12)
1. Food	1,592.90	1,804.00	1,972.70	2,373.50	2,764.90	3,311.40
2. Alcoholic beverages	67.77	89.66	82.53	115.82	124.93	199.44
3. Tobacco	135.05	146.13	151.04	170.22	166.72	153.12
4. Utilities	483.30	534.80	591.20	671.90	738.40	891.20
5. Housing	1,699.56	1,872.23	1,989.17	2,430.00	2,885.93	3,663.97
6. Furnishings	232.52	237.19	294.53	425.47	545.61	770.44
7. Appliances	155.14	164.49	195.37	216.44	248.34	270.96
8. Clothing and jewelry	419.60	506.00	562.40	743.10	934.90	1,366.00
9. Transportation	84.82	91.68	77.15	102.75	140.88	304.84
10. Motor vehicles	880.10	1,195.30	1,317.00	1,564.80	1,891.40	2,373.20
11. Services	854.30	903.64	1,059.10	1,367.96	1,802.96	3,362.58
12. Financial services	546.15	568.11	714.66	774.28	1,021.09	1,749.67
13. Reading, Recreation, and miscellaneous	322.10	395.10	471.50	651.30	915.10	1,193.20
14. Nondurable household items	260.00	303.42	345.54	388.44	452.14	505.44
15. Gas and other fuel	411.40	474.20	556.50	626.80	714.40	767.10

Table 5.3   Thousands of Households in Each Consumer Group

Group Number	Gross Income	Number in Thousands
1.	0 < 3,000	14,149[a]
2.	3 < 4,000	6,863
3.	4 < 5,000	6,236
4.	5 < 6,000	6,107
5.	6 < 7,000	5,042
6.	7 < 8,000	4,755
7.	8 < 10,000	8,563
8.	10 < 12,000	7,565
9.	12 < 15,000	9,774
10.	15 < 20,000	10,220
11.	20 < 25,000	4,589
12.	25,000 +	5,033

[a]Only those of age over twenty. See Section 5.3 for a discussion of this adjustment.

gasoline were $8,283 million. These figures are summarized in column (1) of table 5.4.

In addition to these specific taxes, the July 1976 *SCB*, reports that state and local (S&L) governments collected $30,384.6 million of general and miscellaneous taxes, for which no breakdown among consumer goods is given. Columns (2) through (6) of table 5.4 show our method for allocating these taxes among consumer goods. Column (2) is based on the tax rates in table 5.5, which in turn are based on information from the *Commerce Clearing House State Tax Handbook*. Each of the rates in table 5.5 is a weighted average of the statutory rates in each state, where the weights are the states' proportions of national personal income in 1973. For example, only eight states tax the transportation of persons and property, at rates varying from 2 to 5 percent of purchase price. The sum of each state's rate times its proportion of personal income yields the low national effective sales tax rate of .25 percent.

We then use the nine rates in table 5.5 to generate rates for our classification of consumer goods. These state and local (S&L) rates, t_m ($m = 1, \ldots, 15$), are shown in column (2) of table 5.4. The 3.99 percent rate for "tangible personal property" in table 5.5 applies directly to consumer goods such as appliances in table 5.4. On the other hand, our food category includes some food from restaurants, which is taxed at the full rate of 3.99 percent, some food from stores, which is taxed at the lower rate of 1.82 percent, and some value of food consumed on farms, which is not taxed. The weighted average of these is 2.30 percent, which is the first entry in column (2) of table 5.4.

Column (4) of table 5.4 shows personal consumption expenditures on the consumer good classification, from table 2.6 of the July 1976 *SCB*.

Table 5.4   Consumer Sales Taxes (in millions of 1973 dollars)

Consumer Good	Tax Collections on Which We Have Specific Data (1)	S&L Consumer Sales Tax Rates, t_m, based on Table 5.5 (2)	$\dfrac{t_m}{1+t_m}$ (3)	Consumer Expenditures from July 1976 SCB (4)	Initial Estimate of S&L Tax Collections (3) × (4) (5)	Final Estimate of S&L Tax Collections ($30,384.6 allocated by column 5) (6)	Total Consumer Tax Collections (7)
TOTAL				827,525	16,718.94	30,384.6	52,983.0
Food		.0230	.02248	146,763	3,299.64	5,996.7	5,996.7
Alcoholic beverages	8,684.0	.0399	.03837	21,302	817.34	1,485.4	10,169.4
Tobacco	5,631.4	.0411	.03948	13,134	518.50	942.3	6,573.7
Utilities		.0238	.02325	38,644	898.35	1,632.6	1,632.6
Housing				123,173			
Furnishings		.0399	.03837	31,716	1,216.91	2,211.6	2,211.6
Appliances		.0399	.03837	26,836	1,029.67	1,871.3	1,871.3
Clothing and jewelry		.0399	.03837	68,062	2,611.47	4,746.0	4,746.0
Transportation		.0025	.00249	7,326	18.27	33.2	33.2
Motor vehicles		.0312	.03026	70,607	2,136.29	3,882.5	3,882.5
Services		.0185	.01816	117,219	2,129.15	3,869.5	3,869.5
Financial services				55,894[a]			
Reading, recreation, and miscellaneous		.0274	.02667	39,398	1,050.71	1,909.5	1,909.5
Nondurable household items		.0321	.03110	31,916	922.64	1,804.0	1,804.0
Gas and other fuel	8,283.0			35,535			8,283.0

[a]Includes imputed service charge payments.

Table 5.5   Sales Tax Rates on Selected Consumer Purchases

Consumer Purchase	Percentage of Tax Rate
Tangible personal property	3.99
Food	1.82
Alcoholic beverages	3.99
Tobacco	4.11
Drugs	.99
Utilities	2.38
Services	1.85
Transportation	.25
Other	.00

(This has the same column total as column (1) of table 5.1, although the latter uses the producer good classification.) The figures in column (4) of table 5.4 are *gross* of sales taxes. Consequently, to estimate tax collections, the observed gross-of-tax expenditures in column (4) are multiplied by $t_m/(1 + t_m)$, shown in column (3). This procedure gives us initial estimates of S&L tax collections in column (5). The total in column (5), however, is substantially less than the total of $30,384.6 million found in the *SCB*. Therefore, we allocate the *SCB* total on the basis of the estimated tax collection figures in column (5), in order to get column (6). Finally, adding columns (1) and (6) gives our total for consumer sales taxes, which is shown in column (7). These final figures on tax payments remain unchanged as the construction of the benchmark data set develops. Because of our consistency procedures, however, the tax *rates* may not be unchanged. Personal consumption expenditures are one of the items scaled to match value added. Therefore, a fixed amount of tax will yield different rates, depending on the severity of the consistency adjustment.

5.2.3   Household Savings Data

Each consumer group exhausts its income with expenditures on commodities and saving. As explained in the preceding sections, we consider a saving commodity that feeds through the Z coefficient matrix in the same manner as other consumer goods and is thereby translated into demands for the nineteen producer goods. These coefficients are determined by data on business investment from the *Survey of Current Business*. In this way the total saving of consumers exactly equals the net investment of the business sector.

The 1973 Consumer Expenditure Survey provides data on the net change in assets, less net change in liabilities for each income group. Unfortunately, the resulting saving estimates across our twelve income classes are extremely volatile and unreliable. That is, a graph of saving against income is very irregular in shape, and no alternative data source is

Table 5.6   **Saving per Household in 1973, by Income Class (in dollars)**

Gross Income	Saving
0–2,999	– 18.74
3,000–3,999	64.58
4,000–4,999	106.87
5,000–5,999	174.20
6,000–6,999	239.35
7,000–7,999	309.86
8,000–9,999	419.54
10,000–11,999	596.77
12,000–14,999	835.96
15,000–19,999	1,203.55
20,000–24,999	1,670.55
25,000 +	4,980.27

better. To correct for this irregularity, we manually smoothed the points on the 1973 function.[2] With this procedure we believe we have obtained more reasonable values for saving by income class. The resulting estimates are shown in table 5.6.

5.3 Household Income Sources and Taxes Paid

In chapter 4 we describe industry and government use of labor and capital services. In equilibrium these demands for factors equal the supplied endowments of factors. We must, therefore, estimate the ownership of each factor by each consumer group. The income from these factors will equal the total of expenditures and saving (after the benchmark consistency adjustments that we describe in chapter 6).

The major source of data on income and income taxes is the Treasury Department's Merged Tax File, which is compiled from individual income tax returns. The Merged Tax File classifies individuals by gross income, including nontaxable government transfers. This measure is very similar to the gross income concept used to classify households in the expenditure survey data. The only substantive difference between the two data sources is the treatment of young family members who are wage earners. The Treasury Tax File counts these tax returns in the same manner in which it counts all other individual returns. Most of them fall into the lowest income group. As a result, the source of income for the Treasury's lowest income group is almost entirely wages. The Consumer

2. Data in Projector and Weiss (1966) suggest that saving per household is negative for the lowest-income group(s), increases with income, and increases at a decreasing rate. We wish to obtain this general shape for our twelve income groups, but we wish to use as much of the basic data as possible. Rather than regress savings on income, then, we merely keep the savings amounts for seven of the groups and change the savings data for the five outliers so that they fit on a smooth curve.

Expenditure Survey does not interview these family members separately, so their lowest income group consists primarily of retired persons with relatively low wage income and higher capital income, especially from the owner-occupied home. To correct for this discrepancy, we eliminate from the Treasury sample all tax returns for individuals under twenty years of age.

5.3.1   Household Capital Income

Sources of capital income are shown in table 5.7. All of the income categories in this table are returns to the capital owned by individuals, even if that ownership is implicit. For example, pension funds are a conduit through which individuals earn a return to their own personal saving, while dividends and financial capital gains are the forms in which corporate source income is attributed to individuals.

Partnership net income is a combined return to the investment of capital and labor by the entrepreneur, and so must be apportioned between the two.[3]

The first eight columns of table 5.7 derive from the Treasury Merged Tax File. For imputed net rental information we use Consumer Expenditure Survey data as follows. We take total reported "estimated gross rent" and subtract a figure for "cost of home ownership" that includes maintenance, depreciation, property taxes, and mortgage interest payments. This difference is scaled up by the ratio of the total number of homeowners to the number of households in the group to get average imputed rental income, shown in column (9) of table 5.7. (This procedure is consistent with our imputations for owner-occupied housing expenditures.)

Column (10) provides the estimated imputed interest receipts from ownership of financial assets. These receipts are exactly equal to the imputed service charge payments for financial services, described in section 5.2.1 above. Column (11) shows the totals of columns (1) through (10).

5.3.2   Household Labor Income and Taxes Paid

The data for household labor income also come from the Merged Tax File. Two sources of labor income are shown in the first two columns of table 5.8. Wages and salaries plus the labor share of net partnership income equal total labor income, shown in column (3). When this total is

---

3. In discussing production side data in section 4.2, we describe a procedure to divide these returns for each industry. After totaling all industries, it turns out that 36.66 percent of this income had been attributed to capital. We apply this proportion to the self-employed income of each consumer group in order to estimate capital income from this activity. This assumes implicitly that all consumer groups have the same proportions of activity among industries.

Table 5.7   Average Capital Income per Household by Source (in 1973 dollars)

Consumer Income Class	Private Pensions (1)	Dividends before Exclusions (2)	Interest Receipts (3)	Net Rents (4)	Short-Term Capital Gains (5)	Full Long-Term Capital Gains (6)	Royalties (7)	36.66% of Partnership Income (8)	Net Rent of Owner-Occupied Homes (9)	Imputed Interest Receipts (10)	Total (11)
0–2,999	10	17	43	6	−5	12	1	−14.30	311.23	40.66	421.59
3,000–3,999	38	32	93	14	−3	23	1	1.47	400.73	101.65	701.85
4,000–4,999	52	30	110	9	−9	13	0	0	410.73	127.79	743.52
5,000–5,999	63	36	168	31	−11	17	1	1.47	437.48	148.12	892.07
6,000–6,999	77	51	218	23	−6	32	2	4.40	427.00	159.74	988.14
7,000–7,999	72	46	232	33	−8	44	4	11.00	444.57	171.35	1,049.92
8,000–9,999	105	79	280	36	−38	7	3	4.77	451.45	153.93	1,082.15
10,000–11,999	147	112	328	30	−18	85	8	11.00	518.10	148.12	1,369.22
12,000–14,999	135	110	356	33	−27	128	4	23.83	560.77	182.97	1,506.57
15,000–19,999	163	183	476	38	−33	190	11	29.70	735.37	223.63	2,016.70
20,000–24,999	221	339	721	97	−2	361	27	78.82	913.41	345.61	3,101.84
25,000+	438	2,637	2,154	420	−221	4,552	142	714.52	1,060.80	909.05	12,806.37
Average	99	205	323	44	−24	291	11	43.26	—	—	—

Table 5.8   **Average Labor Income and Income Taxes per Household (in 1973 dollars)**

Consumer Income Class	Wages and Salaries (1)	63.33% of Partnership Income (2)	Labor Income (1) + (2) (3)	Capital Income (4)	Total Income (3) + (4) (5)	Federal Income Tax (6)	S&L Income Tax (7)	Total Tax (6) + (7) (8)	Average Tax Rate (8) ÷ (5) (9)	Marginal Tax Rate (10)
0–2,999	623.3	−24.70	607.60	421.59	1,029.19	6	0	6	.0058	.0100
3,000–3,999	1,640.2	2.53	1,642.73	701.85	2,344.58	74	1	75	.0320	.0608
4,000–4,999	2,586.0	0	2,586.00	743.52	3,329.52	158	3	161	.0484	.1019
5,000–5,999	3,459.2	2.53	3,461.73	892.07	4,353.80	257	6	263	.0604	.1228
6,000–6,999	4,370.6	7.60	4,378.20	988.14	5,366.34	365	13	378	.0704	.1346
7,000–7,999	5,529.0	19.00	5,548.00	1,049.92	6,597.92	516	24	540	.0818	.1570
8,000–9,999	6,925.9	8.23	6,934.13	1,082.15	8,016.28	709	47	756	.0943	.1813
10,000–11,999	8,739.0	19.00	8,758.00	1,369.22	10,127.22	962	90	1,052	.1039	.2078
12,000–14,999	11,169.5	41.17	11,210.67	1,506.57	12,717.24	1,330	143	1,473	.1158	.2215
15,000–19,999	14,294.3	51.30	14,345.60	2,016.70	16,362.30	1,951	270	2,221	.1357	.2618
20,000–24,999	17,443.5	136.18	17,579.68	3,101.84	20,681.52	2,829	449	3,278	.1585	.2897
25,000+	22,549.7	1,234.48	23,784.18	12,806.37	36,590.55	8,049	1,303	9,352	.2556	.4067
TOTAL	6,794.4	74.74	6,869.14	—	—	1,057	139	1,196	—	—

added to capital income in column (4) (which is repeated from table 5.7), we have total factor income in column (5).

The total in column (5) of table 5.8 is the measure of economic income that provides the proper denominator for our calculations of effective average tax rates. In this model, income tax is defined as the sum of federal, state, and local income taxes. These data, which are shown in columns (6) and (7) of table 5.8, were provided by the Treasury Department's Merged Tax File. When we divide total income taxes (column 8) by income (column 5), we get the average income tax rates, which appear in column (9). We use gross-of-tax income in the denominator of these calculations. This differs from our net-of-tax rates on the production side of the model. On the production side we define a unit of a factor to be that which earns a dollar *net* of factor taxes. The rate for factor taxes is tax paid per unit value of the factor used. In order to calculate personal income tax rates, however, we divide taxes by each individual's total factor income.

We should note that the income sources shown in table 5.8 will be scaled to match production side data. (We will describe this consistency adjustment in chapter 6.) The tax collection data, however, are not altered. Consequently, the average tax rates used by the model are slightly different from the rates shown here, although the differences are small, and relative magnitudes are roughly preserved.

The last column of table 5.8 shows estimates of the appropriate marginal tax rates that apply to changes in income for each of the income groups. The Merged Tax File provides information on the federal marginal income tax rate, averaged over all members of an income class, but we require information on state marginal tax rates as well. One might think that state and local income taxes are less progressive than federal income taxes, since the maximum marginal tax rates are reached at relatively low income levels in most states (Maxwell and Aronson 1977). The data on tax collections, however, tell the opposite story. When state and local income tax collections, by income group, are divided through by income, we see that these state and local average tax rates rise faster than the federal average tax rates at all levels of income. For total marginal tax rates we simply scale up each federal marginal rate by the ratio of total income taxes to federal income taxes in the group. This procedure assumes that marginal tax rates in the federal and state income tax systems increase at similar rates.

5.3.3 Household Transfer Incomes

Each consumer's disposable income consists of after-tax factor incomes, plus the (nontaxable) transfer from government. The components of these transfers are shown in table 5.9. These data come from the Treasury Tax File.

We might expect government transfers to accrue to low income groups

Table 5.9   Average Government Transfers per Household by Source (in 1973 dollars)

Consumer Income Class	Unemployment Compensation (1)	Welfare Receipts (2)	Government Employee Pension (3)	Workmen's Compensation (4)	Veterans' Benefits (5)	Social Security (6)	Insurance Value of Medicare (7)	Insurance Value of Medicaid (8)	Insurance Value of Veteran Benefits (9)	Value of Food Stamp Bonus (10)	Total (11)	Transfers as Proportion of Income (12)
0–2,999	20	130	9	4	18	458	123	104	11	36	913	.462
3,000–3,999	38	237	29	10	59	844	164	161	38	51	1,631	.396
4,000–4,999	47	236	48	14	69	805	160	139	37	51	1,606	.309
5,000–5,999	61	165	73	18	55	810	157	92	29	41	1,501	.242
6,000–6,999	65	157	110	31	80	748	133	76	34	36	1,470	.201
7,000–7,999	63	95	109	47	81	585	97	61	31	28	1,197	.142
8,000–9,999	69	49	153	53	81	547	89	35	28	16	1,120	.113
10,000–11,999	64	26	196	56	86	475	83	23	30	9	1,048	.086
12,000–14,999	58	10	208	68	85	341	60	14	31	6	881	.059
15,000–19,999	57	12	300	69	99	301	55	10	33	5	941	.050
20,000–24,999	46	3	510	81	103	303	58	7	37	3	1,151	.048
25,000+	41	4	1,005	80	112	358	76	5	32	2	1,715	.043
TOTAL	45	81	172	37	64	467	91	56	26	21	1,060	.043

more than to those with higher incomes. Column (11) of table 5.9 shows this pattern over much of the income range, with two notable exceptions. The poorest consumer group has the smallest per capita transfer income. This fact may be due to the imprecision of our correction for teenage workers. (See above in section 5.3.) Also, the group with the highest total income has the largest transfers. This is largely the result of the concentration of government employee pensions in the high-income group. Many recipients of these pensions work at other full-time jobs after retiring from the government.[4] Still, if transfers are taken as a proportion of total income for each consumer group, as in column (12) of table 5.9, we have a very progressive pattern.[5]

5.4   Investment Data

5.4.1   Gross Private Fixed Capital Formation and Depreciation

Purchases of investment goods are an element of final demand. The 1972 input-output table contains a column for Gross Private Fixed Capital Formation (GPFCF). Table 5.2 of the July 1976 *SCB* contains a 1973 total for this item. We scale the 1972 input-output column to the 1973 total by the following method. Purchases of structures, which appear in table 5.4 of the *SCB*, are attributed directly to demand for the output of the construction industry. We use purchases of producers' durable equipment for 1973 (table 5.6 of the *SCB*) in conjunction with similar data from the 1972 *SCB* to scale up particular elements of the GPFCF column. For the remaining elements of the column, including the trade and transportation margins, we scale the 1972 input-output entry by the ratio of total GPFCF for 1973 and 1972. Finally, we adjust the column of estimates proportionally to the proper 1973 total of $202,092 million, shown in column (2) of table 5.1. Not surprisingly, construction and metals and machinery account for the bulk of the capital formation. About 57 percent of the total occurs in construction and about 21 percent in metals and machinery.

A major portion of these gross investment purchases is required to replace depreciated capital. We must be careful to distinguish between

---

4. It could be argued that government pension programs should be treated like private pension programs (i.e., that the benefit payments should be considered capital income). Instead, we have chosen to treat all flows to the government (including government retirement contributions) as taxes, and to treat all payments from the government to individuals as transfer payments.

5. If one uses columns (11) and (12) of table 5.9 to calculate the average income for each of the consumer groups, one will notice that these average incomes are greater than the upper limit of the Consumer Expenditure Survey income brackets in many cases. This is because we include imputed rents, which are not counted as income in the Consumer Expenditure Survey.

gross investment and net investment, since, in our model, industries use capital services but do not use up the capital itself. For our estimate of economic depreciation we use figures from table 1.9 of the July 1976 *SCB* to find the total capital consumption allowance with capital consumption adjustment. This comes to $117,652 million in 1973—a figure that is 58.22 percent of total GPFCF of $202,092 million. Using this ratio we assume that 58.22 percent of each gross investment purchase is used to replace capital, leaving 41.78 percent of the GPFCF column as net investment.

5.4.2 Net Inventory Change

The second component of net investment is net inventory change. For this component we once again scale up a column of the 1972 input-output table to a 1973 total. The elements of this vector, however, are more volatile from year to year than are the elements of other sectors. Consequently, we do not scale the entire column by a single ratio of the 1973 total to the 1972 total. Instead, we use subtotals from table 5.8 of the July 1976 *SCB* for five broad categories such as "durable manufacturing." We take the ratio of the 1973 subtotal to the 1972 subtotal for each of the five categories, and then use these five ratios for our scaling. Column (3) of table 5.1 includes the results of these calculations. Net investment demand for each output is 41.78 percent of column (2) plus all of column (3) of table 5.1. Over all industries this net investment demand is $103,070 million in 1973.

5.5 Government Receipts and Expenditures

Expenditures by government (other than those for public enterprises) are an element of final demand. We model the government as a consumer with a Cobb-Douglas utility function. This function is defined over all nineteen producer goods, plus capital and labor services.

5.5.1 Government Purchases of the Nineteen Producer Goods

The 1972 input-output table has four columns for final purchases by government. These four categories are federal defense expenditures, other federal expenditures, state and local education expenditures, and other state and local expenditures. In order to obtain 1973 estimates we multiply each column by the ratio of its 1973 total to its 1972 total. These totals come from table 3.6 of the July 1976 *SCB*. The sum of the four scaled columns is our basic government expenditure column. These expenditures are shown in column (4) of table 5.1. The largest increase from 1972 to 1973 was in state and local expenditures for items other than education, while federal defense expenditures actually decreased in nominal terms. Once again, construction and metals and machinery are important components of these expenditures, along with transport equipment and ordnance, and services. Construction gets about 38 percent of the total, while these other three industries receive around 12 percent to 14 percent each.

Rather than purchasing agricultural output in 1973, the federal government was observed to sell, through price stabilization programs, $1,526 million of goods stored from previous years. Government cannot be assigned a negative Cobb-Douglas expenditure share, so we set government demand for agricultural output to zero. Government is then assigned an endowment of 1,526 million units of agricultural output, which they sell in the benchmark equilibrium. On the other eighteen outputs, general government spends $121,290 million.

5.5.2   Government Use of Labor, and Labor Tax

Table 4.11 shows government purchases of labor services, with a total of $165,785 million. The purchases of labor for government enterprises are equal to $16,723 million. The difference of $149,062 million is the appropriate number for general government. The difference between total contributions for social insurance ($16,056 million) and the estimate of the contributions in government enterprises ($1,557 million) is $14,499 million for general government. When we subtract the contributions figure from the labor purchase figure, we calculate that general government paid $134,563 million for net-of-tax labor services. Division yields an effective tax rate of .1077. This rate differs from the government enterprise rate because the federal rate differs from the state and local rate, while enterprises make up a different fraction of the two.

5.5.3   Government Use of Capital

Capital use estimates for government pose problems, since no return to governmental capital is ever earned. Our previous approach of defining a unit of capital—that which earns a dollar per year—is less appropriate here. If we assume that the interaction of the economy and the governmental process causes a rough equilibration of rates of return, however, we can apply the private rate of return to a government capital stock estimate. We show the calculations for this imputation in table 5.10. John Kendrick's (1976) national wealth estimates provide column (1) of the table.

In column (6) of table 4.2 we show the total capital income for all industries as $181,973 million. If we subtract the imputed earnings of government enterprises, we get $174,162 million for capital income in the private business sector, which is shown in column (2) of table 5.10. When we divide this by Kendrick's figure for business net wealth, we get the return of almost 10 percent. We then impute this rate of return to the government capital stock. Since the government capital stock estimate is for total government, we must subtract the $7,811 million imputed return

Table 5.10   1973 Government Capital Stock Estimates (in millions of dollars)

	Net Worth (1)	Earnings Net of Tax (2)	Rate of Return (3)
Business	$1,747,200	$174,162	.09968
Government	1,081,000	107,755	.09968

in government enterprises. This gives us a $99,944 million imputed return to the capital used by general government. To this we add the $160 million of net rent paid by government as payment for borrowed capital.[6] The total return to capital used by general government is then $100,104 million.

Only part of this capital return is endowed to government, however; the $160 million of net rent paid are for capital owned by individuals, as are the $15,351 million of net interest paid. We assume that all of the capital employed by government enterprises ($7,811 million) is privately owned. Since total government use of private capital is $15,511 million, general government is assigned the residual of $7,700 million.[7] Government's endowment of capital is then $92,404 million ($100,104 − $7,700). The government finances its total expenditures by using the revenue from the sale of this capital endowment plus tax revenues.

5.6 Foreign Trade Data

We treat the foreign sector transactions of the United States in a fairly simple manner, so as to close the model. First of all, we do not deal with capital flows (i.e., we only model commodity trade). Secondly, we do not differentiate between commodities on the basis of place of origin (i.e., automobiles produced in the United States and those produced abroad are considered to be identical).[8]

Despite these simplifying assumptions, it would be incorrect to say that foreign trade has no effect on our model. Foreign trade introduces a difference between the aggregate demands of U.S. consumer groups (broadly defined to include business investment and government purchases) and the demands for products faced by domestic industries in the United States.

We take data on foreign trade from two sources. For merchandise trade we use series B of the 1973 foreign trade statistics of the Organization for Economic Cooperation and Development. These data are presented on a Standard International Trade Classification (SITC) basis, but

6. See section 4.3 and table 4.3 for the derivation of this figure.
7. Note that $160 + 15,351 = 15,511 = 7,811 + 7,700$.
8. Each of these basic assumptions will be relaxed in chapter 11.

we have converted them to the Standard Industrial Classification (SIC) basis of our model. For service items we take data from the 1973 balance-of-payments accounts for the United States. These appear in the December 1974 *SCB*. The balance-of-payments accounts identify transportation as a separate category. This is fortunate, since the merchandise trade-statistics report imports at market value in the country of origin, while exports are reported at market value at the point of shipment.

When we add these two together, we have a total value of exports of $84,598.8 million. The total value of imports is $83,004 million. In this general equilibrium model, however, we impose zero balance of foreign trade activity. To get zero trade balance, we allocate the 1973 trade surplus of $1,595 million proportionately among the imports. When this procedure is complete, we have a total of $84,598.8 million for both exports and imports. The detailed breakdown of these totals is shown in table 5.1.

For most goods, there are substantial trade flows in both directions. In fact, at this level of aggregation, a noticeable correlation exists, by industry, between imports and exports. For example, metals and machinery is by far the most important industry for both imports and exports, with around 30 percent of the total. The largest trade surplus is in agriculture, while the largest deficit is in petroleum and gas.

Appendix

Table 5.A.1   **Correspondences between Our Consumer Goods and Bureau of Labor Statistics (BLS) Categories**

Our Categories	Bureau of Labor Statistics Categories
Food	Food at home Food away Meals as pay Food on vacation
Alcoholic beverages	Alcoholic beverages Alcoholic beverages on vacation
Tobacco	Tobacco
Utilities	Gas in mains Gas in bottles Electricity Gas and electricity combined bills Water, garbage Telephone
Housing	Rent Estimated gross rent Other shelter Owned vacation home Lodging on vacation
Furnishings	Household textiles Furniture Floor coverings Miscellaneous furnishings

Table 5.A.1 (continued)

Our Categories	Bureau of Labor Statistics Categories
Appliances	Major appliances Small appliances Housewares Television
Clothing and jewelry	Clothing, male Clothing, female Clothing, infant
Transportation	Other transportation Other transportation on vacation
Motor vehicles	Vehicle purchase Auto repair
Services	Domestic services Dry cleaning Materials and repair Personal care services[a] Private education Public education Gifts and contributions[b]
Financial services	Vehicle finance charges Health insurance Miscellaneous Life insurance[c] Other personal insurance[c]
Recreation, reading, and miscellaneous	All expense tours on vacation Other vacation expenses Boats, aircraft, wheel goods Other recreation Reading
Nondurable, nonfood household items	Nonprescription drugs[a] Housekeeping supplies[a] Personal care products[a]
Gasoline and other fuels	Fuel oil and kerosene Other fuels Gasoline Gasoline on vacation

Table 5.A.1 (continued)

Our Categories	Bureau of Labor Statistics Categories

[a]Diary survey.

[b]Gifts and contributions include several categories such as appliances for wedding gifts. The majority, however, includes cash gifts to religious and educational institutions, which are part of our service good.

[c]The appropriate measure of expenditure on insurance services is premiums less claims paid. Since only data on premiums are available, we subtract 75 percent in order to approximate the desired expenditure before we add these insurance categories to purchases of financial services. The National Income Division suggested this 75 percent figure.

6 Adjustments to the Data Set and Specification of Parameters

6.1 Introduction

In chapters 4 and 5 we described the basic data that we use in our general equilibrium model. We must adjust these data in several ways, however, before we can use them. In particular, we always assume that the United States economy was in equilibrium in 1973, so the data must satisfy certain equilibrium conditions. Demands must equal supplies for all goods and factors. All industries must earn zero profits. Government receipts must equal government expenditures. In addition, we require certain conditions of consistency of the input-output matrix, of the matrix of goods consumption for consumers, and of the matrix of conversion between producer goods and consumer goods. In section 6.2 we describe these consistency adjustments.

Even after we make these adjustments, we are not yet ready to perform simulations with the model. In order to perform simulations we need parameter values that would describe the behavior of consumers, producers, the government, and our foreign trade partners.

We determine parameter values for the equations in the model using a nonstochastic *calibration* method. The model is calibrated to the base-year equilibrium, such that the adjusted data will be reproduced exactly as an equilibrium solution to the model. An alternative procedure would be to estimate the parameters of the model econometrically. Unfortunately, our model is much too large to be estimated as an econometric system of simultaneous equations. On the other hand, if we were to use single-equation methods to estimate the parameters and then calculate an equilibrium solution for the economy, the solution would not match the adjusted benchmark data.[1]

---

1. For a detailed discussion of these issues, see Mansur and Whalley 1984.

We describe our calibration procedures in section 6.3. When we assume that some type of activity can be characterized by a Cobb-Douglas function, we can calibrate the model merely by looking at the budget shares of consumers or the input purchases of producers. More often, however, we use the more complicated constant elasticity of substitution (CES) functional form. In this case we have to prespecify the value of the elasticity of substitution before we can proceed with the calibration. We describe our choices of elasticities in section 6.4.

Before we discuss our consistency adjustments, one other matter must be discussed. All of our data are in value terms, i.e., they are the products of prices and quantities. For several reasons we will want to deal separately with prices and quantities. To do this we adopt units conventions that tell us, for example, what constitutes a unit of labor and a unit of capital. These conventions allow us to translate data on factor payments by industry into observations on the physical quantities used. We use these observations directly when we determine the production function parameters.

Since we treat factors of production as being perfectly mobile among alternative uses, the allocation of factors by industry in equilibrium will equalize the returns received net of taxes in all industries. It is therefore convenient to adopt a definition of a physical unit of each factor as the amount that can earn in equilibrium a reward of $1 per period net of all taxes in any of the factor's alternative uses. In the case of capital, units are defined as net of both capital use taxes and personal factor taxes. Units for commodities are similarly defined as those amounts that in equilibrium sell for $1 net of all consumer taxes and subsidies. The observed benchmark equilibrium is characterized by an equilibrium price vector of unity for both goods and factors; ownership of a unit of labor or capital services yields a net income of $1.

We should stress the implications of these unit conventions. With labor services, for instance, the number of workers in an industry is an inappropriate measure of the amount of labor used by the industry. Our procedures implicitly assume that more productive individuals are endowed with a greater number of effective labor units. Similarly, we ignore the portfolio composition of capital ownership, since we assume that all assets yield the same real risk-free net rate of return.

6.2   Consistency Adjustments

6.2.1   Factor Payments and Factor Incomes

In order to illustrate our consistency adjustment procedures, it might be best to start with an example. One requirement of the general equilibrium model is that the total net-of-tax payments to labor by industry and

Table 6.1   **Total Labor Income by Consumer Group, before and after Adjustments (all figures in millions of 1973 dollars)**

Consumer Group	Labor Income before Adjustment	Labor Income after Adjustment
1	$8,596.9	$9,719.6
2	11,274.1	12,746.3
3	16,126.3	18,232.1
4	21,140.8	23,901.4
5	22,074.9	24,957.5
6	26,380.7	29,825.6
7	59,377.0	67,130.6
8	66,254.3	74,906.0
9	109,566.5	123,881.5
10	146,605.9	165,757.2
11	80,673.2	91,207.8
12	119,705.8	135,337.4
TOTAL	$687,776.4	$777,603.0

government must equal the total labor income of consumers. In the unadjusted data, the total payments to labor by the nineteen industries come to $643,040 million (see table 4.1). Government's payments to labor equal $134,563 million (see section 5.5.2), and the total of these payments is $777,603 million. On the other side of the ledger, we can multiply the number of households (shown in table 5.3) by the average labor income per household (shown in table 5.8) to get the total labor income of consumers. The total for all twelve consumers is about $687,776 million. In order to reconcile the two figures, we choose to accept the figures for payments to labor, and then scale up the income figures proportionally. The results are shown in table 6.1.

We follow a similar procedure in adjusting the data on net payments to capital and consumer capital income.[2] In table 4.2 we show payments to capital by industry. These figures are gross of the personal factor tax, however, and we subtract personal factor taxes before undertaking the adjustments. The total of personal factor taxes (PFT) paid by industry is $40,932.5 million (see table 4.7). When we subtract this from the $181,973 million of capital income gross of the PFT, we have $141,040.5 million. We then add in the government's use of capital net of the PFT ($5,557.9 million) to get our total of purchases of capital, net of all taxes. This total is $146,598.4 million, and we scale down consumer capital incomes to match it. To do so we first multiply the number of households (table 5.3) by the average capital income before adjustment, shown in

2. Payments for capital would not have to equal domestic capital income in a model with international capital flows. In the standard version of our model, with no international capital flows, we assume that domestic capital is owned by domestic consumers.

Table 6.2   Total Capital Income by Consumer Group, before and after
Adjustments (all figures in millions of 1973 dollars)

Consumer Group	Capital Income before Adjustment	Capital Income after Adjustment
1	$5,965.1	$5,316.2
2	4,816.8	4,292.9
3	4,636.6	4,132.3
4	5,447.9	4,855.3
5	4,982.2	4,440.3
6	4,992.4	4,449.3
7	9,266.5	8,258.5
8	10,358.1	9,231.5
9	14,725.2	13,123.5
10	20,610.7	18,368.8
11	14,234.3	12,686.1
12	64,454.5	57,443.7
TOTAL	$164,490.3	$146,598.4

table 6.2. The total for all twelve consumer groups is $164,490.3 million, which must be multiplied by 0.891 to yield the figure for total net purchases of capital of $146,598.4 million. The capital incomes of consumers after adjustment are also shown in table 6.2.

Whenever we have to reconcile one vector with another, we use this procedure of accepting one vector and scaling the other vector up or down to match.[3] When we have to adjust a matrix, we use the RAS adjustment procedure developed by Michael Bacharach (1971). The RAS procedure adjusts a matrix so that the row sums and column sums simultaneously equal totals that have been estimated separately. We will discuss this procedure in detail below when we discuss the input-output matrix.

Figure 6.1 is a schematic representation of all of the consistency adjustments that are required of the data set. We will now describe the rest of the consistency adjustments. We accept the data on tax collections because they are recent and reliable. Since we have already performed our adjustments on factor returns by industry (and since factor returns plus factor taxes equal value added in each industry), we now have a final series for value added.

6.2.2   Government Revenues and Expenditures

As we said, we accept the data on government tax revenues. We also accept the data on government endowments. We collect the totals for these government income sources from tables 4.1, 4.4, 4.13, and 5.4, and from the text of chapters 4 and 5, and present them in table 6.3.

3. As a check, we compare the adjusted data to the raw data to be sure that we have not unknowingly introduced dramatic changes.

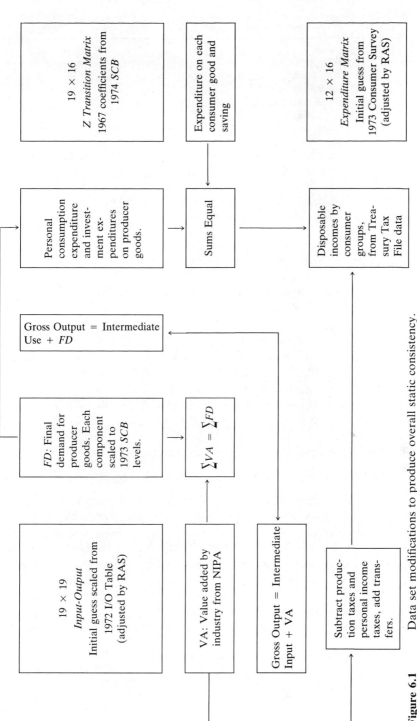

Figure 6.1   Data set modifications to produce overall static consistency.

Table 6.3   Sources of Funds for the Government (in millions of 1973 dollars)

Sources	Amount
Labor taxes from industry	$64,997
Government labor tax	14,499
Capital taxes from industry	136,828
(including personal factor tax)	
Output taxes	15,060
Intermediate taxes	1,656
Sales taxes	52,983
Personal income taxes (on labor)	78,248
TOTAL TAX REVENUE	$364,271
Income from sale of capital endowment	92,404
Income from sale of agricultural endowment	1,526
TOTAL ENDOWMENT INCOME	$93,930
TOTAL GOVERNMENT REVENUE	$458,201

The government spends its total revenue of $458,201 million on purchases of goods and factors and on transfer payments. It spends $97,961.9 million on purchases of capital,[4] and $149,062 million on labor services and labor taxes. If we multiply the number of households by transfer payments per household (table 5.9), we see that total transfer payments are equal to $106,057 million. This leaves $105,120.1 million for purchases of the eighteen commodities other than agriculture. However, table 5.1 indicates that the government spent $121,290 million on these eighteen commodities. We reconcile the two by scaling down the expenditure figures, multiplying each one by the ratio of 105,119 to 121,290. We show the figures for this adjustment in table 6.4.

6.2.3   Final and Intermediate Demands for Producer Goods

We have already adjusted the factor incomes of consumers, and we accepted the data on transfer incomes and income taxes without adjustment. As a result, we have all the ingredients of consumer disposable income. These are shown in table 6.5. The data in the column for the personal taxes are net of personal factor taxes. Consequently, the personal taxes shown here correspond to T_j^I in equation (3.38), including the tax on labor income for each group and the rebate or additional tax at the personal level for capital income of each group.

One of the requirements of the general equilibrium model is that

4. In chapter 5 we found that general government uses $7,700 million of privately owned capital. These interest and rental payments are fully taxed at the personal level, and they include personal factor taxes of $2,142.1 million. We subtract this figure from $100,104 million, the total use of capital by general government, to get $97,961.9 million for net purchases of capital.

Table 6.4   Government Expenditures by Industry, before and after
Adjustments (all figures in millions of 1973 dollars)

Industry	Government Expenditures before Adjustment	Government Expenditures after Adjustment
Mining	$217	$188.1
Crude petroleum and gas	0	0.0
Contract construction	45,690	39,599.3
Food and tobacco	1,522	1,319.1
Textiles, apparel, and leather	699	579.8
Paper and printing	2,178	1,887.7
Petroleum refining	1,501	1,300.9
Chemicals, rubber, and plastics	4,141	3,589.0
Lumber, furniture, stone, clay and glass	927	803.4
Metals, machinery, instruments, and miscellaneous manufacturing	14,117	12,235.1
Transport equipment and ordnance	16,103	13,956.4
Motor vehicles	2,503	2,169.3
Transportation, communications, and utilities	9,961	8,633.2
Trade	2,121	1,838.3
Finance and insurance	884	766.2
Real estate	1,783	1,545.3
Services	16,154	14,000.6
Government enterprises	818	709.0
TOTAL	$121,290	$105,120.7

Table 6.5   Consumer Disposable Incomes, after Consistency Adjustments
(all figures in millions of 1973 dollars)

Consumer	Labor Income	Capital Income	Transfers	Personal Taxes	Total Disposable Income
1	$9,719.6	$5,316.2	$12,918.0	$-1,477.2	$29,431.0
2	12,746.3	4,292.9	11,193.6	-746.6	28,979.4
3	18,232.1	4,132.3	10,015.0	-210.2	32,589.6
4	23,901.4	4,855.3	9,166.6	179.5	37,743.8
5	24,957.5	4,440.3	7,411.7	601.2	36,208.3
6	29,825.6	4,449.3	5,691.7	1,260.4	38,706.2
7	67,130.6	8,258.5	9,590.6	4,047.0	80,932.7
8	74,906.0	9,231.5	7,928.1	5,245.9	86,819.7
9	123,881.5	13,123.5	8,610.9	10,541.0	135,074.9
10	165,757.2	18,368.8	9,617.0	17,301.4	176,441.6
11	91,207.8	12,686.1	5,281.9	11,315.2	97,860.6
12	135,337.4	57,443.7	8,631.6	30,190.1	171,222.6
TOTAL	$777,603.0	$146,598.4	$106,056.7	$78,247.8	$952,010.4

Table 6.6   **Personal Consumption Expenditures, before and after Adjustments
(all figures in millions of 1973 dollars)**

Consumer Group	Personal Consumption before Adjustment	Personal Consumption after Adjustment
Food	$146,763	$150,140.4
Alcoholic beverages	21,302	21,792.2
Tobacco	13,134	13,436.3
Utilities	38,644	39,533.3
Housing	123,173	126,007.6
Furnishings	31,716	32,445.9
Appliances	26,836	27,453.6
Clothing and jewelry	68,062	69,628.3
Transportation	7,326	7,494.5
Motor vehicles, tires, and auto repairs	70,607	72,231.8
Services	117,219	119,916.5
Financial services	55,894	57,180.3
Reading, recreation, and miscellaneous	39,398	40,304.7
Nondurable, nonfood household items	31,916	32,650.5
Gasoline and other fuel	35,535	36,352.8
Savings	103,070	105,441.7
TOTAL	$930,595	$952,010.4

consumer disposable incomes must be exhausted by consumer expenditures on current consumption and saving. Table 5.4 provides a vector of consumer expenditures on the sixteen consumption goods. (The total for the sixteenth good, which is the savings good, is taken from the total of adjusted private fixed capital formation in the nineteen industries.)[5] We list these consumer expenditures in table 6.6. Their total is $930,594.8 million, which does not match the total for consumer disposable income of $952,010.4 million. As usual, our procedure is to scale up the expenditure totals by the ratio of 952,010.4 to 930,594.8, which equals about 1.023. The results of this scaling are shown in table 6.6.[6]

Now that we have a vector of consumption of the sixteen consumer goods, we can proceed to calculate the demands for the nineteen producer goods. We do this by using the Z matrix, which was shown in table 4.10. We do not adjust the Z matrix itself in any way. We premultiply the consumption vector (which is of length sixteen) by the (19×16) Z

5. The procedures whereby we produce these investment data are described in section 5.4.
6. Note that these consumption figures include sales taxes. We will return to this point shortly.

matrix, and the result is a nineteen-element vector for the amounts of producer goods used in consumption and investment.

We have now adjusted all the elements of the final demand for each industry output: consumption, investment, government demand, and net exports.[7] We also have all the elements of value added in each industry: payments to labor, payments to capital, and taxes. We have constructed our consistency adjustments such that the sum over all industries of the final demands equals the sum over all industries of the value added. We still must make one other major adjustment, however, before the production side of the economy is complete. One of the requirements of the general equilibrium model is the zero-profit condition. Receipts must equal expenditures for each of the nineteen industries. Receipts come from the various components of final demand as well as from other industries that pay for intermediate inputs. Expenditures are made for the elements of value added as well as for intermediate inputs from other industries. In terms of figure 6.1, the sum of any given row of input-output matrix plus the sum of the final demands for that industry must equal the corresponding column sum of the input-output matrix plus value added in that industry.

Since the interindustry transactions matrix (table 4.8) was compiled from sources different from either final demand or value added, this consistency condition is not met by the basic data. The first step, as described in section 4.5, is to scale up each column of the 1972 table by the ratio of 1973 value added to 1972 value added. Next we use Bacharach's RAS procedure, which we mentioned earlier. This procedure takes a total of each row plus final demand and compares it to the sum of the corresponding column plus value added. We then adjust upward or downward each element of the row in order to make the totals more nearly equal. (For technical reasons, we only adjust part of the way at each iteration.) The next step is to make the same sort of adjustment on the columns. The problem is that when we adjust the rows, the column totals change, and vice versa. It therefore takes several iterations before the RAS procedure converges to an acceptable degree of accuracy. We iterate until every row sum plus final demand is within $1,000 of the corresponding column sum plus value added.

6.2.4 Expenditures and Sales Taxes on Consumer Goods

We have already adjusted the aggregate vector of sixteen consumption values such that their sum equals the sum of the vector of the twelve groups' disposable incomes. To obtain the matrix of expenditures on each consumer good by each group, we multiply the numbers in table 5.2

---

7. Exports in table 5.1 were not adjusted. Imports were scaled to the same total, as described in section 5.6.

(which represent expenditures per household) by the number of households in each consumer group (table 5.3). The resulting matrix, however, is not consistent with either the aggregate consumption vector or the disposable income vector. The sum of each household's expenditures does not match its disposable income, and the sum of all groups' expenditures on a given product does not equal the appropriate total consumption for that good. We therefore apply the RAS procedure again to this matrix. Rows and columns are scaled successively until each row adds to the correct total consumption and, simultaneously, each column adds to the correct disposable income.

The final step is to divide the expenditure data between net expenditures and payments of sales taxes. We divide total consumer sales tax payments (table 5.4) by total consumer expenditures for each of the sixteen consumer goods, giving us a sales tax rate for each good.[8] We multiply these sales tax rates by the newly adjusted elements of the consumer expenditure matrix, and the result is a matrix of sales tax payments. We then subtract this sales tax matrix from the expenditure matrix to get a matrix of net expenditures.

6.3   Benchmark Calibration

As noted in the introduction to this chapter, we choose parameters for the model by using the calibration method. We assume that producers minimize cost and receive zero excess profits. These assumptions have certain implications that allow us to choose the values of the production function parameters. Similarly, the assumption that households maximize their utility subject to a budget constraint has implications that allow us to choose the values of the utility function parameters. Similar logic applies to the choice of parameters in the government's utility function. We describe these calculations in this section.

When we use CES utility functions or production functions, the assumptions of cost minimization and utility maximization leave us with one free parameter. To deal with this problem we specify the elasticity of substitution parameters on the basis of estimates from the econometric literature. The values of the other parameters then follow from the restrictions imposed by cost minimization and utility maximization. The choices of elasticity parameters are discussed in section 6.4.

Notation in the rest of this chapter corresponds to that of chapter 3 and to the notational appendix of chapter 3.

---

8. We believe it is reasonable to assume that the government does not differentiate among consumers when it levies sales taxes, such that each consumer faces the same sales tax rate.

6.3.1 Calibration of the Value-Added Functions

Consider the CES value-added function in equation (3.2), reproduced here:

$$(6.1) \qquad VA = \phi \left[\delta L^{\frac{\sigma-1}{\sigma}} + (1-\delta)K^{\frac{\sigma-1}{\sigma}} \right]^{\frac{\sigma}{\sigma-1}} .$$

For expositional simplicity, we suppress the i subscripts of all variables and parameters. If producers minimize the cost of a unit of output, they will minimize the Lagrangean:

$$(6.2) \quad \mathscr{L} = P_K^* K + P_L^* L + \lambda \left[\phi \left\{ \delta L^{\frac{\sigma-1}{\sigma}} + (1-\delta)K^{\frac{\sigma-1}{\sigma}} \right\}^{\frac{\sigma}{\sigma-1}} - 1 \right],$$

where P_K^* is the cum-tax cost of capital, $P_K(1 + t_K)$, and P_L^* is the cum-tax cost of labor, $P_L(1 + t_L)$. The first order conditions with respect to L and K are given by:

$$(6.3) \qquad \frac{\partial \mathscr{L}}{\partial K} = P_K^* + \lambda\phi\{ \cdot \}^{\frac{1}{\sigma-1}}(1-\delta)K^{-\frac{1}{\sigma}} = 0$$

and

$$(6.4) \qquad \frac{\partial \mathscr{L}}{\partial L} = P_L^* + \lambda\phi\{ \cdot \}^{\frac{1}{\sigma-1}}\delta L^{-\frac{1}{\sigma}} = 0 ,$$

where $\{ \cdot \}$ is $\left\{ \delta L^{\frac{\sigma-1}{\sigma}} + (1-\delta)K^{\frac{\sigma-1}{\sigma}} \right\}$.

If we divide (6.3) by (6.4), we get:

$$(6.5) \qquad \frac{P_K^*}{P_L^*} = \frac{(1-\delta)K^{-\frac{1}{\sigma}}}{\delta L^{-\frac{1}{\sigma}}} .$$

With a little rearrangement we can solve for δ.

$$(6.6) \qquad \delta = \frac{P_L^* L^{\frac{1}{\sigma}}/P_K^* K^{\frac{1}{\sigma}}}{1 + P_L^* L^{\frac{1}{\sigma}}/P_K^* K^{\frac{1}{\sigma}}} .$$

Recall that, by our unit conventions, the benchmark net-of-tax factor prices P_L and P_K equal one. As a result, equation (6.6) can be rewritten as:

$$(6.7) \qquad \delta = \frac{(1 + t_L)L^{\frac{1}{\sigma}}/(1 + t_K)K^{\frac{1}{\sigma}}}{1 + (1 + t_L)L^{\frac{1}{\sigma}}/(1 + t_K)K^{\frac{1}{\sigma}}}.$$

Our unit conventions further imply that the number of units of each factor equals the *value* of factor use net of tax. Thus, for each industry, L and t_L are available from table 4.1, and K and t_K are available from table 4.7. As a result, when we specify a value for σ (see section 6.4 below), we have all the information necessary to use equation (6.7) and calculate δ.

Once we know σ and δ for each industry, we can calculate ϕ, using the zero-profit condition. This condition implies that

$$(6.8) \qquad P_K^* K + P_L^* L = VA.$$

But since P_K and P_L are unity in the benchmark, we have

$$(6.9) \qquad \phi = \frac{(1 + t_K)K + (1 + t_L)L}{\delta L^{\frac{\sigma-1}{\sigma}} + (1 - \delta)K^{\frac{\sigma-1}{\sigma}}}.$$

In section (6.4) we choose $\sigma = 1$ for some of our industries. In this Cobb-Douglas case,

$$(6.10) \qquad VA = \phi L^{\delta} K^{1-\delta}.$$

The first-order conditions in this case are

$$(6.11) \qquad \frac{\partial \mathcal{L}}{\partial K} = P_K^* + \frac{\lambda\phi(1 + \delta)L^{\delta}K^{1-\delta}}{K} = 0$$

and

$$(6.12) \qquad \frac{\partial \mathcal{L}}{\partial L} = P^* + \frac{\lambda\phi\delta L^{\delta}K^{1-\delta}}{L} = 0.$$

If we follow through with the same of kind of manipulations represented by equations (6.5) and (6.6), we get

$$(6.13) \qquad \delta = \frac{P_L^* L/P_K^* K}{1 + P_L^* L/P_K^* K}.$$

It follows, in the Cobb-Douglas case, that

$$(6.14) \qquad \phi = \frac{(1 + t_K)K + (1 + t_L)L}{L^{\delta}K^{1-\delta}}.$$

Finally, the adjusted input-output transactions matrix discussed earlier is not in the final form we need. We need a matrix of input-output coefficients. To do this, we divide each column of the adjusted 1973 transactions table by gross output in that industry.

6.3.2 Calibration of Household Utility Functions

We set out the details of the structure of preferences for our twelve consumer groups in section 3.4. In order to perform equilibrium calculations with this structure, we need to specify the values of a large number of parameters for each consumer. These include the following: λ_1, λ_2, . . . , λ_{15}, the weighting parameters that determine the choice among the fifteen consumption goods other than saving; σ_1, the elasticity of substitution between present leisure and present consumption of goods; β, the weighting parameter between present leisure and present consumption of goods; σ_2, the elasticity of substitution between present and future consumption; and α, the weighting parameter between present and future consumption.

The first set of parameters that we specify is the set of λ_m ($m = 1, . . . , 15$) budget share parameters for the fifteen consumer goods other than savings. Since the inner nest of the utility function is of the Cobb-Douglas type, we merely take each consumer's adjusted expenditure on each of the fifteen goods and divide by the consumer's total expenditure on all fifteen goods. The resulting values are shown in table 6.7. The trends in table 6.7 are rather unsurprising. For example, the proportion of income devoted to food (good 1), utilities (good 4), and housing (good 5) is larger among poor households than among rich ones. The richest group spends a higher proportion of its income on furnishings, clothing and jewelry, services, and financial services than does any other group.

In order to choose the other parameters, we first specify values for: γ, the after-tax rate of return in the benchmark; ξ, the uncompensated elasticity of labor supply with respect to the net wage rate; η, the uncompensated elasticity of saving with respect to the net rate of return; and ζ, the ratio of labor endowment to the labor supply (E/L where $L = E - \ell$).

We will discuss our choices of these latter parameters in section 6.4. For now let us say that our standard case is to set $\xi = 0.15$, $\eta = 0.4$, and $\zeta = 1.75$ for all consumers. Actual labor supply and ζ together imply knowledge of leisure and total endowment in the benchmark. (We will occasionally alter these parameters when we perform sensitivity analyses.) For γ we start with an average value of 0.04 and then make corrections for each household on the basis of marginal tax rates.

Our calibration procedures begin with the derivation of $\hat{\xi}$, defined as the elasticity of demand for *leisure* with respect to its price P_ℓ, the net wage rate. This derivation proceeds as follows. We know that the labor supply elasticity is

Table 6.7   Consumer Cobb-Douglas Preference Parameters for the Fifteen Consumer Goods Other Than Savings

Good/Consumer	1	2	3	4	5	6	7	8	9	10	11	12
1. Food	0.197	0.202	0.198	0.201	0.189	0.182	0.185	0.185	0.180	0.177	0.169	0.146
2. Alcoholic beverages	0.018	0.023	0.024	0.025	0.025	0.028	0.025	0.029	0.024	0.027	0.024	0.028
3. Tobacco	0.022	0.019	0.018	0.018	0.019	0.019	0.020	0.019	0.017	0.016	0.013	0.008
4. Utilities	0.062	0.059	0.059	0.056	0.056	0.051	0.050	0.048	0.048	0.044	0.040	0.035
5. Housing	0.218	0.200	0.180	0.173	0.162	0.155	0.153	0.149	0.141	0.141	0.137	0.125
6. Furnishings	0.026	0.030	0.031	0.028	0.030	0.032	0.037	0.033	0.037	0.043	0.046	0.046
7. Appliances	0.028	0.029	0.030	0.031	0.032	0.038	0.037	0.035	0.037	0.033	0.031	0.025
8. Clothing and jewelry	0.058	0.067	0.065	0.074	0.072	0.076	0.077	0.082	0.081	0.087	0.090	0.095
9. Transportation	0.011	0.012	0.011	0.010	0.008	0.009	0.009	0.009	0.006	0.007	0.008	0.012
10. Motor vehicles, tires, and auto repairs	0.059	0.065	0.064	0.062	0.086	0.083	0.081	0.097	0.095	0.092	0.091	0.083
11. Services	0.137	0.124	0.133	0.137	0.132	0.133	0.131	0.122	0.127	0.134	0.145	0.195
12. Financial services	0.052	0.060	0.074	0.066	0.070	0.068	0.067	0.062	0.069	0.061	0.066	0.082
13. Reading, recreation, and miscellaneous	0.029	0.033	0.028	0.035	0.032	0.037	0.042	0.045	0.048	0.054	0.062	0.058
14. Nondurable, nonfood household items	0.046	0.042	0.042	0.045	0.044	0.041	0.040	0.041	0.041	0.038	0.036	0.029
15. Gasoline and other fuel	0.038	0.037	0.042	0.040	0.043	0.047	0.046	0.047	0.049	0.045	0.042	0.033

$$(6.15) \qquad \xi = \frac{\partial(E - \ell)}{\partial P_\ell} \cdot \frac{P_\ell}{(E - \ell)} = \left(\frac{\partial E}{\partial P_\ell} - \frac{\partial \ell}{\partial P_\ell} \right) \cdot \frac{P_\ell}{(E - \ell)}.$$

Since $\partial E / \partial P_\ell = 0$, we can define the elasticity of leisure demand as:

$$(6.16) \qquad \hat{\xi} = \frac{\partial \ell}{\partial P_\ell} \cdot \frac{P_\ell}{\ell} = -\xi \cdot \frac{(E - \ell)}{\ell} = -\xi \cdot \frac{1}{(\zeta - 1)}.$$

In the central case where $\xi = 0.15$ and $\zeta = 1.75$, this equation implies that $\hat{\xi} = -0.20$.

The next step is to solve for σ_1, the elasticity of substitution between present consumption and present leisure. We start with equation (3.18), which represents the demand for leisure, reproduced here as:

$$(6.17) \qquad \ell = \frac{\beta(I - SP_S)}{P_\ell^{\sigma_1} \Delta_1}.$$

Notice that β and P_S are the only elements of equation (6.17) that do not depend on P_ℓ. Taking the derivative of this equation with respect to P_ℓ, we get

$$(6.18) \qquad \frac{\partial \ell}{\partial P_\ell} = \frac{-\beta(I - SP_S)\sigma_1}{\Delta_1 P_\ell^{(\sigma_1 + 1)}} + \frac{\beta}{P_\ell^{\sigma_1} \Delta_1} \left[\frac{\partial I}{\partial P_\ell} - P_S \frac{\partial S}{\partial P_\ell} \right]$$

$$- \frac{\beta(I - SP_S)}{P_\ell^{\sigma_1} \Delta_1^2} \cdot \left(\frac{\partial \Delta_1}{\partial P_\ell} \right).$$

Let us take a closer look at $\partial S / \partial P_\ell$, which appears in the middle term of equation (6.18). First, we reproduce equation (3.14), which gave the demand for savings:

$$(6.19) \qquad S = \frac{(1 - \alpha)I}{P_S^{\sigma_2} \left[\dfrac{\bar{P}}{P_K^\gamma} \right]^{\sigma_2 - 1} \Delta_2}$$

The net wage P_ℓ affects S in two ways. First, there is a $P_\ell E$ term in I which corresponds to the income effect of P_ℓ on S. Consequently, $\partial I / \partial P_\ell = E$. Secondly, there is a P_ℓ term in P_H which is in Δ_2, corresponding to the cross-price effect. This latter effect is indirect and can be shown to be very small in this case. Incorporating this effect would require advance knowledge of Δ_2, β, and σ_2, whose derivation in turn depends on σ_1, α, and Δ_1. While the system of nonlinear simultaneous equations in these variables is, in principle, soluble, we ignore the indirect cross-price effect and only consider the income effect. We thus use the approximation

(6.20)
$$\frac{\partial S}{\partial P_\ell} \approx \frac{(1-\alpha)E}{P_S^{\sigma 2}\left(\dfrac{\bar{P}}{P_K\gamma}\right)^{\sigma 2-1}\Delta_2} = \frac{SE}{I}.$$

If we substitute the results of the preceding paragraph into equation (6.18), we get

(6.21)
$$\frac{\partial \ell}{\partial P_\ell} = \frac{-\beta(I - SP_S)\sigma_1}{\Delta_1 P_\ell^{(\sigma_1+1)}} + \frac{\beta}{P_\ell^{\sigma_1}\Delta_1}\left[E - \frac{P_S SE}{I}\right]$$
$$- \frac{\beta(I - SP_S)}{P_\ell^{\sigma_1}\Delta_1^2}\left(\frac{\partial \Delta_1}{\partial P_\ell}\right).$$

Next, we use the equation for leisure, (6.17), to factor this expression.

(6.22)
$$\frac{\partial \ell}{\partial P_\ell} = \frac{-\ell\sigma_1}{P_\ell} + \frac{\beta}{P_\ell^{\sigma_1}\Delta_1}\left[E - \frac{P_S SE}{I}\right] - \frac{\ell}{\Delta_1}\left(\frac{\partial \Delta_1}{\partial P_\ell}\right).$$

Finally, we must evaluate $\partial \Delta_1/\partial P_\ell$. We rewrite equation (3.19), which specifies Δ_1:

(6.23)
$$\Delta_1 = \left[(1-\beta)\bar{P}^{(1-\sigma_1)} + \beta P_\ell^{(1-\sigma_1)}\right].$$

This implies that $\dfrac{\partial \Delta_1}{\partial P_\ell} = \dfrac{\beta(1-\sigma_1)}{P_\ell^{\sigma_1}}$, and, therefore:

(6.24)
$$\frac{\partial \ell}{\partial P_\ell} = \frac{-\ell\sigma_1}{P_\ell} + \frac{\beta}{P_\ell^{\sigma_1}\Delta_1}\left[E - \frac{P_S SE}{I}\right] - \frac{\ell\beta(1-\sigma_1)}{P_\ell^{\sigma_1}\Delta_1}.$$

The elasticity definition implies that

(6.25)
$$\hat{\xi} = \frac{\partial \ell}{\partial P_\ell}\cdot\frac{P_\ell}{\ell} = -\sigma_1 + \frac{\beta P_\ell^{(1-\sigma_1)}}{\ell\Delta_1}\left[E - \frac{P_S SE}{I}\right]$$
$$- \frac{\beta P_\ell^{(1-\sigma_1)}(1-\sigma_1)}{\Delta_1}.$$

We can rewrite equation (6.17) as:

(6.26)
$$\frac{\beta P_\ell^{(1-\sigma_1)}}{\Delta_1} = \frac{P_\ell \ell}{I - SP_S}.$$

With this arrangement, we can derive a new expression for $\hat{\xi}$:

(6.27)
$$\hat{\xi} = -\sigma_1 + \frac{P_\ell E}{I} - \frac{P_\ell \ell(1-\sigma_1)}{I - SP_S}.$$

Finally, solving for σ_1, we get:

$$(6.28) \qquad \sigma_1 = \left[-\hat{\xi} + \frac{P_\ell E}{I} - \frac{P_\ell \ell}{I - SP_S} \right] \bigg/ \left[1 - \frac{P_\ell \ell}{I - SP_S} \right].$$

The parameter $\hat{\xi}$ is derived above, P_ℓ is obtained from the consumer's marginal tax rate, and the other values appear in the benchmark data set, including E, I, and S. The price of savings, P_S, is less than unity because the U.S. tax system allows deductions for certain kinds of savings as described in chapter 9.

Once σ_1 is obtained from (6.28), we can solve for β. First, we reproduce equation (3.17), which gives us the amount of current consumption on goods other than leisure.

$$(6.29) \qquad \bar{X} = \frac{(1 - \beta)(I - SP_S)}{\bar{P}^{\sigma_1} \Delta_1}.$$

Taking the ratio of equation (6.17) to equation (6.29), we have

$$(6.30) \qquad \frac{\ell}{\bar{X}} = \frac{\beta(I - SP_S)/P_\ell^{\sigma_1} \Delta_1}{(1 - \beta)(I - SP_S)/\bar{P}^{\sigma_1} \Delta_1} = \frac{\beta}{(1 - \beta)} \cdot \frac{\bar{P}^{\sigma_1}}{P_\ell^{\sigma_1}}.$$

Solving for β yields

$$(6.31) \qquad \beta = \frac{\ell P_\ell^{\sigma_1}/\bar{X}\bar{P}^{\sigma_1}}{1 + \ell P_\ell^{\sigma_1}/\bar{X}\bar{P}^{\sigma_1}}.$$

We know the λ_m expenditure shares on the fifteen consumer goods, and we know cum-tax prices P_m^* from the unit convention and tax rates, so we can calculate $\bar{X}$ from equation (3.23) and $\bar{P}$ from equation (3.26). Other right-hand parameters have been discussed, so β is now available. In table 6.8 we present the values of σ_1 and β for the twelve consumers.

Our next task is to find values for σ_2, the elasticity of substitution between present and future consumption, and the weighting parameter, α. We first specify a value for $\eta = (\partial S/\partial r)(r/S)$—the elasticity of saving with respect to the real after-tax rate of return. This rate of return r is given by $r = P_K \gamma/P_S$, as discussed in section 3.4. To find σ_2 as a function of η we could, in principle, follow procedures very similar to those above. To find σ_1 as a function of ξ, we differentiated ℓ with respect to P_ℓ. Here we would differentiate the demand for S, equation (3.14), with respect to the rate of return r. Reproduced here,

$$(6.32) \qquad S = \frac{(1 - \alpha)I}{P_S^{\sigma_2} \left(\dfrac{\bar{P}}{P_K \gamma} \right)^{\sigma_2 - 1} \Delta_2}.$$

Table 6.8   Values for the Elasticity of Substitution between Current Leisure and Current Consumption, σ_1, and the Weighting Parameter, β (assuming the labor supply elasticity is 0.15)

Consumer Group	σ_1	β
1	0.569	0.201
2	0.674	0.248
3	0.777	0.287
4	0.838	0.309
5	0.886	0.325
6	0.948	0.343
7	0.983	0.354
8	0.990	0.359
9	1.027	0.371
10	1.005	0.369
11	0.969	0.366
12	0.738	0.350

As a practical matter, it is exceedingly difficult to evaluate $\partial S/\partial r$ analytically. The $\partial \bar{P}/\partial P_K$ and $\partial P_S/\partial P_K$ terms depend on the capital/labor ratios of particular outputs, and there are many other complex interactions as well. Consequently, we evaluate $\partial S/\partial r$ numerically, using an iterative procedure. The object of the procedure is to choose a value of σ_2 that implies a given value for the saving elasticity.[9] Basically, the iterative procedure involves a numerical differentiation. First, we calculate the values of S and r when all prices are equal to one. Then, we arbitrarily increase the value of P_K by 1 percent and recalculate all of the prices, incomes, and demands. The 1 percent change in P_K results in particular changes for r—the rate of return—and for S—the value of saving. These changes are used to obtain $\eta = \Delta S/\Delta r \cdot r/S$ for each consumer. If this η is greater than the desired value, then σ_2 is adjusted downward, and conversely. After few iterations we obtain the vector shown in table 6.9, resulting in $\eta = 0.4$ for every consumer. (A similar procedure of varying the price of labor by 1 percent was used to verify the 0.15 uncompensated wage elasticity of labor supply.)

Once we have values of σ_2, we can calculate values for α for each household. To do so, we need the expressions for H (present consumption of goods and leisure) and C_F (future consumption), which first appeared as equations (3.11) and (3.12). These are reproduced here as:

$$(6.33) \qquad H = \frac{\alpha I}{P_H^{\sigma_2} \Delta_2}$$

9. We usually choose a savings elasticity of $\eta = 0.4$, although we sometimes perform sensitivity analyses with respect to this parameter. For any alternative η, we must iterate again to find the corresponding σ_2.

Table 6.9   **Values for the Elasticity of Substitution between Present and Future Consumption, σ_2, and the Weighting Parameter, α (assuming the saving elasticity is 0.4)**

Consumer Group	σ_2	α
1	1.319	0.980
2	1.531	0.937
3	1.585	0.900
4	1.600	0.857
5	1.618	0.823
6	1.641	0.787
7	1.668	0.739
8	1.673	0.689
9	1.697	0.625
10	1.698	0.580
11	1.675	0.560
12	1.500	0.488

and

$$(6.34) \qquad C_F = \frac{(1-\alpha)I}{P_{CF}^{\sigma_2}\Delta_2},$$

where P_{CF} is the "price" of future consumption, $P_S \bar{P}/P_K \gamma$. Taking the ratio of the two, we get

$$(6.35) \qquad \frac{H}{C_F} = \frac{\alpha I/P_H^{\sigma_2}\Delta_2}{(1-\alpha)I/P_{CF}^{\sigma_2}\Delta_2} = \frac{\alpha}{1-\alpha} \cdot \frac{P_{CF}^{\sigma_2}}{P_H^{\sigma_2}}.$$

Solving for α yields

$$(6.36) \qquad \alpha = \frac{HP_H^{\sigma_2}/C_F P_{CF}^{\sigma_2}}{1 + HP_H^{\sigma_2}/C_F P_{CF}^{\sigma_2}}.$$

From equation (3.7), we can see that

$$(6.37) \qquad C_F = SP_S/P_{CF}.$$

It follows that

$$(6.38) \qquad \alpha = \frac{HP_H^{\sigma_2}/SP_S P_{CF}^{(\sigma_2-1)}}{1 + HP_H^{\sigma_2}/SP_S P_{CF}^{(\sigma_2-1)}}.$$

Since σ_1 and β are already available, H can be obtained from equation (3.15) and P_H from equation (3.27). Savings S and prices are also available for the right-hand side. The resulting values for σ_2 and α are shown in table 6.9.

6.3.3   Calibration of Government Expenditures

As noted in section 3.6, the government has a Cobb-Douglas utility function, which is defined over the nineteen producer goods, plus labor and capital. The adjusted data for government expenditure on the nineteen producer goods were shown in table 6.4. We discussed the government's payments to labor and capital in section 5.5. When we combine all these expenditure data and calculate the expenditure shares, we get the Cobb-Douglas parameters that are listed in table 6.10.

6.4   Elasticities

6.4.1   Value-Added Elasticities

We rely on a literature search to provide estimates of production function substitution elasticities. Since the introduction of the CES function, many economists have estimated the values of elasticities. Estimates have been obtained using a variety of econometric procedures and for various industrial classifications, although in the process some seemingly contradictory estimates have been produced.

Table 6.10   General Government Cobb-Douglas Preference Parameters for the Nineteen Producer Goods, Capital, and Labor

Commodity	Expenditure Share
Agriculture, forestry, fisheries	0.0
Mining	0.004
Crude petroleum and gas	0.0
Contract construction	0.0886
Food and tobacco	0.0029
Textiles, apparel, and leather	0.0013
Paper and printing	0.0042
Petroleum refining	0.0029
Chemicals, rubber, and plastics	0.0080
Lumber, furniture, stone, clay, and glass	0.0018
Metals, machinery, instruments, and miscellaneous manufacturing	0.0274
Transport equipment and ordnance	0.0312
Motor vehicles	0.0049
Transportation, communications, and utilities	0.0193
Trade	0.0041
Finance and insurance	0.0017
Real estate	0.0035
Services	0.0313
Government enterprises	0.0016
Capital	0.3333
Labor	0.4316

Many researchers have attempted to estimate substitution elasticities between capital and labor in U.S. manufacturing. Ernst Berndt paraphrases the disagreements among estimates in the following terms:

Studies based on cross-sectional data provide estimates which are close to unity, but time-series generally report lower estimates. Furthermore, estimates of σ seem to vary systematically with the choice of functional form; regressions based on the marginal product of capital relation generally produce lower estimates of σ than regressions based on the marginal product of labor relation. (1976, p. 59)

Several hypotheses have been advanced to rationalize these discrepancies, but none of the hypotheses has been wholly accepted. The most plausible explanation for the discrepancy between the time-series and cross-section results is that adjustments take place with a lag.

Our procedure is to use the hundreds of estimates reviewed by Vern Caddy (1976) and arrange these estimates on the producer good classification used in this study. For each group of estimates (for one elasticity parameter), we calculate the mean and variance of the group. These are reported in table 6.11, with a further partition into cross-section and time-series estimates.

In either the cross-section or time-series estimates of table 6.11, agriculture and food have elasticities somewhat lower than the manufacturing industries. Because of the difference between the two sets of estimates, we use the "overall" elasticities in the last columns of table 6.11. For those industries for which estimates are not available, we set the elasticities at unity, meaning that we employ a Cobb-Douglas production function.

6.4.2   Labor Supply Elasticities

In the general equilibrium model in its present form, consumers balance the competing objectives of increasing leisure by working less and of increasing consumption opportunities by working more. The uncompensated net-of-tax wage rate elasticity of labor supply, ξ, measures how this work choice is affected by changes in the net-of-tax wage. In subsection 6.3.2 we described the way in which a prespecified value of ξ is converted into the relevant parameters of the consumer's utility function.

Once again we appeal to the econometric literature in our search for the value of ξ. The econometric literature gives many estimates for population subgroups, since different individuals will typically have different rates of response to a new net-of-tax wage. Finegan's (1962) occupational study found managers, craftsmen, and clerical workers varying from a $-.29$ to a $+.42$ labor supply elasticity, while Boskin's (1973) division by sex, race, and age found estimates from $-.07$ (for prime-age white males) to $+1.60$ (for elderly black women). In table 6.12

Table 6.11 Central Tendency for Estimates of Elasticity of Substitution by Industry Reported by Caddy (1976)

	Cross-Section			Time-Series			Overall		
	a	b	c	a	b	c	a	b	c
Agriculture, forestry, fisheries	.8312	(.1078	27)	.3971	(.0688	15)	.6759	(.1369	42)
Mining	No information								
Crude petroleum and gas	No information								
Contract construction	No information								
Food and tobacco	.8912	(.1160	24)	.5322	(.1072	24)	.7117	(.1439	48)
Textiles, apparel, and leather	1.0530	(.1198	65)	.5773	(.1063	30)	.9025	(.1643	95)
Paper and printing	1.0468	(.0857	49)	.4895	(.0795	17)	.9033	(.1435	66)
Petroleum refining	.9342	(.1000	14)	.5479	(.1227	9)	.7830	(.1444	23)
Chemicals, rubber, and plastics	1.1482	(.2321	64)	.5086	(.1194	27)	.9603	(.2808	91)
Lumber, furniture, stone, clay, and glass	1.0218	(.1142	88)	.5585	(.1800	31)	.9123	(.1656	118)
Metals, machinery, instruments, and miscellaneous manufacturing	.8719	(.1183	109)	.4844	(.1057	58)	.7373	(.1479	167)
Transport equipment and ordnance	1.0534	(.3470	14)	.3407	(.0388	7)	.8159	(.3572	21)
Motor vehicles	1.1782	(.3755	18)	.4631	(.0770	10)	.9228	(.3863	28)
Transportation, communications, and utilities	No information								
Trade	No information								
Finance and insurance	No information								
Real estate	No information								
Services	No information								
Government enterprises	No information								

Notes: For each column the numbers reported are a) the mean of the estimates, b) the variance among the estimates, and c) the number of estimates available.

we list the results of a number of econometric studies. Table 6.12 is based primarily on the review by Mark Killingsworth (1983).

A certain injustice is perpetrated against these authors by reporting their results in such summary fashion. Each study has its own mesure of the wage, its own data year or time period, and its own functional form. Also, the studies differ as to how they account for participation rates. The numbers in table 6.12 are provided only to give the reader a framework for choosing a plausible aggregate labor supply elasticity.

Elasticity estimates for males are mostly small and negative, ranging from $-.40$ to 0. Borjas and Heckman (1978) review the econometrics of these studies and reduce the bounds to $-.19$ and $-.07$. The estimates for females are more often positive, and can be large in absolute value. Killingsworth finds that females' elasticity estimates are mostly between $.20$ and $.90$ in cross-section studies. To obtain the model's aggregate labor supply elasticity of 0.15, which we use for each of the twelve consumer groups, we perform a rough numerical calculation. The *Statistical Abstract* (U.S. Department of Commerce, Bureau of the Census, 1973) shows that the median money income of male employed civilians has consistently been twice that of females. It also shows about a 1.7 ratio of males to females in the labor force—a ratio that is decreasing with time. In any case, the ratio of male to female income should be at least 3.0 (though decreasing). Taking a male elasticity of $-.10$ and a female elasticity of $+.90$, the three-to-one weighted average is a 0.15 aggregate elasticity.

We need to specify one other parameter dealing with the labor/leisure choice, and that is ζ, the ratio of labor endowment to actual labor supply in the benchmark. This is the parameter that we use to convert from a labor supply elasticity to a leisure demand elasticity (see section 6.3.2). In the absence of concrete data, we choose 1.75 for ζ, to reflect that individuals typically work a forty-hour, out of a possible seventy-hour week. This parameter is surprisingly important, however, since its value affects the difference between the compensated and uncompensated labor supply elasticities. Consider equations (6.28) and (6.16), which together show how ξ and ζ determine σ_1, the elasticity of substitution between consumption goods and leisure. With other parameters given, a higher ζ raises E in equation (6.28). It therefore raises σ_1, a crucial parameter in determining the distorting effects of taxes on labor. Without empirical estimates of ζ, then, it is particularly important to perform sensitivity analyses.[10]

---

10. Welfare costs of distorting labor taxes increase with σ_1 and therefore with ζ. When we integrate corporate and personal taxes, as in chapter 8, and replace lost revenue with additional taxes on labor, the net gains are inversely related to ζ. Fullerton, Henderson, and Shoven (1984) report results when ζ is set to 1.25, the standard 1.75, and a final value of 2.25. The present value of net welfare gains are $512.5 billion, $344.4 billion, and $244.6 billion, respectively.

Table 6.12   Estimates of the Uncompensated Labor Supply Elasticity

A. Males

Authors	Data Subset	Type of Data	Range of Estimates
Finegan (1962)	Male family heads	Interoccupational	−.35 to −.25
Rosen (1969)	Male family heads	Interindustry	−.30 to −.07
Kalachek-Raines (1970)	Male family heads	U.S. cross-section	+.05 to +.30
Owen (1971)	Male family heads	U.S. time-series	−.24 to −.11
Greenberg-Kosters (1973)	Poor male family heads	U.S. cross-section	−.16 to −.05
Boskin (1973)	Different male subgroups	U.S. cross-section	−.07 to +.18
Hill (1973)	Poor male family heads	U.S. cross-section	−.32 to −.07
Ashenfelter-Heckman (1973)	Male family heads	U.S. cross-section	−.15
Fleisher-Parsons-Porter (1973)	Males age 45–59	U.S. cross-section	−.25 to −.10
Ashenfelter-Heckman (1974)	Married males	U.S. cross-section	0
Burtless-Hausman (1978)	Low-income males	Gary NIT cross-section	0
Hausman (1981)	Married males	U.S. cross-section	0

B. For Females

Authors	Data Subset	Type of Data	Range of Estimates
Finegan (1962)	Females	Interoccupational	−.095
Leuthold (1968)	Females	U.S. cross-section	−.067
Kalachek-Raines (1970)	Females	U.S. cross-section	+.20 to +.90
Boskin (1973)	Different female subgroups	U.S. cross-section	−.04 to +1.60
Ashenfelter-Heckman (1974)	Married females	U.S. cross-section	.87
Hausman (1981)	Married females	U.S. cross-section	.9
Hausman (1981)	Female household heads	U.S. cross-section	.5

C. Aggregate

Authors	Data Subset	Type of Data	Range of Estimates
Winston (1966)	Aggregate	International cross-section	−.11 to −.05
Lucas-Rapping (1970)	Short-run aggregate	Time-series	1.35 to 1.58
Lucas-Rapping (1970)	Long-run aggregate	Time-series	0 to 1.12

6.4.3   The Saving Elasticity

Our parameter η represents the uncompensated elasticity of saving with respect to changes in the real after-tax rate of return. To see what economic theory tells us about η, consider saving as an expenditure on future consumption. An increase in the net rate of return lowers the price of future consumption. The compensated quantity demanded must rise, but the percentage increases may exceed or fall short of the percentage decrease in price. The resulting expenditure on future consumption (saving) may rise or fall, so the sign of η is ambiguous.

Empirical estimates of η have hardly narrowed the range of plausible values. Denison's law states that η is zero, following Edward Denison's (1958) observation that saving as a fraction of income in the United States has been a historical constant. Econometric estimates by Michael Boskin (1978) suggest that η is significantly positive. Using eight different regressions, Boskin finds values for η that range from 0.2 to 0.6, but that cluster between 0.3 and 0.4. Howrey and Hymans (1978) use Boskin's data but find that estimates of η are sensitive to (1) the measure of expected inflation, (2) the sample period, (3) the definition of saving, and (4) the interest rate variable chosen for the regression. They cannot reject the hypothesis that η is zero.

More recently, Lawrence Summers (1981) builds a model in which lifetime consumption plans depend upon several factors, including parameters for intertemporal substitution in utility, time until retirement and death, the rate of time preference, rates of growth, and the rate of return to saving. The model is then solved for the saving elasticity. Plausible values for these other parameters imply values for η that range from 1.5 to 3.0, much higher than those of the econometric estimates described above. Finally, David Starrett (1982) and Owen Evans (1983) show how amendments to Summers's model could widen these bounds still further, but they argue for values of η that are lower than those found by Summers.

Given the wide range of estimates, the saving elasticity is a particularly important candidate for sensitivity analyses. In our standard set of parameters, used for calculations in later chapters, we employ Boskin's central estimate of 0.4 for η. We then report additional results for alternative values of this saving elasticity.

6.4.4   Commodity Demand Elasticities

We use Cobb-Douglas forms for the subutility function that determines the allocation of consumption expenditures among consumer good categories. As a result, there is no need to specify substitution elasticities. All own-price elasticities are -1, all income elasticities are unity, and all cross-price elasticities are zero. Cobb-Douglas exponents are given from data on expenditure shares (see table 6.7).

6.4.5   External Sector Parameters

Specification of parameter values for our foreign trade functions (3.46) involves the unit terms M_i^0, E_i^0, and the elasticity parameters μ and ν.

Since the benchmark equilibrium is characterized by prices of unity and overall trade balance, the unit terms M_i^0 and E_i^0 are equal to the benchmark trade values shown in table 5.1.

Equations (3.50) and (3.51) define the foreign price elasticities of export demand (ϵ_E^{FD}) and import supply (ϵ_M^{FS}). We reproduce these here as:

$$(6.39) \qquad \epsilon_E^{FD} = \frac{\nu(1 + \mu)}{(\mu - \nu)}$$

and

$$(6.40) \qquad \epsilon_M^{FS} = \frac{-\mu(1 + \nu)}{(\mu - \nu)}.$$

Once we have values for ϵ_E^{FD} and ϵ_M^{FS}, therefore, we can calculate implied values for ν and μ. An approximate central case value for ϵ_E^{FD} is -1.4, as seen in the compendium of trade elasticities provided by Stern, Francis, and Schumacher (1976). If we accept this value for ϵ_E^{FD}, we can rewrite equation (6.39) as:

$$(6.41) \qquad \mu = \frac{0.4\nu}{1.4 + \nu}.$$

Of course, this equation is satisfied by an infinite number of combinations of μ and ν. Because the demand for U.S. exports in equation (3.41) should be highly sensitive to price, we postulate a high negative value for ν. As a practical matter, we set $\nu = -10$, so μ must be 0.465. Together, these figures imply 0.40 for the import supply elasticity ϵ_M^{FS}.

7   Dynamic Considerations

7.1   Dynamic Sequencing of Static Equilibria

Thus far we have discussed the economic model and data with which we can calculate a static general equilibrium for 1973. However, we think that tax policy evaluations based on single-period, static equilibria can be misleading. In particular, meaningful welfare calculations can be based on neither H—the utility of present consumption in 1973—nor U—the overall utility measure that includes expected consumption in later years.

First, consider a welfare measure based on H and consider a tax change that increases the net return to saving. If consumers respond to increasing saving incentives, then the utility H from current consumption will fall. Only over time will the additional savings provide enough capital deepening to allow for higher future consumption. Thus a policy that looks harmful in the short run can provide substantial welfare gains in the long run.

Second, consider a welfare measure, based on U, from 1973. This utility function includes expected future consumption for each household group. The expectations are myopic in that our consumers assume that the current price of capital will remain unchanged in the future.[1] Thus a tax change that raises the net rate of return also raises expectations about the amount of future consumption that can be obtained from a given amount of current saving. Actual capital deepening will bring the net return down; thus expected future consumption overstates actual future consumption. Expected utility, U, therefore overstates the utility from actual consumption.

---

1. In fact, the price of capital can change substantially over time, as we shall see when we consider some large policy changes in chapters 8 and 9.

The myopic expectations turn out to be correct if the economy is on a balanced growth plan. They are incorrect in any transition to a higher or lower capital/labor ratio, and they become more accurate as the economy settles down to a new steady-state path. Consequently, it is appropriate to look explicitly at the future path of the economy. In so doing we base our welfare measures on current consumption H from each year in a sequence of static equilibria. Preferences based on U and expected future consumption are used only insofar as they generate actual consumption and savings for any particular year.

The first equilibrium in every sequence is for the 1973 benchmark year. The later equilibria in a sequence can represent any later years. It would be possible to calculate one equilibrium for every year. However, computational expenses increase with the number of equilibria to be calculated. We usually calculate equilibria that are five or ten years apart, and we usually calculate enough equilibria to look fifty years beyond 1973. For example, we frequently calculate a sequence of equilibria representing the years 1973, 1983, 1993, 2003, 2013, and 2023.[2] Later in this chapter we discuss the sensitivity of our results to such choices.

The equilibria in any sequence are connected to each other through capital accumulation. Each single-period equilibrium calculation begins with an initial capital service endowment. Saving in the current period will augment the capital service endowment available in the next period. As we move through our sequence, the capital stock grows because of saving. When the capital endowment grows at the same rate as the effective labor force, the economy is on a *balanced growth path*.

In fact, we *assume* that, in a base-case sequence, the economy is on a steady-state, balanced growth path. This assumption is crucially important. Just as the assumption that the economy is in equilibrium in 1973 is central to the development of the static version of the model, so the assumption of a balanced growth path is central to the development of the dynamic version.

To be more precise, the definition of a steady-state growth path is a situation where tax policy is unchanging and

2. When we make our dynamic welfare calculations (as discussed below in section 7.2), we need to have the values of certain variables for every year, even though we do not usually make an equilibrium calculation for every year. In order to calculate the values of these variables for the intermediate years, we assume that the path between equilibria is characterized by smooth exponential growth. For example, assume that we have calculated the value of the H function (defined in chapter 3) for 1973 and 1983. If we assume that the growth rate between the two years is constant, then it must be that $H_{1983} = H_{1973}(1 + GR)^{10}$ where GR is the growth rate. We can then solve for GR as

$$GR = \left[\frac{H_{1983}}{H_{1973}}\right]^{\frac{1}{10}} - 1.$$

Then, for the intermediate years, we calculate H as $H_{1973+t} = H_{1973}(1 + GR)^t$.

(7.1)
$$\frac{\dot{E}}{E} = \frac{\dot{K}}{K} = n,$$

where

E = labor endowment,
$\dot{E}$ = increase in labor endowment,
K = capital endowment,
$\dot{K}$ = increase in capital endowment, and
n = growth rate of effective units of labor.

Moreover, we separate the growth of effective labor units into components that reflect population growth and Harrod-neutral technical change (increase in productivity of existing labor). Thus,

(7.2)
$$n = (1 + h)(1 + g) - 1,$$

where

g = growth rate of natural units of labor,
h = growth rate of output per worker hour.

On the steady-state path, all relative prices remain constant. Tax policy changes will alter the steady-state path and set the economy on a transition path (which may be rather lengthy). Eventually the economy approaches a new steady state. Figure 7.1 illustrates the transition for a tax policy change which results in increased saving. Without the change, consumption per capita is growing at a constant rate. With the change, consumption is at first lower than it would have been. Consumption will then rise at a faster rate, however, as a result of the greater amount of capital accumulation. The level of consumption under the new regime

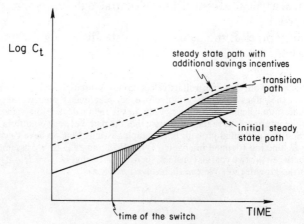

Fig. 7.1   The transition for a tax policy change that stimulates savings.

eventually surpasses the level under the old set of taxes, and consumption approaches a new balanced growth path asymptotically. By calculating a sequence of equilibria, we are able to study the transition in detail.

We choose the parameters for the dynamic version of our model in the following way. First, we observe the amount of saving and the size of the capital stock in the benchmark year. This gives us the rate of growth of capital. We then assume that the effective labor force grows at the same rate.

Using the notation in chapter 3, the expression $n = \dot{K}/K$ in equation (7.1) can be rewritten as

$$(7.3) \qquad n = \frac{S\gamma}{CAP(1 - \bar{f}\tau)},$$

where S is total savings, γ is the factor of conversion from stock to flow units, and CAP is capital income net of corporate and property taxes.[3] The multiplication by $(1 - \bar{f}\tau)$ is necessary because we define units of capital as being net of personal factor taxes.

If we plug the appropriate values from the consistent 1973 data set into equation (7.3), we can calculate n, the steady-state growth rate:

$$(7.4) \qquad n = \frac{(105441.7)(.04)}{(189672.9)(1 - (.816058)(.278288))} = 0.028770.$$

The endowment of effective labor must also grow at this rate. For simplicity we assume that the growth of effective labor is divided evenly between population growth and increased productivity. We therefore assume that $g = h$ in equation (7.2), and we solve the equation:

$$(7.5) \qquad g = h = \sqrt{1.02877} - 1 = 0.014283.$$

The importance of the division of n between g and h will become clearer later in this chapter, when we describe our dynamic welfare calculations. In particular, we are able to consider the effect of tax changes on a population that is the same size as the initial population. If we were to include the utility of additional individuals in later years, our welfare measure would be weighted in favor of future periods.

When all endowments and incomes increase at the rate n, and when demand functions are homogeneous of degree one in income, the government's tax receipts also grow proportionately. Transfer income will grow at the same rate because consumers are each given a share of government revenue in the benchmark. The only problem is presented by progressive personal income taxes. This problem is solved by scaling the (B_j) intercept of each linear tax schedule by the steady-state growth rate n. With a larger negative intercept and larger incomes subject to the same marginal

---

3. We choose $\gamma = .04$. We will discuss this choice later in this chapter.

tax rate, each consumer will experience a constant average rate of tax as income grows through time. The personal income tax remains progressive, however, in the sense that high-income consumers still have higher average and marginal tax rates than low-income consumers.

7.2   The Comparison of Dynamic Sequences

In this section we describe our procedures for the evaluation of alternative sequences of equilibria.

A well-known concept in static welfare analysis is the *compensating variation*, defined as the amount of additional income at new prices that would be necessary in order to allow the consumer to reach his old level of utility. The *equivalent variation* is defined as the amount of additional income at old prices that would enable the consumer to reach the new utility level.

We can derive the static compensating and equivalent variations for the H utility function (the CES composite of current consumption and leisure). The H function might be called an *evaluation function*, distinguishing it from the overall utility function, U, which we use to determine saving behavior. The H function is the appropriate one to use in our dynamic welfare evaluations. Since savings are used to buy future consumption, we would be double counting if we included savings in our evaluation of utility in the current period.

The first step in deriving compensating and equivalent variations is to solve for the expenditure function that corresponds to H. The budget constraint was provided in equation (3.8), which we reproduce here:

$$(7.6) \qquad\qquad I = P_H H + P_S S.$$

In equation (7.6), I is expanded income, as defined in equation (3.39). When we subtract $P_S S$ (the amount spent on saving), we have the income left over for current consumption and leisure. Let us call this I_H. Substitution implies

$$(7.7) \qquad\qquad I_H = H \cdot P_H.$$

The evaluation function H is a combination of goods and leisure, similar to a utility function. For present purposes, however, it is also useful to think of H as a composite commodity, a physical combination or aggregation of goods and leisure. Each unit of H costs P_H, provided in equation (3.27) as a composite of prices for goods and leisure. The expenditure function is $H \cdot P_H$, a function of the required utility level and prices.[4]

---

4. This equation does not hold exactly for the first of our twelve consumer groups, because we use a negative minimum purchase requirement to account for their negative savings.

Assume we have old values H^o, I_H^o, and P_H^o and new values H^n, I_H^n, and P_H^n. The compensating variation for any single period is defined as the additional income required to obtain old utility levels at new prices:

(7.8) $$CV = H^o P_H^n - H^n P_H^n = (H^o - H^n) P_H^n.$$

It is customary to reverse the sign of this welfare measure, such that the CV is positive for a welfare gain.

In similar fashion, we write the equivalent variation as

(7.9) $$EV = (H^n - H^o) P_H^o.$$

These measures can be applied to any consumer in any period, since we calculate each consumer's income and utility in each time period under each tax regime. A problem arises, however, in trying to sum a stream of compensating or equivalent variations, because these are measured in prices of different years from different sequences. Fortunately, the benchmark sequence is on a steady-state path, so its prices remain stable with no tax change. Thus a natural choice is to measure welfare gains in benchmark prices, equal to actual 1973 prices. For the ith period, then, the constant dollar difference between revise-case consumption and benchmark consumption is $(H_i^n - H_i^o) P_H^o$. If we use PV to denote a present value operator to be described below, then the present value of this stream of welfare gains is

(7.10) $$PVWG \equiv PV\left[(H_i^n - H_i^o) P_H^o\right] = P_H^o \cdot \left[PV(H_i^n) - PV(H_i^o)\right],$$

since P_H^o is a constant. Also, since $(H_i^n - H_i^o) P_H^o$ is just the EV for period i in unchanged prices, this measure might be interpreted as the present value of equivalent variations. This is the measure used to report all welfare gains in results below.

Because this measure is so important for our welfare evaluations, let us further describe and justify the choice in several ways. First, suppose that we want the present value of a CV measure that is comparable to the EV measure above. Since we need to add together the compensating variations for different periods, and since these are measured in all different prices P_{Hi}^n, we could convert them to constant prices P_H^o through the use of a price index P_{Hi}^n / P_H^o. Then the present value of these "real" CVs (with sign reversal) is:

(7.11) $$PV\left[\frac{(H_i^n - H_i^o) P_{Hi}^n}{P_{Hi}^n / P_{Hi}^o}\right],$$

which reduces to $PVWG$ from (7.10). The point is that compensating and equivalent variations are defined so as to express welfare changes in different prices, so the conversion to common prices eliminates any useful distinction between the two concepts. The welfare change $(H_i^n -$

H_i^o) could be multiplied by a price such as P_H^o or any price level from the revise-case sequence. Thus we merely use P_H^o.

Second, since $PVWG$ is in base-period prices, the welfare gains from one tax proposal can be compared directly to the welfare gains from a different tax proposal. That is, since $PVWG$ reduces to the present value of equivalent variations from each period, we have an argument analogous to that of John Kay (1980). The EV is preferred to the CV for comparing alternative replacement policies, since the CV are each measured in the new prices of each different replacement equilibrium.

Third, suppose that our model contained a lifetime utility function of the form $U(H_0, \ldots, H_T)$, where consumers could substitute consumption among the various periods in a CES function for U with a composite price P_U. Then there would exist a comprehensive expenditure function of the form $U \cdot P_U$ and a comprehensive CV or EV of the form $(U^n - U^o)P_U^n$ or $(U^n - U^o)P_U^o$. Additional discounting in this case would not be necessary. Either the CV or EV would be a valid measure of the number of additional dollars in one set of lifetime prices that would be required to attain a different total lifetime utility. We do not have a lifetime utility function, however. Our welfare measure provides enough additional dollars in one set of prices to allow the consumer to reach a particular pattern of $H_0, \ldots, H_T$, more than enough to reach the same lifetime utility if there were substitution among the H_i. Our welfare measure for each consumer may be biased for this reason.

Finally, since the $PVWG$ are dollar measures of welfare change, they can be summed across consumer groups to provide an estimate of the total welfare effect (efficiency gain or loss) of any policy change.[5] Because the utility from government expenditures is held constant, as described in section 3.5, these measures represent all welfare changes for U.S. consumers. The gains and losses of foreigners are excluded. Therefore, the $PVWG$ measures represent changes in domestic welfare levels, rather than worldwide levels. We should recognize that a tax change could have terms of trade effects, such that worldwide welfare increased while U.S. consumer $PVWG$ measures were all negative.

7.3 Present Value Calculations

Now let us discuss the details of the calculations of present values in equation (7.10). We have a problem in evaluating the welfare gains of a growing economy because an overly high weight might be placed on outcomes occurring in the distant future. For example, if the economy is

5. We take the unweighted sum of the $PVWG$ for the various consumers, so we might be said to be using a Benthamite social welfare function. It would be possible to employ a concave social welfare function by weighting poorer consumers more highly, but we have not done so.

growing at 3 percent per year (due to labor force growth), and we are discounting our social welfare measure at 4 percent, then a 2 percent improvement in consumption seventy-five years hence is weighted at half the importance of an immediate 2 percent improvement. We believe this does not sufficiently discount the distant future because of the spurious effect of population growth. The approach we have taken is to consider the impact of the tax policy change on a population the size of the original 1973 population. That is, we do not consider population growth per se as a reason to assign additional weight to the outcomes of future years. Rather, we determine the effect of our plan on a per capita basis and then multiply by our initial population size.

In base- and revise-case calculations we compute a value of H for each year for each consumer. If we consider a sequence of equilibria extending fifty years past our benchmark (i.e., from 1973 to 2023), the present value of the stream of H values for those five decades is given by:

$$(7.12) \qquad PV = \sum_{t=0}^{50} \frac{H_t}{(1 + g)^t (1 + \rho)^t},$$

where g is the population growth rate and ρ is the consumer's rate of time preference. We discount by g because we want our calculations to consider only the initial-sized population.

Equation (7.12) is fine for the first fifty years. However, it neglects the utility accruing more than fifty years after the tax change. Before we can use equation (7.12), we must add a *termination term*. In general, we will have a series of equilibrium calculations that extend T years past the starting year, 1973. Over the course of the T years in a revise-case calculation, the economy asymptotically approaches a new steady state. However, it will not actually reach the new steady state. In the case of a policy designed to increase saving, the economy will still be experiencing a small amount of capital deepening, even after many years. In order to calculate the termination term, we *assume* that the capital in the economy has reached the steady state in period T. In the case of a capital-deepering policy, we thus assume a slight decrease in saving and increase in H from the amount that we actually calculated for period T.

The actual saving in period T might be called S_T, but we get the steady-state level of saving for period T, S', by rearranging equation (7.3) to obtain

$$(7.13) \qquad S' = \frac{nCAP_T(1 - \bar{f}\tau)}{\gamma}.$$

Actual consumption expenditure in period T is I_{HT}, but steady-state expenditure for period T is then calculated as $I'_H = I_T - P_S S'$. From these values we need to calculate the H' that would result from expenditure I'_H.

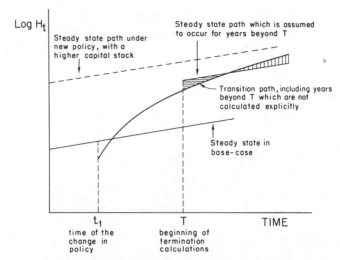

Fig. 7.2   The approximation involved in calculations of the termination term.

Since H is homogeneous of degree one in expenditure I_H, we can multiply actual H by the ratio I'_H/I_{HT} to obtain steady state H' as:[6]

$$(7.14) \qquad H' = H_T \left(\frac{I_T - P_S S'}{I_T - P_S S_T} \right).$$

In the case of a capital-deepening policy, I'_H/I_{HT} exceeds unity, so we increase H_T. We then assume that H grows at the steady-state rate from period T to infinity. These assumptions are illustrated in figure 7.2.

We are now able to calculate the present value of a sequence of values of H. The present value formula consists of equation (7.12) plus the termination term:

$$(7.15) \quad PV(H) = \sum_{t=0}^{T} \frac{H_t}{(1+g)^t (1+\rho)^t} + \frac{H'}{(\rho - h)(1+g)^T (1+\rho)^T}.$$

Note that the second term on the right-hand side of equation (7.15) (the termination term), is divided by $(\rho - h)$ where ρ is the discount rate and h is the growth rate of labor efficiency. When we divide by $(\rho - h)$,

6. An alternative would be simply to assume that H_T was close enough to the new steady state. Since H approaches the new steady state from below, the direct use of H_T would understate welfare gains. Instead, we assume that capital is close enough to the steady state. Savings S' (enough to increase that capital at rate n) is less than savings S_T (enough to continue towards the true steady state). Since $S' < S_T$, equation (7.14) scales *up* H_T to approximate the higher steady-state welfare. It thus avoids understating the gains as would occur with the use of H_T.

we are in effect taking a stream growing at the rate of h per person but discounted at the rate ρ, and transforming it into a present value at time T. This present value in period T is also discounted to the present by the $(1 + \rho)^T$ division. Furthermore, the initial population becomes a smaller fraction of the economy through time because of population growth at the rate g. We reduce the termination term to the initial population size when we divide by $(1 + g)^T$. This fixed population size still enjoys ever-increasing absolute economic power due to the exponential growth in labor productivity at rate h.

When we evaluate a tax policy change, we use equation (7.15) to calculate the present value of the base-case sequence and the present value of the revise-case sequence. This gives us $PV(H^o)$ and $PV(H^n)$, which we plug into equation (7.10) to get our present value of welfare gains or losses for each consumer.

Our procedures do *not* guarantee that our measures of the change in welfare will be invariant with respect to the number of years between the first and last equilibrium. In general, the longer is our calculated sequence of equilibria, the closer are the final values of income, consumption, and utility to the actual steady-state values. In table 7.1 we test the sensitivity of the model to changes in the number of periods. In each of these runs the policy change is the switch to a consumption tax. (This policy proposal and the way in which we model it are discussed in much greater detail in chapter 9.) All of the runs use additive replacement for equal revenue yield, and all of the equilibria are spaced five years apart.

As seen in table 7.1, the results become fairly robust when we carry out the calculations for fifty years or more. A fifty-year simulation of the consumption tax provides a welfare gain of $556 billion, while a hundred-year simulation provides $569 billion, which is not much different.

Our welfare measure also depends somewhat on the number of years between any two equilibria in a sequence, although our assumption of smooth, exponential growth between equilibria helps to reduce the size of this effect (see footnote 2, this chapter). Table 7.2 shows our tests for this type of sensitivity. Since all of these simulations cover a total of fifty years, the $556 billion for five-year spacing matches the number from the previous table. When equilibria are separated by only one year, the same tax change implies a $491 billion welfare gain.[7]

7.4   Important Parameters for Dynamic Sequencing

Several of the parameters necessary to implement our dynamic sequencing procedures were presented and described in earlier chapters or in earlier sections of this chapter. These parameters include the growth

---

7. See Ballard and Goulder 1982 for further discussion of these effects.

Table 7.1   Effect of Number of Equilibrium Periods on Welfare Gain from Adoption of a Consumption Tax (in billions of 1973 dollars)

Number of Equilibria	Number of Years beyond 1973 Covered by Those Calculations	Welfare Gain (Loss)
2	5	$(−61)
3	10	144
4	15	272
5	20	365
6	25	431
7	30	476
8	35	507
9	40	530
10	45	545
11	50	556
12	55	563
13	50	567
14	65	570
15	70	572
16	75	572
17	80	572
18	85	572
19	90	571
20	95	570
21	100	569

Table 7.2   Effect of Number of Years between Equilibria on Welfare Gain from Adoption of a Consumption Tax (in billions of 1973 dollars)

Number of Equilibria	Number of Years between Equilibria	Welfare Gain (Loss)
6	10	$641
11	5	556
26	2	505
51	1	491

Note: Because the first equilibrium represents the initial year, each of these sequences covers exactly fifty years.

rates of population and technical progress, (g and h), set in equation (7.5), and r, the real net-of-tax rate of return. While the average net-of-tax rate of return is set to 4 percent, each consumer group has a net rate of return that depends on its own marginal tax rate. Any group with a marginal tax rate less than the average earns a net return higher than 4 percent, while any group with a marginal tax rate greater than the average earns a net return of less than 4 percent.

We must now discuss two more parameters: γ, the annual rate at which capital services are augmented as a result of additional saving, and ρ, the discount rate. We assign to γ the same value that we assign to r in the benchmark—0.04. If each unit of capital earns a 4 percent rate of return net of taxes in the benchmark, then an additional unit of capital acquired through savings can be expected to earn the same return. That is, S will contribute .04 units of capital services, each earning a dollar per period net of taxes in the benchmark.

Now let us consider the discount rate. In order to calculate present values for consumption sequences, we want to use the discount rate, ρ, implied by the utility function evaluation of present and future consumption. In general, for each consumer, this will also be equal to the real net rate of return, r. To see this, represent the choice between present consumption (C_0) and future consumption (C_1) by the indifference-curve diagram of figure 7.3. Suppose that the individual has I_0 of income in the present period, and faces consumption prices of P in either period. Any income not consumed in the present period can earn the return r before being spent in the future period, so the effective price of C_1 is $P/(1 + r)$, which is less than P. The individual maximizes utility subject to his income I_0 by setting the ratio of marginal utilities equal to the price ratio. His marginal rate of substitution at the tangency is therefore $(1 + r)$, implying a discount rate of r in the benchmark. As a result, each consumer's H stream is discounted at its own rate of return to measure dollar present values that can be added up across groups.

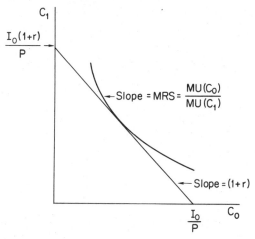

Fig. 7.3   The choice between present and future consumption.

7.4   Revenue Yield Equality in the Dynamic Model

In order to analyze tax policy changes intelligently, it is important to maintain the assumption of equal revenue yield. This is true in the dynamic case as well as in the static case. In the dynamic case, however, we could apply more than one standard of yield equality. We invoke a strong form of yield equality in that we require that the government collect the same revenue in each period of the revise sequence as it collected in the corresponding period of the base sequence. This requirement can cause some problems, most notably with a switch from an income tax to a consumption tax. (See chapter 9 for more discussion of the consumption tax.) Since the consumption tax base is less than the income tax base for at least the first few periods of a consumption tax, unchanged rates of tax would provide substantially reduced revenue in those periods. Our strong form of yield equality implies that the tax rates must be substantially higher with a consumption tax in the initial periods. These higher tax rates exacerbate the already distorted choice between work and leisure. As time goes on, however, the economy will grow faster under the consumption tax, since this type of tax policy leads to faster capital accumulation. In fact, the consumption tax base might ultimately exceed the income tax base.

We could consider a weaker form of yield equality under which the present value of the revenues under the two systems would be equated. The differences in the pattern of tax collections would be made up with deficits or surpluses. In order to do this, however, we would need to deal explicitly with the government bond market. We have not done so, although we should note that the treatment of financial assets in general equilibrium models is receiving more and more attention. (For example, see Auerbach and Kotlikoff 1983, Feltenstein 1984, or Slemrod 1983).

8 Integration of the Corporate and Personal Income Taxes

It has long been recognized that the existence of separate taxes on corporate income and personal income may reduce the efficiency of the allocation of capital. This recognition has given rise to proposals to integrate the two taxes in a variety of ways. This chapter presents estimates of static and dynamic general equilibrium resource allocation effects for four integration plans for the United States. Our results indicate that total integration of personal and corporate taxes would yield an annual *static* efficiency gain of around $4 billion to $8 billion, in 1973 dollars. Partial integration plans yield less of a gain. Our analysis indicates that full integration may yield *dynamic* gains whose present value is at least $300 billion, and could be as large as $695 billion. This is about 1.4 percent of the discounted present value of consumption and leisure in the U.S. economy, after correction for population growth. The plans differ in their distributional effects. Both the distribution and efficiency results depend on the replacement taxes used to preserve government revenues.

8.1 The Taxation of Corporate Income

A corporate tax that operates separately from the personal income tax is widely acknowledged to lead to a number of problems associated with the "double" taxation of corporate income (see McLure 1979). Dividends are paid out of corporate profits net of corporate taxes. Dividends are further taxed under the personal income tax. Retained earnings are also taxed twice, to the extent they are capitalized in higher share values.

This chapter is a revised version of an article by Don Fullerton, A. Thomas King, John B. Shoven, and John Whalley, "Corporate tax integration in the United States: A general equilibrium approach," *American Economic Review* 71 (September 1981): 677–91. Reproduced by permission.

(However, the capital gains resulting from retained earnings are not fully taxed by the personal income tax, and they are taxed on a deferred basis.)

One problem with this double taxation is that it may reduce overall rates of return and affect capital accumulation adversely. A second problem is that the deferral advantage given to retained earnings impairs the efficiency of capital markets. This is sometimes referred to as the "lock-in" effect. Firms can invest retained earnings in projects with a below-market yield, and their shareholders can still earn a higher net-of-tax return than if the funds were distributed as dividends and invested elsewhere.

A third problem is that there is a bias toward debt finance, since only equity returns are subject to corporate taxes. This bias may distort corporate financial policies. A fourth distortion may exist to the extent that firms can choose whether or not to incorporate, as in Ebrill and Hartman (1982).

A final problem is that the corporate tax introduces higher effective tax rates in some industries than others, due to special provisions in the corporate tax law and to the varying degrees to which industries are incorporated. These tax rate differentials further disrupt an efficient allocation of capital. Refer back to figure 2.1, in which a fixed amount of capital is allocated between two sectors such that the net-of-tax rate of return is equalized. Here we can interpret sector X as the corporate sector and sector Y as the noncorporate sector. Without any partial capital taxes, the equalized rate of return (on value of marginal product) is $\bar{r}$ and the capital allocation is K_x^0 and K_y^0. If a tax is imposed on capital in sector X, the new allocation is given by K_x^1 and K_y^1 with the equalized net rate of return being r_n. The tax is the difference between r_g and r_n in sector X. The value of the foregone output in sector X is given by the area $ABK_x^0 K_x^1$, whereas the value of the increasing output in sector Y is $EFK_y^1 K_y^0$. The difference is the area of the two triangles in area ABCD. This is the efficiency cost or deadweight loss of the differential tax.

As we noted in section 3.2 when we described our modeling of the corporation tax, economists disagree on the importance and even the direction of these biases. Stiglitz (1973), for example, points out that a corporate tax on properly measured income could have a neutral effect on incentives if the marginal investment is entirely financed by debt. For equity finance, Feldstein and Slemrod (1980) point out that the corporate tax system can *shelter* income for a high-bracket stockholder. Especially when personal tax brackets extended up to 70 percent, the owners of corporations could have their total taxes reduced by paying only the corporate rate on retained earnings. Even the extra tax on dividends may not distort investments at the margin, if the market values of shares already reflect the fact that these taxes must be paid eventually when profits are distributed. For elaboration of this argument, see Auerbach (1979b), Bradford (1981), and King (1977). Finally, we note here that the corporate tax may be greatly reduced or eliminated by some depreciation allowances and by interest deductions on the part of the marginal investment financed by debt.

In our model, personal taxes combine with corporate taxes to raise effective tax rates in industries that are highly incorporated, but observed corporate taxes are still reduced by the extent to which each industry makes use of credits, deductions, and allowances. Also, we note that our model considers intertemporal and intersectoral distortions in the allocation of real capital, but does not include endogenous financial decisions or distortions in the choices among debt, retained earnings, or dividend policy.

Integration plans seek to remove or mitigate the adverse effects of the two separate tax systems by linking the personal income tax liabilities of stockholders to the corporate tax liabilities of the firms. In this chapter we consider four corporate tax integration alternatives. The plans differ in the extent to which they remove the undesirable features of the present corporate income tax.

For three of the four plans, we consider two "subplans." In one case the second distinction has to do with whether we index capital gains for inflation. In the other cases the subplans differ from each other according to the way in which we model corporate dividend/retention policies. Finally, we consider the case in which capital tax rates are made equal for all industries. This last case is not being offered as a realistic policy proposal. Rather, we consider it as a basis for comparison.

Thus, while we have four main types of plans for integration of the corporate and personal income taxes, we will present results for seven integration plans and one plan for complete capital tax rate equalization. We will now describe each of the integration plans in turn.

Plan 1: Total Integration. Under this alternative, the corporate income tax is eliminated, and the personal income tax is modified to tax total shareholder earnings, rather than just dividends. When capital gains are realized, the tax basis is set at the original purchase price plus the retained earnings accumulated during the holding period. This feature avoids a double tax on retained earnings capitalized in higher stock prices. However, if the basis is not reset for inflation, capital gains taxes will be assessed on purely nominal appreciation. This amounts to a capital wealth levy. We evaluate this total integration plan with and without inflation indexation of capital gains.

These total integration plans are the most comprehensive we consider. They contain modifications to the income tax which, if they had been made originally, would have dispensed with the need for a separate corporate tax. Industrial distortions through the corporate tax are removed, as is the corporate tax distortion of intertemporal consumption choice.

Plan 2: Dividend Deduction from Corporate Income Tax Base. This approach simply removes the "double" taxation of dividends by making them deductible from taxable corporate income. Capital gains taxation of individuals is unaltered, and the corporate income tax is effectively converted into a tax on retained earnings. Unless differences in retention policies by industry were to disappear, the corporate tax would continue to result in some discrimination among industries. Plan 2 would result in an incentive to pay out more dividends. In section 8.3, we will discuss the dividend/retention behavior of corporations. We will also present a model alternative that will test the sensitivity of our results to changes in corporate financial policies.

Plan 3: Dividend Deduction from Personal Income Tax Base. An alternative way of removing the "double" taxation of dividends is to allow a dividend deduction from the personal income tax rather than from the corporate income tax. Capital gains taxation is again unaltered. As with plan 2, differences in retention policies by industry will perpetuate the industrial discrimination caused by the corporate tax. However, it will also once again be true that corporations will have an incentive to pay out more dividends. As mentioned earlier, we will discuss this in section 8.3.

Plan 4: Dividend Gross-Up. This was the plan most actively discussed in the U.S. tax reform debate during 1977. It only seeks a partial reduction of the double taxation of dividends. The taxable incomes of individual shareholders are "grossed up" by some proportion of the corporate income taxes paid by corporations. Then the shareholders receive a corresponding tax credit. Individuals whose personal tax rates are lower than the corporate tax rate will effectively receive a rebate. Individuals with higher personal tax rates will end up paying additional taxes at the personal level. Because of the partial nature of the credit, none of the distortions listed above will be removed entirely.

8.2   Representing the Tax Integration Plans in Model Equivalent Form

Each of the four tax integration plans described in section 8.1 must be represented in model equivalent form for the purpose of analyzing its general equilibrium effects. Each plan implies a different set of values for the capital tax rates and for f_i, the proportion of capital income from industry i which is taxable at the personal level (see chapter 3).

Plan 1: Total Integration. Under this plan, corporate taxes are eliminated from the numerator of the new capital tax rate calculation. The personal income tax is changed to tax all earnings rather than just dividends. This means that g_{RE}, the fraction of retained earnings taxed at the personal level, is set to one. We calculate new f_i parameters using this new g_{RE}, but with the same capital income weights as before. These changes imply new personal factor taxes and thus new capital tax rates by industry.

Plan 2: Dividend Deduction from Corporate Income Tax Base. This plan's corporate income tax base is the undistributed profits of corporations. It is represented in model equivalent terms for each industry by removing a portion of the corporate tax paid from the 1973 capital taxation figures and recalculating the capital tax rate. The portion of corporate tax removed is given by the ratio of dividends to net-of-tax corporate profits by industry (U.S. Dept. of Commerce, BEA 1976b). (We thus assume no change in corporate financial policy.) The f_i and the personal income tax functions do not change.

Plan 3: Dividend Deduction from Personal Income Tax Base. This plan removes dividends from the income tax system. In model equivalent terms it is specified by considering the effect of dividend deductibility on the income tax functions of households. We set g_D, the proportion of dividends taxable by the personal income tax, to zero, and all f_i are recalculated. Other adjustments are analogous to those made for plan 1.

Plan 4: Dividend Gross-Up. This scheme gives stockholders an income tax credit of 15 percent of the corporate taxes paid by the firms in which they own an interest. It is most satisfactorily modeled as a reduction in the corporate taxes of each industry by the amount of the credit. This amount is then treated as an increase in dividends in the calculation of new f_i values. The new effective tax rates include 85 percent of corporate income taxes and the new personal factor taxes. The higher dividends relative to retained earnings result in higher f_i and $\bar{f}$ values, so that consumers experience an increase in taxable capital income.

8.3 Corporate Financial Policies

Our model does not consider corporate financial policies directly, although we have made some attempts to examine the sensitivity of our findings to alternative assumptions about these policies.

In recent years a number of authors (Stiglitz, 1973, 1976; King, 1974) have viewed the corporate tax as a differential tax on the various financial instruments that are available for transferring capital income from firms to individuals. According to this view, the capital income of corporations can be "paid" to the owners of capital by interest payments, dividends, or retentions (which are assumed to be converted into capital gains). Each of these instruments has tax and nontax advantages and disadvantages that govern its relative use by industry. The firm that uses debt finance can deduct interest from its corporate tax base. This tax advantage is counteracted by the disadvantage that a heavily debt-financed company has a higher probability of bankruptcy and/or takeover. Equity financing cannot avoid corporate taxation. However, equity financing may result in a large reduction in personal taxes if earnings are retained. Dividends may be paid for a variety of reasons, even though they do not have any tax advantage. For a recent study of the reasons for dividends, see Feldstein and Green (1983).

For the purposes of this chapter, the important point is that when the tax laws change, firms can be expected to modify their financial policies. For example, if plan 2 (dividend deduction from the corporate tax) encourages firms to pay out all earnings in dividends, then plan 1 (total integration) and plan 2 are identical in their effects.

We do not have good estimates of the elasticities of financial policies with respect to changes in the tax law. Therefore, we model various extreme behavioral reactions and calculate the effects of the integration plans, given these extreme assumptions. The two assumptions we will use are, first, that corporate policies do not change, and second, that all corporate income is paid in dividends. We cannot claim that we have a "true" general equilibrium treatment of corporate financial policies. This is because we adjust the dividend/retention ratio to estimate model equivalent tax rates *before* we make our general equilibrium calculations. Endogenous financial behavior in general equilibrium models has been explored by a number of authors in recent years (see, for example, Slemrod 1983, Feltenstein 1984, and Galper and Toder 1982).

8.4 The Lock-in Effect

The deferral advantage under the existing personal and corporate tax structure gives a tax preference to retention by existing firms. This is the *lock-in effect*. New firms entering financial markets must borrow at higher interest rates than the required rate of return on retentions of existing firms. Thus, if existing firms are more slowly growing and less efficient, the proper allocation of resources to new firms may not take place.

Our general equilibrium model employs constant returns to scale technology. We do not incorporate an explicit theory of individual firm behavior, and a reallocation of capital among firms within an industry does not affect the industry production function. Therefore, we are unable to model the efficiency aspects of the lock-in effect.

Our analysis of integration of the corporate and personal taxes will consider interindustry and intertemporal distortions. Interindustry distortions enter through differences in rates of tax on capital income by industry. Intertemporal distortions enter through the taxation of saving generally.

8.5 Results

In table 8.1 we present the static efficiency effects of the integration plans. Table 8.2 contains the static distributional effects. In table 8.3 we present our calculations of dynamic effects.[1]

To obtain the static measures of efficiency changes displayed in table 8.1, we first calculate the changes in national income plus leisure, valued at prices before the policy change and after the policy change. We use these Passche and Laspeyres quantity indexes (rather than compensating or equivalent variations) because the consumers may assess the utility contribution of saving inaccurately, due to their myopic expectations. Instead of showing both the Laspeyres and Passche indexes, we merely report the geometric mean of the two.

The main effect of corporate tax integration is that the capital stock is allocated more efficiently among the industrial sectors. To get some idea of the magnitude of these changes, let us focus on eight industries. Four of these (agriculture, petroleum refining, real estate, and government enterprises) have low rates of capital tax under the current law. The other four (chemicals and rubber, metals and machinery, transportation equipment, and motor vehicles) have high capital taxes. The differences are due largely to differences in the degree of incorporation in these industries.

When the corporation income tax is removed, capital in the industries that were previously more heavily taxed becomes a better buy than it was before. Table 8.4 shows how capital gets reallocated among industries. Seven industries end up using less capital in the first equilibrium under corporate tax integration than they had used in the base case. These are agriculture, mining, crude petroleum and gas, petroleum refining, real estate, services, and government enterprises. Some 6.5 percent of the total capital stock is reallocated in the first period under integration from these seven industries to the other twelve industries.

Table 8.4 shows that the outputs of industries that were previously treated more favorably have increases in price as a result of the tax

---

1. The figures in tables 8.1 and 8.3 are presented in billions of 1973 dollars. It may be useful to give some idea of how large a 1973 dollar was. The Commerce Department's GNP deflator stood at 105.8 in 1973 (with the 1972 value set to 100.0). By 1982 the GNP deflator had risen to 213. Thus, if the structure of the economy were unchanged in the intervening seven years, the welfare gain figures in tables 8.1 and 8.3 would have to be increased by about 100 percent in order to bring them up to 1982 levels. However, we must urge caution in making this kind of extrapolation.

Table 8.1   Static Welfare Effects: Change in Annual Real Expanded National
                 Income (in billions of 1973 dollars)

	Tax Replacement			
Plan	Lump-Sum Scaling	Multipli-cative Scaling	Additive Scaling	VAT Scaling
Plan 1: Full integration with indexing	9.671	2.192	2.695	4.917
Plan 1: Full integration without indexing	7.855	4.234	4.381	5.291
Plan 2: Dividend deduction from corporate income tax[a]	3.580	0.063	0.230	0.985
Plan 2: Dividend deduction from corporate income tax, with extreme behavior assumption[a]	8.061	4.230	4.388	5.380
Plan 3: Dividend deduction from personal income tax[a]	4.068	2.873	2.928	1.841
Plan 3: Dividend deduction from personal income tax, with extreme behavior assumption[a]	4.539	2.903	2.965	3.390
Plan 4: Dividend gross-up	3.450	2.455	2.486	2.719
Equal capital tax rates on industry[b]		10.912		

Notes: Real expanded national income incorporates the change in the valuation of leisure through induced variations in labor supply. The numbers reported are the geometric means of Paasche and Laspeyres index numbers, for each tax replacement, as described in the text.
[a]The standard simulations for dividend deduction plans 2 and 3 assume that corporate financial policies do not change. In particular, the new f_i parameters are calculated with the old levels of dividends and retained earnings as weights for g_D and g_{RE}. However these dividend deduction plans might encourage greater distribution of corporate profits. The extreme behavior assumption uses the sum of dividends and retained earnings as the weight on g_D, with no weight on g_{RE}.
[b]This result is for complete equalization of capital tax rates by industry. The property tax, corporate franchise tax, corporate income tax, and personal factor tax are included in this equalization. This result is presented for comparison purposes.

change. It is not surprising that these price changes lead to changes in the prices of consumer goods. Two consumer goods have large increases in their relative prices. These are housing and gasoline and other fuels. Among the consumer goods with the largest *decreases* in relative prices are nondurable, nonfood household items, motor vehicles, appliances, and clothing and jewelry.

Because the total capital stock has not changed in just the first period of the revised-case simulation, the social marginal product or gross return to capital changes only slightly. However, overall taxes are reduced as a result of corporate tax integration, so the net return to capital (P_K) rises sharply. Capital also earns a higher net return because it is allocated more

Table 8.2   Percentage Changes in Expanded Real Income after Income Taxes and Transfers by Income Class, for Each Tax Replacement

Income of Consumer Group (1973 dollars)	Equal Capital Tax Rates on Industry[b]	Plan 1 Full Integration with Indexing (additive scaling)	Plan 1 Full Integration with Indexing (multiplicative scaling)	Plan 2[a] Dividend Deduction from Corporate Income Tax (multiplicative scaling)	Plan 2[a] With Extreme Behavior (multiplicative scaling)	Plan 3[a] Dividend Deduction from Personal Income Tax (multiplicative scaling)	Plan 3[a] With Extreme Behavior (multiplicative scaling)	Plan 4 Dividend Gross-Up (multiplicative scaling)
0–2,999	1.763	1.935	3.981	2.393	3.632	0.270	0.291	0.897
3,000–3,999	1.329	1.210	2.939	1.767	2.647	0.283	0.311	0.685
4,000–4,999	1.063	0.592	2.045	1.239	1.863	0.258	0.285	0.519
5,000–5,999	1.055	0.624	1.946	1.166	1.789	0.272	0.296	0.504
6,000–6,999	1.118	0.595	1.830	1.061	1.693	0.284	0.317	0.488
7,000–7,999	1.036	0.431	1.468	0.839	1.406	0.269	0.296	0.425
8,000–9,999	0.920	0.244	1.033	0.587	1.070	0.238	0.253	0.344
10,000–11,999	0.961	0.478	0.991	0.523	1.031	0.274	0.294	0.336
12,000–14,999	1.035	0.527	0.888	0.420	0.945	0.283	0.311	0.325
15,000–19,999	0.938	0.741	0.608	0.214	0.686	0.312	0.338	0.266
20,000–24,999	1.012	1.310	0.809	0.223	0.730	0.426	0.486	0.296
25,000+	0.651	6.501	3.970	1.125	1.330	1.992	2.515	0.656

Notes: Expanded real income includes leisure, valued at the household net-of-tax wage rate. Numbers shown are the arithmetic means of percentage changes to income based on Paasche and Laspeyres price indexes.

[a]See footnote a, table 8.1.

[b]See footnote b, table 8.1.

Table 8.3   Dynamic Welfare Effects: Present Value of Equivalent Variations Over Time (in billions of 1973 dollars)

Plan	Tax Replacement			
	Lump-Sum Scaling	Multiplicative Scaling	Additive Scaling	VAT Scaling
Plan 1: Full integration	695.0	310.6	418.2	559.6
with indexing	(1.394)	(0.623)	(0.839)	(1.122)
Plan 1: Full integration	473.5	288.2	339.7	408.6
without indexing	(0.950)	(0.578)	(0.681)	(0.819)
Plan 2: Dividend deduction				
from corporate	259.8	57.6	114.5	188.6
income tax[a]	(0.521)	(0.115)	(0.230)	(0.378)
Plan 2: Dividend deduction				
from corporate income tax,	492.9	295.8	351.0	424.0
with extreme behavior assumption[a]	(0.989)	(0.593)	(0.704)	(0.850)
Plan 3: Dividend deduction				
from personal	263.7	208.1	222.4	238.4
income tax[a]	(0.529)	(0.417)	(0.446)	(0.478)
Plan 3: Dividend deduction				
from personal income tax,	315.7	236.1	256.9	286.8
with extreme behavior assumption[a]	(0.633)	(0.475)	(0.515)	(0.575)
Plan 4: Dividend gross-up	179.0	128.8	142.3	160.8
	(0.359)	(0.258)	(0.285)	(0.323)
Equal capital tax rates		544.8		
on industry[b]		(1.093)		

Notes: We consider eleven equilibria, five-years apart, in order to project annual consumption values over the fifty intervening years. For consumption beyond year fifty, we have an appropriate treatment of the terminal conditions. The dynamic equivalent variations are analogs of static concepts applied to the consumption sequence over time, assuming the first-period discount factor is unchanged.

The numbers in parentheses represent the gain as a percentage of the present discounted value of welfare (consumption plus leisure) in the base sequence. The value is $49 trillion for all comparisons, and only accounts for a population the size of that in 1973.

[a]See footnote a, table 8.1.
[b]See footnote b, table 8.1.

efficiently. In the base sequence of equilibria, all prices are equal to unity in all periods by our units convention and the assumption that the benchmark equilibrium lies on a steady-state growth path. In the first equilibrium period under full corporate tax integration, the relative price of capital rises to 1.208 (we normalize by setting the price of labor equal to 1.0). However, the price of capital does not stay so high in later periods because more saving occurs under integration than in the base case. In the first equilibrium period, the higher net rate of return to capital leads to a 14.5 percent increase in saving. By the second equilibrium period, which occurs five years after the first period, the relative price of capital

Table 8.4 Changes Resulting from Full Corporate Tax Integration for Selected Industries, in First Equilibrium Period

Industry	Capital Tax Rates		Relative-Output Prices (price of labor = 1.0)		Percentage of Total Capital Stock Used by Given Industry	
	Before Integration	After Integration	Before Integration	After Integration	Before Integration	After Integration
Industries currently lightly taxed						
Agriculture	0.54	0.46	1.0	1.059	15.4%	13.5%
Petroleum refining	0.46	0.44	1.0	1.060	4.8	4.5
Real estate	0.63	0.56	1.0	1.084	36.1	32.7
Government enterprises	0.26	0.26	1.0	1.051	4.4	3.8
Industries currently heavily taxed						
Chemicals	1.87	0.60	1.0	0.943	2.0	2.8
Metals and machinery	1.72	0.67	1.0	0.959	5.4	6.9
Industries heavily taxed						
Transport equipment	23.50	4.88	1.0	0.936	0.04	0.10
Motor vehicles	1.29	0.47	1.0	0.941	2.5	3.2

drops to 1.188. In the third period it reaches 1.171, in the fourth 1.151, and so on. By the tenth equilibrium period, the price of capital services stands at 1.111, and it drops to 1.107 by the eleventh and final period. Notice that the decreases in the relative price of capital become smaller over time as the economy approaches a new steady-state growth path asymptotically.

The distributional effects reported in table 8.2 depend upon both the sources side and the uses side of each consumer's budget. As we have indicated, the price of capital rises in the simulated equilibrium. It turns out that low-income consumers tend to spend a large proportion of their income on consumer goods that are produced by lightly taxed, capital-intensive industries such as agriculture and real estate. For example, the poorest group spends 19.7 percent of its net money income on food and 21.8 percent on housing, while the richest group spends 14.6 percent on food and 12.5 percent on housing. Therefore, the uses side of the consumer's budget has some regressive effects on the income distribution, when corporate tax integration occurs.

On the sources side, the distributional impact of any policy change is driven by the fact that the capital/labor ratio of income is bowl-shaped across our twelve consumer groups. That is, the very-low-income groups and the highest-income group have factor endowments that are more heavily weighted by capital. The capital/labor ratios for the incomes of the twelve consumer groups are shown in table 8.5. With corporate tax integration, the various consumers have slightly higher capital/labor ratios, but the overall picture is preserved almost precisely. The higher price of capital leads to U-shaped gains by consumer groups when we

Table 8.5   Ratio of Capital Income to Labor Income
for Twelve Income Classes

Income Class (1973 dollars)	Capital Income/ Labor Income in Base Case
0–2,999	0.547
3,000–3,999	0.337
4,000–4,999	0.227
5,000–5,999	0.203
6,000–6,999	0.178
7,000–7,999	0.149
8,000–9,999	0.123
10,000–11,999	0.123
12,000–14,999	0.106
15,000–19,999	0.111
20,000–24,999	0.139
25,000+	0.424

simulate corporate tax integration (see the columns under plan 1 in table 8.2).

The U-shaped character of the gains from corporate tax integration is interesting, but it may be more important to bear in mind that *all groups gain*. Thus, we have a Pareto improvement. However, although the simulated equilibrium is a Pareto improvement over the benchmark 1973 equilibrium, we have said nothing about the possible paths between the two. Short-run losses and transition costs should be considered before enacting such a change. Our model is essentially comparative static and does not measure these disequilibria or temporary influences.

We now report further results for each of the integration plans.

Plan 1: Total Integration. This plan only removes part of the industrial discrimination in the taxation of capital income, because property taxes remain as differential capital taxes by industry. Property taxes are particularly important in the agriculture and real estate industries.

Interindustry discrimination is reduced enough to provide a $4 billion annual static welfare gain in each year (table 8.1, in 1973 dollars) for the cases with either multiplicative or additive scaling and inflation indexation of capital gains taxes. Without this correction for inflation, the efficiency gains are slightly less. Table 8.3 shows that dynamic gains are sensitive to the replacement yield–preserving tax considered. With additive scaling a gain of $418 billion occurs, and with multiplicative scaling a gain of $311 billion occurs. To give the reader a better feel for the relative magnitude of these numbers, we should mention that the discounted present value of the future income stream for the population living in 1973 is about $49 trillion under the present tax system. (This figure is also in 1973 dollars.) The sensitivity of these dynamic results to the replacement tax can be explained by the positive correlation between income and the proportion of income saved. Since multiplicative scaling collects more tax revenue from high-income groups, it creates a greater distortion in their intertemporal choices. Less saving occurs, and the new balanced growth path has a lower capital/labor ratio than it would have had with other kinds of replacement.[2]

Before going on, let us give a somewhat fuller indication of the relative magnitude of these gains. As shown in table 8.3, the $311 billion gain resulting from integration with multiplicative scaling is equal to about

2. The reader may wonder exactly how much effect the multiplicative or additive scaling schemes have on marginal income tax rates. The marginal rates in the base case can be found in table 5.8. They range from .01 for the poorest consumer to .41 for the one with the highest income. Under additive replacement, in the first period, all marginal rates are increased by 3.98 percentage points. Thus, the new rate schedule ranges from 5 percent to 45 percent. By the eleventh period, the additive tax scalar is slightly lower, at 2.90 percentage points. Under multiplicative replacement, in the first period, all marginal rates are multiplied by the same factor of 1.163. Under this scheme, the marginal rates on the lowest groups hardly increase, whereas the marginal rate on the top income class rises to over 47 percent.

0.62 percent of the present value of expanded national income (including the value of leisure) after correction for population growth. (See chapter 7 for the details of our dynamic welfare analysis.) It is also equal to about 0.91 percent of the present value of population-corrected national income. These figures may not be striking. However, when we see that the gain is 16.5 percent of the present value of the revenue that the corporate income tax would collect, is appears that the gains are quite substantial.

We do not need to consider changes in financial policies under this plan. With full integration, all forms of corporate capital income are taxed identically. The tax does not depend on whether corporate capital income is paid in interest, paid in dividends, or retained. Therefore, a change in either the debt/equity or dividend/retention ratio will not alter the new effective tax rates or the new f_i for the revised equilibrium calculation. The resulting solution would be the same even if the ratios changed.

Plan 2: Dividend Deduction from Corporate Income Tax Base. Here dividends are treated like interest for tax purposes, and we first assume that corporations continue to retain the same portion of income. The reduction of the corporate income tax base causes some leveling of capital tax rates and results in a small increase in yearly welfare. Dynamic gains under multiplicative scaling of tax rates are $58 billion. Under lump-sum replacement, dynamic gains are $260 billion. The reduced spread of dynamic results is due to the smaller revenue loss associated with plan 2. When the amount of revenue to be replaced is small, the additive or multiplicative replacement schemes do not add as much distortion of intertemporal choice.

Under our "standard" treatment of plan 2, the dividend/retention ratio is assumed constant even though an incentive exists to replace retained earnings with dividends, which are no longer taxed. For this reason we also consider the extreme case where all corporate earnings are distributed. The corporate income tax would thus be effectively eliminated, and f_i calculations would proceed on the assumption that all corporate earnings are multiplied by the higher .96 for g_D, the proportion of dividends that is taxable at the personal level. The static gain for such a tax replacement is around $8 billion per year under lump-sum replacement, $4 billion under additive or multiplicative scaling, and $5 billion under a sales tax replacement. The dynamic gains are comparable to the gains under full integration. These welfare gains are substantially above the gains calculated using the assumption of fixed dividend/retention policies. This is because corporate decision makers have, in effect, reduced the distortion of the corporate income tax with its differing effective capital tax rates. The Plan 2 extreme-behavior case leads to U-shaped gains among consumers, similar to those for the case in which corporate financial policies are assumed to remain unchanged.

Plan 3: Dividend Deduction from Personal Income Tax Base. The reduced tax on dividends again implies lower tax rates on heavily incorporated industries and a leveling of all rates in general. This occurs through the lower f_i for dividend-paying industries. Static welfare gains are about $3 billion per year. With multiplicative scaling, dynamic gains are $208 billion. Under lump-sum replacement the gains here are about $264 billion, which is about the same as under plan 2. The multiplicative results reflect the importance of the deduction from the upwardly scaled income tax. As might be expected, table 8.2 shows that plan 3 has less progressive effects than the second plan, since dividend income is all taxed at the corporate rate instead of at progressive personal tax rates.

Under extreme financial policy behavior, where firms no longer retain earnings, both the static and dynamic gains are somewhat larger. The corporate tax remains the same, but the new f_i include all corporate earnings as dividends with a g_D of zero. Less corporate income is subject to the personal income tax. The difference between results with and without the extreme-behavior assumption is less than for plan 2, because the personal income tax deduction does less to eliminate interindustry discrimination than does the corporate income tax deduction for dividends. The distributional effects for the extreme-behavior case of plan 3 are generally regressive, although the middle groups all have similar relative improvements. This pattern is similar to the pattern for the case in which we assume no change in financial policies.

Plan 4: Dividend Gross-Up. All plans that decrease the corporate income tax only on dividends can be termed partial integration plans. The fourth plan might be called a partial partial plan, because it reduces only part of the tax on dividends. The static welfare gain is $2.5 billion per year when personal tax rates are scaled upward in order to maintain real government expenditure. Dynamic gains under multiplicative scaling are $129 billion, under additive scaling are $142 billion, and under VAT replacement are $161 billion. Here, again, the spread between the dynamic welfare gains is less than that of full integration because this plan involves smaller revenue loss than full integration. Multiplicative scaling makes up most revenue from high-income, high-saving consumers, and it thus reduces future capital stocks and incomes. The dynamic lump-sum and additive cases show that the dividend gross-up does substantially less to improve the interindustry resource allocation than other plans.

As a basis for comparison we will now report the effects of complete equalization of capital tax rates by industry. We report these results even though we realize that complete equalization of capital tax rates is not a realistic policy proposal. In this case we eliminate all tax discrimination on capital use among industries, use a single tax rate for all industries, and tax equally all capital income at the personal income tax level. Capital tax rates are set to a common rate, providing government with enough revenue to maintain its real purchases. The f_i parameters are all reset to $\bar{f}$—the overall fraction of capital income that is effectively fully taxed by the personal income tax system. The resulting efficiency gains are larger than those of the four integration plans. These gains represent the maximum possible increase in expanded national income from the elimination of *interindustry* capital tax distortions.

Results in table 8.1 indicate that the efficiency gain from equalizing capital taxes by industry is about $10.9 billion per year in 1973 dollars. Table 8.2 shows that the gain turns out to be distributed in such a way that every group experiences an increase in real income. Thus, this change would be a Pareto improvement. Dynamic gains in this case (table 8.3) are $545 billion, which is about 1.1 percent of the discounted present value of the future U.S. income stream after correction for population growth. It is also about 14.7 percent of the discounted present value of the revenues from all taxes on capital (including corporate taxes and property taxes).

The capital tax equalization removes all interindustry distortions, but it leaves intertemporal distortions because the common capital tax rate is scaled to preserve total tax revenue. Full integration with lump-sum replacement, described above, has larger efficiency gains in table 8.3, because it removes some interindustry distortions *and* some intertemporal distortions.

The last results we will report deal with inflation and inflation indexing. As we explained in chapter 3, our model treats nominal capital gains and real capital gains separately. The effects of indexation of nominal capital gains depend on the rate of inflation. We specify the rate of inflation as an exogenous parameter, and we assume that the same rate of inflation persists throughout each sequence of equilibrium calculations. Our standard case sets the inflation rate at 7 percent. In table 8.6 we present the

Table 8.6   **Sensitivity of Dynamic Welfare Effects Due to Full Integration with Indexing, to the Assumed Rate of Inflation (in billions of 1973 dollars)**

	Type of Scaling to Preserve Equal Yield			
	Lump-Sum	Multiplicative	Additive	VAT
2 percent inflation	475.9	220.6	283.0	377.2
	(0.974)	(0.451)	(0.579)	(0.772)
7 percent inflation	695.0	310.6	418.2	559.6
	(1.394)	(0.623)	(0.839)	(1.122)
12 percent inflation	949.4	430.3	593.5	781.1
	(1.862)	(0.844)	(1.164)	(1.532)

Note: Numbers in parentheses represent the gain as a percentage of the present value of welfare in the base sequence.

Table 8.7   Sensitivity of Dynamic Welfare Effects Due to Indexing of Nominal Capital Gains, to the Assumed Rate of Inflation (in billions of 1973 dollars)

	Type of Scaling to Preserve Equal Yield			
	Lump-Sum	Multiplicative	Additive	VAT
2 percent inflation	66.2	29.6	38.0	51.4
	(0.135)	(0.060)	(0.078)	(0.105)
7 percent inflation	254.0	123.0	158.4	205.8
	(0.509)	(0.247)	(0.318)	(0.413)
12 percent inflation	474.5	245.8	314.9	397.5
	(0.931)	(0.482)	(0.618)	(0.780)

Note: Numbers in parentheses represent the gain as a percentage of the present value of welfare in the base sequence.

dynamic welfare gains from full integration with indexing (plan 1), for different levels of the inflation rate. It should not be surprising that the gains are greater when the inflation rate is greater, since a higher inflation rate leads to greater distortionary taxation, which can be removed if we index.

In table 8.7 we show that the economy can derive substantial welfare gains from merely indexing nominal capital gains, without integrating the corporate and personal income taxes. Once again, the gains depend on the method of equal yield replacement and on the rate of inflation.

8.6 Conclusion

In this chapter we have analyzed four plans for corporate and personal income tax integration in the United States.

Total integration of the personal and corporate income taxes is shown to yield static efficiency gains of about $4 billion to $8 billion per year, in 1973 dollars. The present value of the dynamic gains range from $311 billion to $695 billion, depending on the yield-preserving tax. Without indexing, these gains ranged from $288 billion to $474 billion. The dynamic gains results from the other plans are generally lower, although they exceeded $100 billion in every case.

The static distributional effects vary among plans. Full integration with multiplicative scaling leads to a progressive change in the distribution of real income over most of the income range. In addition, every class is better off. Dividend deductibility from the personal income tax has a beneficial effect that is more advantageous to high-income groups. Dividend deductibility from the corporate income tax redistributes from upper-middle-income groups to low-income groups and the highest-income group. The dividend gross-up plan is roughly proportional, with slightly greater gains at the top and bottom of the income scale. We want to emphasize the sensitivity of dynamic gains to the yield-preserving tax. This suggests that the potential gains under integration from removal of intertemporal distortions would be significantly reduced if marginal income tax rates are raised, particularly if the higher-income groups, who are also larger savers, face larger tax rate increases.

We have tried to emphasize that our analyses of dividend deductions from *either* tax are not fully general equilibrium analyses. This is because we cannot estimate the change in corporate financial policies. As a partial remedy for this shortcoming we have analyzed the dividend deduction plans under two assumptions about corporate dividend policies. The first assumption is that these policies do not change. The second is that all corporate income is paid out in dividends. The second assumption leads to greater gains in both the static and dynamic cases and under all three kinds of equal yield replacement. The gains are greater because complete dividend payout implies greater equalization of tax rates on capital.

Finally, we have analyzed the effects of complete equalization of the tax rates on capital for all industries. The resulting gains are the largest that can result from the removal of interindustry distortions. Our results suggest that the gains from such tax rate equalization would be substantial. In the static case we found the gains to be almost $10.9 billion, in 1973 dollars. All consumer groups share in the gains. In the dynamic case, the present value of the gains was in excess of $545 billion.

Among the most interesting of the results in this chapter are the dynamic results, which suggest that there are significant potential gains from corporate tax integration, provided that replacement taxes do not excessively interfere with intertemporal consumption choice. A trade-off appears to occur between achieving progressive or proportional income gains through multiplicative scaling and maximizing the dynamic efficiency gain. Larger intertemporal gains can be secured by keeping the taxes on high-income groups low, because these are the groups that do the most saving.

9 Replacing the Personal Income Tax with a Progressive Consumption Tax

9.1 Introduction

In the last several years there has been renewed interest in the progressive consumption tax as an alternative to the federal personal income tax. This interest is reflected in *Blueprints for Basic Tax Reform* (1977), published by the U.S. Department of the Treasury, Office of Tax Analysis (hereafter referred to as *Blueprints*), and tax reform documents in other countries, such as the Meade Report (Meade 1978) in the United Kingdom. Several recent papers by public finance economists have also advocated the adoption of consumption tax (e.g., Bradford 1980, Feldstein 1978, Boskin 1978, and Summers 1981).

In this chapter we use our model to evaluate the movement from the current U.S. tax system to a progressive consumption tax. Since our model incorporates a labor/leisure choice, where leisure is an untaxed commodity, our results will reflect the fact that *both* the consumption tax and the present tax system are distortionary. The task of this chapter is to quantify the relative efficiency of these two second-best tax systems, using our model and its 1973 benchmark data set.

We are mainly concerned with intertemporal distortions. Consequently, all of our simulations will use the dynamic model. Our dynamic sequences describe the transitions between the base-case steady-state growth path and the new steady-state paths that result from various policy changes. By comparing capital/labor ratios in the base case and the revise case at various points in time, we can get an idea of how long it takes for the economy to approach its new steady-state capital/labor ratio.

This chapter is a revised version of an article by Don Fullerton, John B. Shoven, and John Whalley, "Replacing the U.S. income tax with a progressive consumption tax," *Journal of Public Economics* 20 (February 1983): 3–23. Reproduced by permission.

The next section of this chapter summarizes the philosophical and analytical arguments used to support consumption taxation. Section 9.3 describes briefly some of the features of a practical consumption tax proposal. We emphasize the fact that the present U.S. tax system is far from a pure income tax. Section 9.4 describes the manner in which policy alternatives are put into model equivalent forms, while the following section contains the empirical results. Section 9.6 discusses the sensitivity of our results, and the last section includes a brief conclusion and summary.

9.2   The Progressive Consumption Tax

The idea of taxing consumption rather than income has a long history and is frequently credited to John Stuart Mill. In more recent times, Irving Fisher (1942) and Nicholas Kaldor (1957) have been strong advocates. The arguments in favor of a consumption tax can be separated into three broad categories. These are equity, economic efficiency, and administrative efficiency.

On equity grounds the philosophical argument says that it is more reasonable to base relative tax burdens on withdrawals from the economic system rather than on additions to the economic system. It may be viewed as more fair to tax the use of economic resources rather than the provision of resources.

The second argument in favor of consumption taxation is that a welfare loss occurs because the income tax distorts intertemporal consumption choices. Saving must be made out of net-of-tax income, and the earnings of investments are further taxed before future consumption can occur. Consider an individual with fixed incomes (Y_1, Y_2) who must choose a consumption sequence (C_1, C_2). Suppose the individual can both borrow and lend at a given real interest rate r, and that his marginal tax rate is t. A consumption tax will result in a parallel inward shift of the consumer's budget constraint, while the income tax will lead to a nonparallel shift. If all tax revenues were returned to the individual in a lump-sum form, intertemporal consumption choice would remain undistorted under the consumption tax. A lump-sum return of revenues under the income tax would leave the consumer on a lower indifference curve.

The case in favor of consumption taxes on grounds of economic efficiency is not as strong as the preceding paragraph would make it appear, however. In an economy with positive net saving by taxpayers, the tax base will be lower with a consumption tax than with an income tax. This smaller base will, in general, necessitate higher tax rates, exacerbating other distortionary consequences of taxation. Thus, while the consumption tax involves one less distortion (the intertemporal consumption choice), the efficiency loss on the remaining margins, particularly the labor/leisure margin, may be greater than with an income tax. This is another example of the well-known proposition that we cannot rely on economic analyses that merely count distortions.

The administrative efficiency argument in favor of consumption taxation is that many of the present deficiencies in the measurement of income would be removed if we were to adopt a consumption tax. With a redistributive tax on all expenditures, there would no longer be any need for separate taxes on corporate income, capital gains, and welfare transfers. For a discussion of many of these points, see Andrews (1974).

Under one version of a consumption tax, each taxpaying unit would have a *qualified account*. All financial savings that qualify for a tax deduction would go through such an account. Interest, dividends, and sales of corporate stock might remain in the account. They would not be taxed until they were withdrawn and spent. Measuring the tax base would be easy since it would only include labor and rental income and withdrawals from the qualified account. This device has a comparative advantage in an inflationary economy because it avoids completely the need to define real income or measure economic depreciation. Regardless of the amount of income that accrues to a taxpaying unit, the tax is based on nominal withdrawals in the same year. If we have an income tax and if we use the Haig-Simons definition of income, then it is necessary to tax inheritances as they are received. With a consumption tax, this requirement would also disappear. However, we would still have to concern ourselves with the issue of whether bequests should be taxed as consumption.

9.3   The Existing and Proposed Tax Systems

All of the recent consumption tax policy proposals have recognized the great administrative difficulty of taxing the expenditures of individuals as they occur. Thus the recent proposals have opted for a consumption tax that would be operated as an income tax with a saving deduction. *Blueprints* is a representative consumption tax proposal. Broadly speaking, the proposed tax base is yearly income with a deduction for financial saving.

The *Blueprints* proposals are a mixture of two methods of consumption taxation. These are sometimes called the *prepayment* method and the *deferral* or *postpayment* method. The qualified account, which would apply only to financial saving, is an example of the deferral method. With this method, assets are purchased with dollars that have been shielded from tax. Taxes are not levied until the assets are withdrawn from the qualified account for the purpose of consumption. The prepayment method already applies to consumer durables, such as housing, under the present tax system. Durables are purchased with after-tax dollars, but the stream of imputed income that follows is not taxed. If we assume perfect competition, the prepayment and postpayment methods are equivalent. Taxing the acquisition price of an asset is equivalent (in a present value sense) to taxing the rents as they accrue. This is because, with competition, the purchase price of an asset will equal the present value of its imputed net returns. The prepayment approach and the deferral approach both remove the distortion of intertemporal choice, which we discussed in section 9.2.

We have not been able to capture all features of the *Blueprints* proposal, but we have used the concept of a consumption tax as an income tax with a savings deduction as our basis for considering alternative tax plans. We begin with our model representation of the U.S. income tax and consider the alternative where the existing marginal tax rates are applied to consumption rather than income. Marginal rates are then scaled in our equilibrium calculations to preserve tax revenues. We do not consider the base-broadening features of the *Blueprints* proposals (including the elimination of deductions for medical expenses, charitable contributions, and state and local taxes). However, we do consider cases in which the corporate tax is abolished along with the movement to a consumption tax, as well as cases in which the corporate tax is maintained.

It is important to note that we are comparing the U.S. income tax system with and without full deductibility of saving. For the most part our analysis does not deal with either a pure income tax or a pure consumption tax. The U.S. tax system is very complex and does not even vaguely approximate a true income tax. In fact, in its aggregate treatment of saving, it is roughly halfway between an income tax and a consumption tax. Many forms of saving are already taxed on a consumption tax basis. We have just discussed one important example of consumption taxation, namely, the treatment of consumer durables and owner-occupied housing. According to the *Flow of Funds Accounts* (1976), roughly 20 percent of net saving is made through net accumulation of owner-occupied housing. Our model already accounts for the light taxation of capital income in the housing industry. This industry has an f_i parameter that is much lower than average. We also already account for the tax treatment of imputed returns to consumer durables other than housing, because we do not distinguish between consumer durables and other consumer goods.

A significant amount of savings also flows through private, state, local, or federal government pension plans (excluding Social Security), and through cash-value life insurance policies. Some of these are taxed on a deferral basis, and some are taxed on the prepayment basis.

The *Flow of Funds Accounts* indicate that, in recent years, approximately 30 percent of savings flows through these vehicles and are thus taxed on a consumption tax basis. Our model accounts for the tax treatment of these forms of saving by allowing households to deduct 30 percent of savings in our tax simulations of the current tax policy. In our analysis of consumption tax alternatives, we examine the effects of increasing this deductible fraction of saving.

9.4 Representing Consumption Tax Plans in Model Equivalent Form

In order to evaluate the efficiency of adopting a consumption tax as the major broadly based U.S. tax source, we consider a number of alternative plans that differ in rate structure and in the accompanying tax changes. Before we can perform our simulation experiments, we must represent each plan in model equivalent form. Since we model the light taxation of housing at the industry level, and since saving in housing amounts to 20 percent of total net savings, a complete move to a consumption tax would mean that the remaining 80 percent of net savings would be deductible against personal taxes. The increased deduction of savings would, however, lead to a substantial reduction in tax revenues if all other taxes were left unchanged. So, once again, we preserve revenue yield by lump-sum, multiplicative, or additive increases in taxes.

The amount of extra savings that would result from the deduction would depend upon the elasticity of savings with respect to the real, after-tax rate of return. We discussed estimates of this parameter in chapter 6. We use Boskin's estimate of 0.4 in most of our simulations. (All of the results reported in chapter 8 employed this estimate.) However, it should be clear that the effects of a consumption tax will depend critically on the value of the savings elasticity. Therefore, we also report in this chapter some simulations with different values of the elasticity, in order to test the sensitivity of our results.

We will examine eight different tax modification packages. The features of each of these are shown in table 9.1. Alternative 1, labeled Consumption Tax, would simply raise the fraction of sheltered savings in the federal personal tax from 30 percent to 80 percent. With the current sheltering of the imputed return to housing, this would effectively remove all of savings from the tax base. This policy could be accomplished by greatly liberalizing the provisions governing savings vehicles such as Keogh Plans and Individual Retirement Accounts. The second tax modification policy, which is presented here for purposes of comparison, is integration of corporate and personal income taxes, accompanied by full integration of capital gains. We discussed this plan extensively in chapter 8. The third plan is the consumption tax (80 percent of savings deductible) combined with corporate tax integration. The fourth plan corresponds most closely to a pure consumption tax, in that all income is taxed (including the imputed income from housing), while all savings are

Table 9.1   Tax-Modification Packages

Description	Fraction of Saving Deduction from Taxation	Preferential Treatment of Income from Housing Capital at Industry Level	Fraction of Dividends Taxable	Fraction of Nominal Capital Gains Taxable at Personal Level	Separate Corporate Income Tax
0. Current U.S. system	.3	Yes	.96	.25	Yes
1. Consumption Tax	.8	Yes	.96	.25	Yes
2. Corporate tax integration with indexation of capital gains	.3	Yes	1.0	1.0	No
3. Consumption tax with integration	.8	Yes	1.0	1.0	No
4. Pure consumption tax with integration	1.0	No	1.0	1.0	No
5. Partial consumption tax	.55	Yes	.96	.25	Yes
6. Full savings deduction with housing preference	1.0	Yes	.96	.25	Yes
7. Pure income tax without integration	0.0	No	1.0	1.0	Yes
8. Pure income tax with integration	0.0	No	1.0	1.0	No

deductible. The corporate income tax is eliminated with this plan also. Plans 5 and 6 represent possible policy outcomes, although they do not correspond to particular proposals. Plan 5 represents a partial movement towards a consumption tax, where the 55 percent savings deduction represents a point halfway between the current system and the 80 percent deduction of plan 1. In plan 6 all savings are deductible, and the existing preferences on income from housing capital are retained. The outcome would involve a net subsidy to savings. Plans 7 and 8 investigate whether the present U.S. federal "income" tax system (which is about halfway towards a consumption tax) is better or worse than a "pure" income tax. A pure income tax would remove the special treatment of capital gains and of the imputed income to homeowners who occupy their own homes. It would also eliminate the tax shelters offered by pension funds and other retirement savings vehicles. While savings would be taxed more heavily, many of the interindustry distortions of the present tax system would be eliminated. Plan 8 would go further and remove the corporate income tax as well.

9.5 Results

We have calculated the present value of the compensating variations over time for each of the twelve consumer groups. We described the procedure for these calculations in chapter 7. We use precisely the same procedure here as we used in chapter 8. The individual results are summed over the twelve groups, and are presented in table 9.2.

The consumption tax (plan 1) leads to an efficiency gain of $616 billion if the revenue shortfall caused by the additional savings deductions is made up using the lump-sum tax. The gain is reduced to $537 billion if marginal tax rates are increased in a multiplicative manner, and to $556 billion if an additive surtax is applied to the marginal rates. With sales tax scaling, the gain is $564 billion. The figures in parentheses in table 9.2 give the efficiency gain of each of our plans as a fraction of the present value of future expanded national income, after correction for population growth (estimated at $49 trillion). The consumption tax yields gains that range from 1.08 percent to 1.24 percent of this present value. The gains range from 1.58 percent to 1.81 percent of the present value of national income excluding leisure. A more important comparison is made by comparing the gains with the present value of the revenue that would be raised by the income tax in the base case. The gains from adopting a consumption tax range from 11.6 percent to 13.4 percent of income tax revenues.

Some results regarding corporate income tax integration are presented in row 2 of table 9.2. These results were shown earlier in table 8.3. They indicate that this policy promises a gain for the economy of about the

Table 9.2   Dynamic Welfare Effects in Present Value of Equivalent Variations over Time (in billions of 1973 dollars)

Tax Replacement	Lump-Sum	Types of Scaling to Preserve Tax Yield		
		Multiplicative	Additive	VAT
1. Consumption tax	615.8 (1.235)	536.9 (1.077)	556.1 (1.115)	573.6 (1.150)
2. Corporate tax integration with indexation of capital gains	695.0 (1.394)	310.6 (0.623)	418.2 (0.839)	559.6 (1.122)
3. Consumption tax with integration	1303.6 (2.614)	836.0 (1.677)	976.1 (1.958)	1080.6 (2.167)
4. Pure consumption tax with integration	1431.6 (2.871)	1175.5 (2.357)	1246.2 (2.499)	1254.9 (2.517)
5. Partial consumption tax (55% savings deduction)	299.0 (0.600)	259.3 (0.520)	267.1 (0.536)	280.6 (0.563)
6. Full savings deduction with housing preference	877.3 (1.759)	789.2 (1.583)	806.7 (1.618)	792.2 (1.589)
7. Pure income tax without integration	−544.6 (−1.092)	−238.0 (−0.477)	−317.8 (−0.637)	−447.5 (−0.897)
8. Pure income tax with integration	236.8 (0.475)	152.8 (0.306)	177.0 (0.355)	210.8 (0.423)

Notes: The numbers in parentheses represent the gain as a percentage of the present discounted value of consumption plus leisure in the base sequence. This number is $48.978 trillion for all comparisons, and accounts for only the initial population.

same order of magnitude as that which would be caused by the consumption tax. Our estimates indicate that the present value gain is roughly $695 billion 1973 dollars, with lump-sum replacement taxes. When the lost revenue is regained by increases in distortionary taxes, the gains range from $310 billion to $560 billion.

At this point, let us compare the consumption tax and corporate tax integration more closely. These policies deserve extra attention because they have been the centerpieces of an active public policy debate over the past few years.

One of the important effects of corporate tax integration, which we discussed in chapter 8, was the increase in the net rate of return to capital. This net rate of return, r, was defined in section 3.4 to depend on the price of capital services, P_K, the conversion factor, q, and the cost of investment goods, P_S. The exact relationship is $r = P_K q/P_S$. Since we modeled integration as a cut in taxes on industry use of capital, the price of capital services increased from 1.0 to 1.208 in the first period of the revised-case sequence. The net rate of return increased accordingly. The consumption tax, however, is modeled as a subsidy on savings and the purchase of investment goods (a fall in P_S). The resulting increase in r generates the same kind of savings response, but not through an increase in P_K. In the first equilibrium period under the 80 percent saving deduction, with additive replacement, the price of capital actually drops to 0.988, compared with a price of labor of 1.0.

This drop can be explained by the relative factor intensities in the production of consumer goods and capital goods. In the first equilibrium period, the consumption tax (with additive replacement) leads to a 32.8 percent increase in the quantity of saving. This saving is used directly for investment. It turns out, however, that investment is more labor-intensive than the other components of aggregate demand. In the base case, the total value added in all industries consists of 82 percent labor and 18 percent capital. If we weight the labor intensities of the various industries by the quantities of investment goods produced in each industry in the base case, we find that investment goods consist of 91.6 percent labor and only 8.4 percent capital.[1] The increase in savings generates an indirect increase in the relative demand for labor and thus an indirect decrease in the relative price of capital.

After the first period, the price of capital continues to fall as capital deepening occurs. By the second equilibrium five years later, the relative price of capital drops to 0.952. It continues to drop, and by the eleventh equilibrium (fifty years into the future), it reaches 0.831. (If we were to

---

1. This difference is caused primarily by two industries: construction, and metals and machinery. Some 98.5 percent of valued added in the construction industry comes from labor. Metals and machinery is 92.1 percent labor. Together, these two industries account for 73.4 percent of the total amount of investment.

carry the calculations out for another fifty years, the price would drop to 0.811.)

Another feature of the corporate tax integration was the large sectoral reallocation of capital and the large degree of relative price changes among sectors. This phenomenon is not repeated in the first equilibrium under the consumption tax, because the price of capital is still close to unity. In the first period, the largest relative price change for consumer goods is only 0.6 percent. However, as capital deepening causes the price of capital to drop farther, we get greater changes in relative prices. This time it is the capital-intensive industries, such as agriculture and real estate, that have price decreases and quantity increases. This pattern is just the opposite from the one that emerged from our simulations of corporate tax integration. It is important to remember that the intersectoral changes that follow the consumption tax are due primarily to the change in the price of capital, rather than to improved intersectoral efficiency.

The third plan combines the features of plans 1 and 2, and our estimates indicate that the efficiency improvement is almost precisely additive. This combination of tax changes was advocated in *Blueprints*. The plan offers an efficiency gain of $976 billion, even with an additive surcharge to marginal rates. (The additive surcharge is substantial, since both the consumption tax and corporate tax integration reduce revenues. In the first period, marginal tax rates are increased by 8.6 percentage points. The additive surcharge falls over time to 4.0 percentage points in the eleventh equilibrium.) This gain of $976 billion is well over 60 percent of national income for 1973, and nearly 2 percent of the total present value of population-corrected national income and leisure. It is about 15 percent of the present value of the revenue that would be collected from the corporate income tax and personal income tax in the base case.

The effect on the price of capital is a mixture of the effects we discussed when we looked at the consumption tax and corporate tax integration separately. In the first period the relative price of capital rises to 1.186. However, it falls below unity by the fifth period (twenty years after the policy change). By the eleventh equilibrium, the price of capital stands at 0.884.

The fourth plan treats housing as any other investment and taxes its return, but the plan allows deductions for all net savings (including housing). In any particular year there is no necessary equivalence between the income from housing and investment in housing, so the efficiency results are not the same for plans 3 and 4. Plan 4 also better captures the industrial neutrality of a consumption tax/corporate tax integration policy. The efficiency surplus of plan 4 relative to the current tax system is roughly $1.43 trillion with lump-sum revenue replacement, $1.18 trillion with multiplicative marginal rate surcharges, and $1.25

trillion with additive marginal rate surcharges. When revenues are replaced with increased sales taxes, the gain is also about $1.25 trillion.

At first this plan causes a reallocation away from the real estate industry and the housing commodity. But over time the deduction for net saving in housing has a stimulating effect on the sector. In the base case, 8.2 percent of total domestic demand for the nineteen producer goods goes into the real estate industry, and consumers spend 14 percent of their net money incomes on housing. In the first period under plan 4, these figures drop to 6.5 percent and 10.5 percent, respectively. By the fifth equilibrium (twenty years into the sequence) these sectors have recovered somewhat, so that the corresponding figures are 7.3 percent and 12.0 percent. The recovery continues, but these sectors never reach the shares they had in the base case.

The adoption of plan 5, which is a move halfway toward a consumption tax from the current system, would result in efficiency gains roughly half those involved in plan 1. The decrease in the price of capital and the increase in savings are roughly half of what occur under the 80 percent savings deduction plan.

Plan 6 exempts all savings from taxation and leaves the housing preference unchanged. It thus results in a net subsidy to savings. However, the total efficiency gain is even larger under this plan than under the 80 percent savings deduction, because the subsidy to savings acts to offset somewhat the distortionary effects of the corporate tax.

The gains for multiplicative scaling are typically smaller than those for additive scaling, because multiplicative scaling implies greater increases in the tax rates of high-income consumers. Since these individuals are already the most highly taxed, this scaling causes greater distortions in their labor/leisure choice. Generally speaking, efficiency losses increase with the square of the tax rate, so we would expect very high tax rates on some to be more distorting than somewhat higher rates for all. However, high-income consumers also have higher propensities to save, so the savings deduction benefits these groups most. As a consequence, even though it is less efficient, multiplicative scaling may be viewed as necessary to maintain vertical equity and relative tax burdens of different income groups when savings deductions are increased.

The results of table 9.2 regarding plans 7 and 8 indicate that we could move to a pure income tax with no loss in efficiency, but only if we also integrate the corporate and personal income taxes. The tax base actually increases under plan 7, because the imputed income from housing is included and existing savings deductions are eliminated. Consequently, the tax rate structure is *lowered* in order to maintain government revenues. As a result, the usual relationship between the change in efficiency under lump-sum, multiplicative, and additive replacement is reversed. When we increase taxes in order to maintain the revenue yield, a lump-sum change is always the best way to raise the required revenue. However, under plan 7, a lump-sum decrease in taxes is not as good for the economy as a reduction in the distortionary income tax rates.

Table 9.2 shows that plan 7 is a losing proposition, despite the tax reductions that are necessary to maintain equal revenue yield. Moving to a pure income tax alone, without corporate tax integration, results in a $545 billion loss if there is a lump-sum tax reduction. Even with a multiplicative reduction in income tax rates, the loss is still almost $240 billion. These losses come about primarily because the intertemporal distortions of the current system are made worse. Under the pure income tax, no savings vehicles exist that earn more than $(1 - \text{tax rate}) \times$ (marginal product of capital). The improvement in the interindustry allocation of capital (resulting primarily from the taxation of the return to owner-occupied housing) is more than offset by the deterioration in intertemporal efficiency.

Plan 8 is a comprehensive income tax plan involving corporate tax integration. The revenue losses from integration outweigh the revenue gains from taxing the imputed income from owner-occupied housing and eliminating savings deductions. Thus, we need tax increases in order to preserve equal yield. Plan 8 involves a substantial reduction in intertemporal efficiency, coupled with a substantial improvement in interindustry efficiency. The net effect is a welfare improvement—although a smaller one than most of the other plans investigated. With lump-sum replacement we have an efficiency gain of about $237 billion. If the equal yield replacement taxes are distortionary, the increase in welfare ranges from $153 billion to $211 billion.

9.6   Sensitivity of Results to Alternative Assumptions

Because economists have not agreed on a narrow range for the elasticity of saving with respect to the real after-tax interest rate, we have done some sensitivity analysis of our results with respect to this parameter. The efficiency gain numbers for plan 1 (consumption tax) are shown in table 9.3 for three different elasticity estimates. In addition to the 0.4 figure used previously, we have run our simulations with saving elasticities of 0.0 (consistent with Denison's law; Denison 1958) and 2.0, a magnitude roughly comparable to those derived in Summers (1981). The results of table 9.3 indicate that the efficiency gain increases with the saving elasticity. With the higher value for the saving elasticity, we get results consistent with the lower range of Summer's results. For example, we find that the welfare gain with an additive marginal tax surcharge is $395 billion with a saving elasticity of 0.0, while it is $556 billion or $988 billion if the parameter is 0.4 or 2.0, respectively. This last $988 billion figure is 71 percent of 1973's national income. Note that the taxation of capital

Table 9.3   **Sensitivity of Dynamic Welfare Effects to the Savings Elasticity in Present Value of Equivalent Variations over Time (in billions of 1973 dollars)**

Full Consumption Tax (80% savings deduction)	Types of Scaling to Preserve Tax Yield			
	Lump-Sum	Multiplicative	Additive	VAT
Savings elasticity = 0.0	474.3	365.1	394.7	431.3
	(0.951)	(0.732)	(0.792)	(0.865)
Savings elasticity = 0.4[a]	615.8	536.9	556.1	573.6
	(1.235)	(1.077)	(1.115)	(1.150)
Savings elasticity = 2.0	998.8	987.3	988.2	940.4
	(2.003)	(1.980)	(1.982)	(1.886)

Notes: The numbers in parentheses represent the gain as a percentage of the present discounted value of consumption plus leisure in the base sequence. This number is $49 trillion for all comparisons, and accounts for only the initial population.
[a]This row is also presented in table 9.2.

income would be nondistortionary only if the elasticity of substitution between present and future consumption were zero. A zero elasticity for savings corresponds to a unitary own-price elasticity for future consumption.

The results shown in table 9.4 give us some information regarding how long the economy takes to resettle into a steady-state growth path. Once the economy has completely adjusted to the new policy regime, all relative prices will again remain constant. In the case of consumption tax programs, the new steady state is characterized by a higher capital intensity and a lower relative return to capital. The results of table 9.4 indicate that for the cases with a 0.4 saving elasticity, roughly 40 percent of the adjustment is completed after ten years, 80 percent after thirty years. The economy then asymptotically approaches the new steady-state growth path. The transition is accomplished more rapidly with a savings elasticity of 2.0, despite the fact that the total adjustment is larger. In this case, 70 percent of the adjustment is completed in ten years, with 89 percent adjustment accomplished in twenty years. There is a high variance to previous estimates of the length of the long run, with R. Sato's (1963) figure being extremely long (greater than one hundred years) and those of Summers (1981) and Hall (1968) being surprisingly short (around five years). It is also difficult to reconcile these various findings completely but it is clear that the prime determinant is the degree of substitution throughout the model used for the analysis.

It is interesting to note that, when the savings elasticity is 2.0, the method of equal yield tax replacement makes very little difference. When the savings elasticity is so high, the 80 percent savings deduction generates a tremendous increase in savings. Table 9.5 shows the relationship

Table 9.4   Time Path for the Ratio of the Rental Price of Capital to the Wage Rate

Plan Number	Savings Elasticity	Revenue Replacement	Pre-change	Factor-Price Ratios Time Period (years)										
				0	5	10	15	20	25	30	35	40	45	50
1	0.4	Lump-Sum	1.000	1.002	0.965	0.936	0.913	0.894	0.879	0.867	0.857	0.848	0.841	0.836
1	0.4	Additive	1.000	0.988	0.952	0.923	0.902	0.889	0.870	0.859	0.850	0.842	0.836	0.831
3	0.4	Additive	1.000	1.186	1.108	1.052	1.009	0.977	0.951	0.931	0.916	0.903	0.892	0.884
1	0.0	Additive	1.000	0.988	0.964	0.944	0.927	0.913	0.900	0.890	0.881	0.873	0.866	0.860
1	2.0	Additive	1.000	0.987	0.891	0.847	0.823	0.809	0.800	0.795	0.791	0.789	0.788	0.787
7	0.4	Additive	1.000	0.904	0.921	0.935	0.948	0.961	0.970	0.978	0.986	0.993	0.998	1.004

Table 9.5   **Percentage Increase in Savings in the First Equilibrium Period, Moving from Base Case to 80 Percent Savings Deduction**

	Types of Scaling to Preserve Tax Yield			
	Lump-Sum	Multipli-cative	Additive	VAT
Savings elasticity = 0.0	20.0	21.3	21.4	21.7
Savings elasticity = 0.4	30.8	32.7	32.8	31.6
Savings elasticity = 2.0	83.3	89.6	89.9	77.3

between the savings elasticity and the increase in the amount of savings. The economy grows more rapidly when the savings elasticity is high. As a result, the increases in tax rates necessary to preserve equal yield in the later periods are much smaller when the savings elasticity is high. Thus, multiplicative and additive replacements do not actually cause much distortion in this case.

The changes enacted in the United States tax law in 1981 included several moves that allow greater deductions for certain types of savings. However, the plans as they now stand do not correspond well to the model of the consumption tax we have employed in the simulations in this chapter. In particular, there is a maximum amount that can be deducted in any one year for contributions to IRA and Keogh accounts. This limitation raises two problems. The first problem is only a transitional one: when an individual has a large amount of wealth, he or she can transfer existing wealth into the new accounts without doing any new saving. When a ceiling is placed on the amount of deductions, it may take many years before the individual exhausts his or her wealth. The second problem is that, when a ceiling on deductions does exist, there may be no *marginal* incentive to save. If the individual would have saved $5,000 under the old law, a new law that allows deduction for saving up to $3,000 will not have the desired effect on savings. This point is important and often overlooked in popular discussions of tax policy. In such discussions it is often assumed that a decrease in *average* tax rates will have a desired *marginal* effect.

Martin Feldstein and Daniel Feenberg (1983) investigate both of these issues by looking at a microdata set for 1972, and they reach relatively optimistic conclusions. They make two main points. First, most of the individuals in their sample have little or no financial wealth, so the transitional problem would be negligible for these taxpayers. Second, most of their taxpayers save very little, thus even a low ceiling on deductions would still preserve marginal incentives.

After studying Feldstein and Feenberg's tables we find ourselves less sanguine about the prospects for the current tax structure. Our main objection stems from a point, made earlier, about the importance of wealthy individuals to any consumption tax proposal. It is true that 69 percent of the taxpayers in the Feldstein-Feenberg sample have one year of transferable assets or less. However, most of these are low-income taxpayers who do not do the bulk of the saving in the economy. In the income range above $30,000, only 27 percent of the sample have one year of transferable assets or less. The really eye-catching statistic is that, among the taxpayers in the high-income group, fully 42 percent have twenty years of transferable assets or more.

The story that emerges from a look at saving behavior is similar, though less dramatic. Some 80 percent of the taxpayers in the sample save 6 percent of their wage and salary income, or less. However, the corresponding figure for the highest-income group is only 67 percent of the taxpayers. This suggests that a large number of taxpayers who would be expected to save a great deal would not, in fact, be subject to a marginal incentive to save under current laws.

It is difficult to simulate plans with ceilings in a general equilibrium model, since the *price* of the commodity (savings in this case) depends on the quantity consumed. But, of course, the quantity depends on the price. This simultaneity is difficult to model, and we have not attempted to do so here. We must conclude, however, that plans with ceilings would lead to smaller welfare gains than plans without ceilings. In a sense, the worst thing a policymaker can do is to give away revenue without eliminating distortions. After all, the lost revenue must be made up somehow, presumably with distortionary taxes elsewhere in the economy.

Instead of putting a ceiling on deductible savings, it makes more sense to put a floor under them. If an individual were allowed to deduct savings over and above 5 percent of income, for example, there might still be a

Table 9.6   Dynamic Welfare Effects of Adopting a Consumption Tax, with and without a Minimum Required Level of Saving, in Present Value of Equivalent Variations over Time (in billions of 1973 dollars)

	Types of Scaling to Preserve Tax Yield		
	Multiplicative	Additive	VAT
No minimum (our standard case)	536.9 (1.077)	556.1 (1.115)	573.6 (1.150)
Deductions allowed only for savings in excess of base savings	700.1 (1.404)	635.0 (1.273)	602.9 (1.209)

Note: The numbers in parentheses represent the gain as a percentage of the present discounted value of consumption plus leisure in the base sequence. This number is about $49 trillion for all comparisons, after correction for population growth.

marginal incentive, without a large revenue loss. (Of course, it would be very important to set the floor at a level that is not too high.)

An ideal system would tax savers on their previous or planned saving and would shelter from taxation additions to saving. The practical problem for the government, of course, is the inability to ascertain what individuals would have saved in the absence of the tax exemption. We modeled this ideal system by taxing households on their base saving, but allowing a deduction for changes from base saving. The welfare gains of this idealized policy are shown in table 9.6, for a saving elasticity of 0.4. The plan with a minimum-required level of saving leads to greater welfare gains in every case. The larger improvement results because the inframarginal tax on savings means that other tax rates do not need to be raised as much in order to preserve revenue.

9.7 Conclusion

The analysis of this chapter indicates that sheltering more savings from the current U.S. income tax could improve economic efficiency even if marginal tax rate increases are necessary in order to maintain government revenue. The present value of welfare gains for a policy of complete savings deduction with marginal rate adjustments (a consumption tax) is around $500 billion to $600 billion in 1973 dollars. Gains of this magnitude are very significant. These gains are of the same order of magnitude as the efficiency gains we have estimated for corporate tax integration. The gains are smaller under the consumption tax when revenues are replaced with distortionary taxes, but larger when lump-sum scaling is used. We find that a combined policy of tax integration and savings deductions offers an even greater welfare improvement, with the present value figure lying between $975 billion and $1.3 trillion.

This chapter also shows that while only half of net savings is currently taxed in the United States, room exists for very great improvement. We have included some sensitivity analysis of our results to the elasticity of savings with respect to the real after-tax rate of return. The results are indeed sensitive to this parameter, and further efforts to narrow the profession's consensus on its value would aid policy evaluation a great deal. We also have investigated the length of time it takes the economy to adjust to these policy changes in this model. Roughly, we estimate the "long run" to be thirty years, although this figure is also sensitive to the savings elasticity.

10   The Relationship between Tax Rates and Government Revenue

10.1   Introduction

Since 1974, when Arthur B. Laffer first drew his famous curve on a napkin in a Washington restaurant, there has been considerable public debate about the possibility of an inverse relationship between tax rates and government revenue. Pictured in figure 10.1, the Laffer curve plots total revenue against the tax rate and claims to show that two rates exist at which a given revenue can be collected. The tax rate of figure 10.1 generally refers to any particular tax instrument, while revenues generally refer to total tax receipts. An increase in the payroll tax rate, for example, could affect not only its own revenue, but work effort and thus personal income tax revenues.

The upward-sloping portion of the curve is called the "normal" range and the downward-sloping segment is the "prohibitive" range. No rational government would knowingly operate on the latter range in the long run, because the same revenue could be obtained with a lower tax rate. However, with adjustment lags in the private sector and a high social discount rate, such tax rates might be used in the short run. The prohibitive range is said to exist because the high tax rates stifle economic activity, force agents to barter, and encourage leisure pursuits.

The debate has been conducted mostly in the spheres of politics and journalism, and it includes a wide variety of unsupported claims and opinions. These range all the way from the assertion that the prohibitive range does not exist to the claim that "we are well within this range at

This chapter is a revised version of an article by Don Fullerton, "On the possibility of an inverse relationship between tax rates and government revenues," *Journal of Public Economics* 19 (October 1982): 3–22. Reproduced by permission.

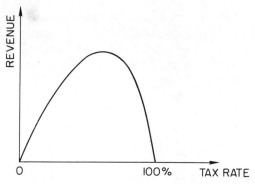

Fig. 10.1   The Laffer curve.

present.''[1] Simple theoretical models can show that the prohibitive range does indeed exist, but the U.S. position on the curve is clearly an empirical matter. Despite the obvious importance of this issue for fiscal policy, no serious estimation of the curve, using an economic model, has been made.[2]

Our original equilibrium model is well suited to answering questions related to the Laffer curve. First, we can attempt to determine where on the Laffer curve the United States economy is today, and we can get an idea of the shape of the entire curve. Second, we can learn about the relationship between the curve and critical parameters, such as the elasticities of supply of factor inputs.[3]

In the next section we offer a brief review of some salient points from the debate. A common aspect of previous studies is that a prohibitive range for some local or national economy is always associated with particularly high tax rates, high factor supply elasticities, or both. In section 10.3 we establish the conditions under which a lower tax rate

1. Michael Kinsley (1978) correctly claims that there is no logical necessity for revenues to be zero at 100 percent tax rates, due to nonmonetary incentives for work effort, but he incorrectly infers that "there's no logical reason to assume without proof that the Laffer curve ever reverses direction at all" (p. 38). Laffer (1980) points out that even if a motivated person still works with a 100 percent tax rate, there must be some higher rate that will make him stop. The curve will still have the shape of figure 10.1. The quote in the text is from Laffer 1977, p. 79.

2. Several papers have described models in which there exists the possibility of a prohibitive range. See Canto, Joines, and Laffer 1978 and Beck 1979 for examples. Other empirical papers have found governments operating in this range, as seen in the next section. Also, Kiefer (1978) provides estimates of revenue effects from the DRI, Wharton, and Chase Econometric models. None of these papers plot out the Laffer curve, however, nor do they estimate its relationship to various elasticity parameters.

3. In general, the location of the curve depends on both supply and demand elasticities, consumption and production parameters, and other circumstances in the economy. In wartime, for example, individuals might be willing to work harder at high tax rates to generate larger tax revenues.

could result in higher revenues. These conditions are summarized in a new curve, plotting the appropriate factor supply elasticity against the tax rate. In section 10.4 we use the model to estimate the position of the Laffer curve for various values of the labor supply elasticity. We also plot the combinations of labor supply elasticities and tax rates that put the economy on the boundary between the normal range and the prohibitive range.

10.2 A Brief Literature Review

The idea of an inverse relationship between tax rates and revenue is not entirely new. In *The Wealth of Nations*, Adam Smith could hardly be more explicit: "High taxes, sometimes by diminishing the consumption of the taxed commodities, and sometimes by encouraging smuggling, frequently afford a smaller revenue to government than what might be drawn from more moderate taxes" ([1776] 1976, 5:414).

The trade literature, as exemplified by Caves and Jones (1973), has always understood the existence of a revenue-maximizing tariff. This pre-Laffer edition contains a hump-shaped tariff revenue curve that looks just like figure 10.1. With respect to internal taxes, Jules Dupuit in 1844 states: "By thus gradually increasing the tax it will reach a level at which the yield is at a maximum . . . Beyond, the yield of tax diminishes. . . . Lastly a tax [which is prohibitive] will yield nothing" (1969, pp. 281–82).

Recent literature has examined this relationship more closely. Canto, Joines, and Laffer (1978) build a simple equilibrium model with one output, two factors, and a labor/leisure choice on the part of a single consumer group. Their utility function includes discounted consumption and leisure of each future period—a formulation very similar to our larger empirical general equilibrium model. Another similarity is that capital is inelastically supplied in any one period, but can grow over time. Labor taxes in these models place a wedge between the wage paid by producers and net wage received by workers. Individuals react to this wedge with an income effect and a substitution effect. In their model, however, government revenues are returned through transfers or are used to buy goods that are perfect substitutes for private goods. This modeling cancels out the income effect and leaves the economy with an unambiguously positive substitution effect and an upward-sloping labor supply.

This way of modeling the economy raises three points. First, as recognized by Canto, Joines, and Laffer, if transfers are given to individuals other than those who pay taxes, and if individuals have different preferences, then income effects do not necessarily cancel. Second, if a government does nothing other than place a distorting wedge into the labor/leisure choice of homogeneous consumers and then return revenues in lump-sum fashion, it necessarily follows that output and welfare would both fall. These authors have not allowed for any positive contribution of a government budget. Their model does not account for the income effect of an efficiency gain that can be associated with correcting market failure by providing a public good. Third, they fail to allow for any complementarity between private and public outputs. Clearly there are public goods such as police protection and transportation systems which act to encourage private production. This complementarity may more than offset the adverse effects of the necessary tax wedge. Thus the "balanced budget" labor supply curve does not have to be upward sloping as these authors insist.

These shortcomings in the Canto, Joines, and Laffer theoretical model are not explicitly corrected in our model. By allowing the labor supply elasticity to take on positive or negative values, however, our model does implicitly take these considerations into account.

We said, above, that no one has used an economic model to estimate the shape of an entire Laffer curve. However, several empirical studies have sought to determine whether some specific tax is being operated at a point where a decrease in tax rates would lead to an increase in revenue collections. For example, Ronald Grieson et al. find the possibility of an inverse relationship between tax rates and revenues for local government in New York: "The inclusion of state taxes lost when economic activity leaves both the city and state would . . . raise the possibility of a net revenue loss as a result of an increase in business income taxes" (1977, p. 179). They find that the nonmanufacturing sector has fewer alternatives to the New York City location and should be taxed more heavily relative to the manufacturing sector, whose response to tax is more elastic. Grieson (1980) finds that this relationship between the two sectors is reversed for Philadelphia, where the nonmanufacturing sector is under greater competitive pressure. As for Philadelphia's position on its own Laffer curve, Grieson finds that "Philadelphia may have been at or very close to the revenue maximizing point . . . before the recent income tax increase, which raises the possibility of it having been in excess of the socially optimal one" (p. 135).

Why a local government might find itself in or close to the prohibitive range of tax rates is not difficult to understand. When a government serves a very small geographic area, and when transportation out of the area is inexpensive, then the possibility of migration can result in very high factor supply elasticities.

Perverse revenue effects are more likely from selective tax cuts than from general tax cuts, if the selective cuts can be directed at individuals or activities that are unusually sensitive to tax rates. Hausman (1983) simulates tax cuts separately for husbands and for wives. He does not find that tax rates are in the prohibitive range, but he does find that tax cuts for wives result in a smaller loss of revenue because wives exhibit higher labor supply elasticity. Feldstein, Slemrod, and Yitzhaki find that capital realizations are very sensitive to the effective tax rate: "An important implication of this high coefficient is that a reduction in the tax rate on capital gains would actually increase the total revenue collected" (1980, p. 786). Two points serve to mitigate the strength of this result. First, a capital gains tax cut might unlock a flood of realizations in the short run, without necessarily increasing revenues in the long run. Second, the capital gains tax cut is likely to increase corporate-retained earnings, decrease the dividends paid out, and thus reduce personal tax revenue from dividends.

The general impression one gets from these empirical studies is that taxes on individual sectors, or small geographic areas, or special groups may be in or close to the prohibitive range. For particular economic activities with high elasticities, tax rates approach the prohibitive range sooner than they would elsewhere in the economy.

One study that deals with the United States as a whole is the study by Canto, Joines, and Webb (1979). They evaluate the 1964 tax cuts, which included the reduction of the top marginal rate in the personal income tax from 91 percent to 70 percent. They determine that it was equally likely that the Kennedy tax cuts may have increased or decreased revenues. For Sweden, Charles Stuart (1981) finds tax rates in the prohibitive range. Using a fairly simple two-sector model, he concludes that Sweden's current 80 percent marginal tax rate exceeds the revenue-maximizing rate. Thus, we have a reason for perverse revenue behavior other than high elasticities for particular economic activities. In these studies, perverse revenue effects are explained by particularly high tax rates.[4]

10.3 Another Simple Curve

We have stressed that this debate focuses on high marginal tax rates, high factor supply elasticities, or a combination of both. By emphasizing the large incentive effect of tax cuts, the "supply siders" imply that they believe the relevant elasticities are large. The entire debate reduces to the empirical matter of determining the relevant parameter values. If supply elasticities are high enough, the economy could be in the prohibitive range.

The very location of Laffer's curve in the rate-revenue space of figure 10.1 depends on the supply elasticity of the factor being taxed. If that

---

4. Other themes from this literature include minimum wage laws, regulation of business, nonmarket activity, and the complexity of tax rules. The Laffer curve itself focuses on tax rates, however, so this chapter will consider different tax rates and assume unchanged complexity. The relevant elasticity for this exercise would provide not just the response of labor supply, but the response of taxable labor supply.

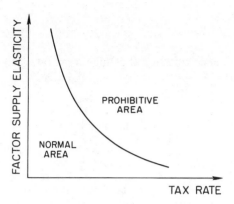

Fig. 10.2   Elasticities, tax rates, and the Laffer curve.

elasticity were fairly low, the total revenue maximizing point would be at a high tax rate for that factor, and the converse. One can imagine a third dimension on that diagram giving different elasticity values. The hill would then be converted into a ridge, running from a low tax rate and high elasticity combination to a high rate and low elasticity pair. The crest of that ridge is plotted in figure 10.2. Everything to the southwest of that curve signifies the normal area, where raising rates increases revenue, and northeast of the curve is the prohibitive area, where no rational government would knowingly operate. Each point on the curve shows the tax rate that maximizes total revenue for a given elasticity.

Suppose, for a simple example, that homogeneous labor L is taxed at the proportional rate t. Labor demand and supply are based, respectively, on the gross-of-tax wage w and the net-of-tax wage $w(1 - t)$, in constant elasticity forms:

(10.1) $L_d = Aw^{\epsilon_d}$, $\epsilon_d < 0$;

(10.2) $L_s = B[w(1 - t)]^{\epsilon_s}$, $\epsilon_s > 0$.

Tax revenue R is equal to twL, so differentiation and algebra provide:

(10.3) $\dfrac{\partial R}{\partial t} = wL\left[1 + \dfrac{\partial L}{\partial t} \cdot \dfrac{t}{L} + \dfrac{\partial w}{\partial t} \cdot \dfrac{t}{w}\right].$

Setting equation (10.3) equal to zero, we have three equations that can be solved for w, L, and the revenue-maximizing tax rate t. Since $L_s = L_d$ in this partial equilibrium system, we can use equations (10.1) and (10.2) to express w as a function of t. Substituting that w back into equation (10.1), we can also express L as a function of t. Differentiating these expressions, substituting into equation (10.3), and solving for t, we have:[5]

5. Equation (10.4) is derived somewhat differently in Blinder 1981.

(10.4)
$$t = \frac{\epsilon_d - \epsilon_s}{\epsilon_d(1 + \epsilon_s)} \, .$$

If $\epsilon_d > -1$ (demand is inelastic), then higher tax rates can always achieve more revenue. If $\epsilon_d < -1$, however, then the relationship between t and ϵ_s will look like figure 10.2:

(10.5)
$$\frac{\partial t}{\partial \epsilon_s} = \frac{-1}{(1 + \epsilon_s)^2}\left(\frac{1 + \epsilon_d}{\epsilon_d}\right) < 0, \text{ and}$$

(10.6)
$$\frac{\partial^2 t}{\partial \epsilon_s^2} = \frac{2}{(1 + \epsilon_s)^3}\left(\frac{1 + \epsilon_d}{\epsilon_d}\right) > 0,$$

so the curve slopes down and is convex to the origin. The easiest case to see is where $\epsilon_d = -\infty$ so that $t = 1/(1 + \epsilon_s)$. Then the revenue-maximizing rate approaches one as ϵ_s goes to zero (inelastic supply), and it approaches zero as ϵ_s becomes infinite (infinitely elastic supply).[6]

In summary, those who find an inverse relationship between tax rates and revenues must believe that the relevant elasticity is high, that the relevant tax rate is high, or both. Those who find a normal range must believe that one or both of these parameters is low. Finally, those who deny the existence of an inverse relationship at any tax rate might really just believe that the uncompensated supply elasticity is zero or negative (or that demand is inelastic).[7]

10.4   Estimation of Laffer Curves

Supply side advocates refer to several different types of taxes when they claim an inverse relationship between a particular tax rate and government revenue. The curve in figure 10.2 could be plotted by varying a product tax rate against the price elasticity of demand for that product, or by plotting capital tax rates against the elasticity of savings with respect to the net-of-tax return to capital.

Over forty simulations were performed in seeking a prohibitive area for capital taxes. Using the dynamic version of the model, tax rates were

6. Several points are manifest. First, this analysis oversimplifies by using a given elasticity for all tax rates to find the revenue-maximizing point. As the tax rate varies, so would equilibrium prices, incomes, and preference parameters like the factor supply elasticity. Second, a given time frame is implied since elasticities might increase as more time is allowed for adjustment. Third, neither elasticities nor tax rates have to be positive. The southwest quadrant contains a symmetrical curve showing the maximum revenue loss from a subsidy. Finally, note that similar analyses can be performed with respect to ϵ_d, the labor demand elasticity.

7. A zero uncompensated elasticity can mask a high compensated elasticity, however. Hausman (1981) points out that while the former is relevant to determine actual factor supply (and thus the tax base and revenues), the latter is relevant for the efficiency cost of distortions.

raised to 83 percent of gross capital income, savings elasticities were increased to 4.0, and equilibria were calculated out fifty years in the future. Normally, discount rate problems arise in determining whether the present value of revenues has increased or decreased. In this case, however, not a single period of the raised-tax sequence of equilibria had lower revenues than the corresponding period of the benchmark sequence. Inverse relationships may exist for high effective rates of tax on certain types of real capital income for certain individuals. No overall inverse relationship was discovered in this model, however, because the tax distortion applies to the savings decision, while savings are only an increment to the capital tax base. More than fifty years would be required for the tax base reduction to offset a tax rate increase and result in lower revenues. For this reason, the example used here is the labor tax against the labor supply elasticity.

In our basic model, the tax on labor used by industry averages 10 percent of net factor payments. The personal income tax takes another 24.9 percent of marginal labor income, weighting the twelve marginal tax rates by labor income of each group. The total wedge thus takes 31.8 percent of marginal labor income gross of all tax.[8] This overall marginal rate is the relevant single parameter for summarizing incentive effects in the model, and this is the parameter varied in simulations for the horizontal axes of figures 10.1 and 10.2. The overall average rate is 19.2 percent, dividing total labor taxes by gross labor income.

Marginal tax rates determine incentives, but average tax rates by definition determine revenues. A more progressive tax structure will therefore attain an earlier revenue maximum. For this reason, progressivity should not be altered in simulating alternative tax rates. Unfortunately, however, there is no unambiguous measure of progressivity. Simulations in this chapter will hold constant the first of three possible progressivity measures defined in Musgrave and Musgrave (1980). The effect of this selection is that the same number of percentage points are added to or subtracted from all average *and* marginal labor tax rates of all consumers when a rate change is simulated. Such changes are summarized by referring to changes in the 31.8 percent overall marginal rate on gross labor income. Thus labor tax rate changes can be thought of as changes in the proportional payroll tax rate or as changes in all average and marginal personal tax rates, on labor income only.

---

8. The model defines labor income as net of the 10 percent factor tax on industries, but gross of the personal income tax on individuals. For a marginal dollar of this labor income, $1.10 is the gross-of-tax payment, $.10 is the payroll tax, and $.249 is the marginal personal tax paid, averaged over the twelve groups. The total marginal tax rate is thus $(.1 + .249)/1.10$, which equals 31.8 percent except for rounding. By the same formula for different groups, personal marginal rates between 1 percent and 40 percent imply total marginal rates between $(.1 + .01)/1.10$, which equals 10 percent, and $(.1 + .4)/1.10$, which equals 45.5 percent.

Government transfers are modeled as lump-sum payments to consumer groups in proportion to their observed 1973 receipts from Social Security, unemployment compensation, food stamps, and other welfare programs. We recognize that supply side advocates may prefer to model these payments as additional work disincentives, increasing the wedge between labor's marginal product and leisure's implicit price. Though lawmakers probably do not intend to subsidize leisure, some programs have that effect. The incentive depends on the program's ability to isolate important characteristics such as age, disability, and number of dependents who make the recipient unable to work. If this intention is successful, the payments will not have a substitution effect. The income effect of transfer programs could also reduce labor supply, but this effect is captured in the model.[9]

The 1973 data set shows total tax revenue of $362.54 billion. Because of the parameter calibration procedures described in chapter 6, this amount of revenue will be collected in the first period of *any* base-case sequence, so long as tax rates are unchanged. Simulations with labor tax rates other than 31.8 percent will have revenues that depend on the elasticity, and it becomes necessary to specify the disposition of extra revenues. One possibility is simply to allow a budget surplus or deficit. If a surplus implies lower future taxes, however, individuals may react to an effective tax rate different from the specified rate for the simulation. Higher revenues must eventually be spent or returned. A second possibility is to increase public expenditures on the nineteen industry outputs of the model. Though government spending has no macroeconomic effects on inflation or unemployment in this model, it does have a microeconomic effect on the pattern of demands for commodities. It indirectly affects the demand for capital and labor through the different factor ratios of production. Instead, we return additional revenues to consumers in lump-sum fashion, in proportion to their original after-tax incomes.[10]

9. The difference between paying people who don't work and paying people not to work is the difference between a marginal payment with incentive effects and a lump-sum payment. Legally, an employee must be laid off to be eligible for unemployment compensation. A worker can ask to be laid off, but employers may be reluctant to circumvent the intent of the law. These transfers are not automatically and fully available to nonworkers. Similarly, AFDC payments are designed to select recipients by particular characteristics, maximizing the lump-sum effect and minimizing disincentive effects. Social Security payments are higher for the blind or disabled. Finally note that these transfers, to the extent that they are disincentives, do not always apply to marginal hours. Most individuals who take an extra hour of leisure do not become eligible for transfers at all. Laffer (1980) is correct, however, that if transfer payments include a means test, work disincentives can be large for some individuals.

10. This lump-sum rebate has no direct effect on prices since no tax rates are altered. It could have an indirect effect on prices of the simulated equilibrium, however, since consumers include the income in their expanded budgets for purchase of commodities and leisure according to their own preference patterns. This disposition of revenues corresponds exactly to that of Canto, Joines, and Laffer (1978), reviewed in section 10.2. By symmetry, a decrease in revenue is accompanied by a lump-sum charge on consumers in the same

The results from over sixty simulations are summarized in table 10.1. The first column shows the total revenue resulting from different labor tax rates using the basic model's value of .15 for the labor supply elasticity with respect to the net-of-tax wage. The "observed" total revenue of $362.54 billion corresponds to the basic tax rate of 31.8 percent, and total revenues are positively related to tax rates, up to a tax that is 70.0 percent of gross labor income. Beyond that rate, revenues start to fall.

Like Canto, Joines, and Laffer (1978), this model ignores production-encouraging aspects of any public goods made possible through increased revenue. As a result, national income (GNP) falls by $223 billion when the elasticity is .15 and the tax rate is raised to 70.0 percent. Though the return to the fixed capital stock rises, labor supply falls off by 30 percent. The gross-of-tax wage rises, but the net-of-tax wage falls in the new equilibrium. If the increased leisure is valued at the net-of-tax wage, then the $223 billion income fall is offset by a $173 billion leisure gain, with $50 billion net loss in real terms. These calculations use the geometric mean of the Paasche and Laspeyres price indexes.

Any column of data from table 10.1 can be used to plot an example of figure 10.1, as was done in figure 10.3 for the .15 elasticity. In any of these Laffer curve diagrams, the actual 1973 U.S. economy is represented by .318 on the labor tax rate axis. If the various tax rates, transfers, and elasticities are reasonable as modeled, then the U.S. economy is well down the normal range of the curve. For those who prefer a high elasticity, figure 10.4 plots another Laffer curve. The 4.0 labor supply elasticity and current tax rates place the United States well onto the prohibitive range.

In the 4.0 elasticity case, even the small jump from a 31.8 percent labor tax rate to a 34.7 percent rate causes an 8 percent fall in labor supply, a $65 billion reduction in national income, a $45 billion increase in the value of leisure, and a net welfare loss of $20 billion in real terms. A small tax cut with this high elasticity results in symmetrical increases in labor supply, output, and welfare. All tax cuts increase welfare in this model because revenue is replaced with lump-sum charges as in Canto, Joines, and Laffer (1978). Such opportunities may not in fact be available.

Underlined in each column of table 10.1 is the maximum revenue point for that elasticity. These tax rate and elasticity combinations correspond to points on a curve like figure 10.2. When plotted for this example, the curve is shown in figure 10.5. On this curve, with tax rates as modeled, the labor supply elasticity would have to be at least 3.0 to put the United States over the peak and into the prohibitive range. Alternatively, if the supply elasticity were at least 1.0 and the true overall tax rate were at least

---

proportions. Total government tax revenues are defined to be inclusive of income returned to consumers, and exclusive of any lump-sum charges necessary to keep government spending on commodities constant.

Table 10.1   Total Revenue Associated with Each Labor Tax Rate (in billions of 1973 dollars)

Rate on Gross Labor Income[a]	Labor Supply Elasticity with Respect to Net-of-Tax Wage										
	.15	.50	1.00	1.50	1.75	2.00	2.50	3.00	4.00	5.00	6.00
.166									332.06		
.209									350.30		
.249									360.59	366.55	371.37
.267									363.16	367.74	371.45
.285								360.28	364.27	367.43	369.94
.301								361.99	364.00		
.318	362.54	362.54	362.54	362.54	362.54	362.54	362.54	362.54	362.54	362.54	362.54
.332							363.36	362.04			
.347					367.96	366.25	363.21	360.62	356.35		
.361					369.50	366.87					
.374				374.07	370.30	366.76	360.58		346.58		
.387					370.38						
.399				375.78	369.92	364.60					
.411				375.79							
.422	433.36		393.37	375.30	367.42				318.61		

Rate			
.444			395.79
.464			396.73
.473			396.72	263.94
.482			396.37
.499	477.25		394.89
.558	509.35	448.11
.571		448.50
.583		448.36
.625	526.41
.659	533.36
.687	536.35
.693	536.64
.700	536.75
.705	536.74
.722	535.95
.741	533.50
.750	531.82
.785	520.46
.850	477.06
.875	449.23

[a]Simulations were made selectively to save computational expense. Not all possible rates are reported. These rates on gross income include Social Security taxes and personal income taxes at the overall marginal rate, all as a fraction of gross labor income.

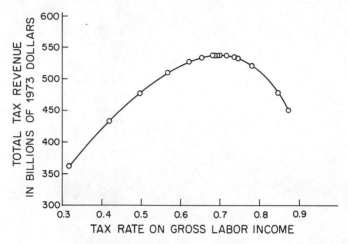

Fig. 10.3   Laffer curve for a labor supply elasticity of 0.15.

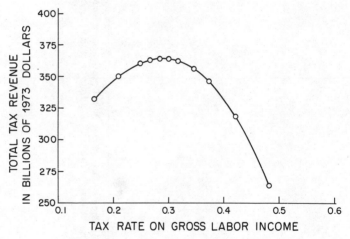

Fig. 10.4   Laffer curve for a labor supply elasticity of 4.0.

46.4 percent, then again U.S. taxes could be operating irrationally. The continuum of figure 10.5 allows the reader to select a plausible tax rate and elasticity combination to determine whether the United States is now in the prohibitive area. We must say, however, that our knowledge of labor supply behavior leads us to believe that it is extremely unlikely that the United States is now operating in the prohibitive range of tax rates.[11]

11. See chapter 6 for our review of the literature on labor supply elasticities.

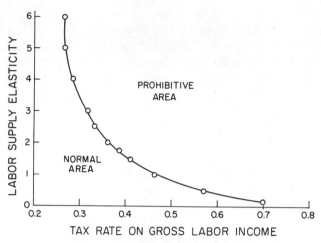

Fig. 10.5   Combinations of elasticities and tax rates that generate maximum revenue.

10.5   Conclusion

In this chapter we considered a number of analytical and empirical arguments about the relationship between tax rates and government revenues. Using our general equilibrium model we were able to plot this relationship for a variety of values of the labor supply elasticity. We found that the U.S. economy *could* conceivably be operating in the prohibitive range for taxes on labor, but that reasonable estimates of an aggregate labor supply elasticity and of an overall marginal labor tax rate are both low enough to suggest that broad-based cuts in labor tax rates would not increase revenues.

The tax rate and elasticity relationship can be applied to other federal, state, or local taxes to find circumstances where a particularly high tax rate on real income or a particularly high elasticity could place a tax in the prohibitive area. A tax on purely nominal capital gains, for example, or an underallowance for depreciation can result in high effective tax rates on some types of real capital income. Future research could investigate the responsiveness of these particular investments to high effective rates. The "marriage penalty," which places a secondary worker in the higher marginal tax bracket of his or her spouse, may represent another high rate of tax on an elastically supplied factor.[12] Welfare programs that make recipients ineligible at a given income level imply effective marginal tax

12. Feenberg and Rosen (1983) simulate the effects of four proposals to reduce or eliminate the marriage penalty. Each has its own welfare effects and redistributions, but none imply higher revenue.

rates of 100 percent or higher. Also, the high elasticity argument is particularly applicable for state and local governments since factors are generally more mobile within national boundaries. McGuire and Rapping (1968, 1970) find labor supply elasticities of 20 to 100 for particular states or industries. This mobility implies that one jurisdiction cannot charge higher tax rates than its neighbors and may apply increasingly to international factor flows.

Finally, though the results of this chapter tend to reject the notion of an inverse relationship between major U.S. tax rates and government revenues, they do not necessarily invalidate the claim that these tax rates and revenues should be lowered. Even on the normal range, taxes may be higher than desired by voters. Preferences can change over time, fewer public goods may now be demanded, and the electorate can legitimately request a tax decrease. Though incentive effects can still be important without perverse revenue effects, the point is that the economics of the tax revolt are less the economics of incentive effects and more the economics of public choice.

11   Alternative Models of
the Foreign Sector

11.1   Introduction

In chapter 3 we described our basic treatment of foreign trade. The standard version of the model uses constant elasticity excess demand functions to describe the merchandise trade of the rest of the world with the United States. The standard version of the model has two variants. The first variant deals only with net trade flows. In this case, none of the nineteen commodities can be exported and imported simultaneously. However, as described in section 3.6, this treatment conflicts with the empirical observation that many products are crosshauled. We allow for crosshauling under the gross trade flows variant of the model. The gross trade flows variant seems to us to be the more realistic one. Consequently, all of the results reported until now were obtained using the constant elasticity gross flows formulation.

There are two reasons for examining more sophisticated models of trade behavior. First, we would like to be able to analyze realistically those tax policy issues that are believed to have their principal effects on the foreign sector. Second, we would like to see how sensitive the findings of our earlier chapters are to the specification of the external sector.

In this chapter we develop some alternative treatments of the international economy. The first of these is a formulation in which we treat certain imports as imperfect substitutes for comparable domestic products. We then present two formulations that model capital mobility between the United States and the rest of the world. The first of these

This chapter is a revised version of a paper by Lawrence H. Goulder, John B. Shoven, and John Whalley, "Domestic tax policy and the foreign sector: The importance of alternative foreign sector formulations to results from a general equilibrium tax analysis model," in *Behavioral Simulation Methods in Tax Policy Analysis*, ed. Martin Feldstein (Chicago: University of Chicago Press, 1983), © 1983 by the National Bureau of Economic Research.

formulations introduces international flows of capital services which depend on the difference between U.S. and foreign rates of return to capital. An elasticity parameter controls the sensitivity of the capital service flows to rate-of-return differentials. The second of these formulations is similar, but involves capital goods rather than capital services.

In order to, evaluate the sensitivity of the model to these different specifications, we analyze the integration of corporate and personal income taxes (see chapter 8) and the introduction of a consumption tax in the United States (see chapter 9) under each of these alternative formulations. We also consider the effects of adopting alternative forms of a value-added tax (VAT) in the United States. We consider VATs of both the income and consumption type, and on both the destination and origin basis. We have delayed looking at the VAT until now, partly because much of the debate on the VAT has centered on foreign trade issues.

It does not appear that the formulation with imperfectly substitutable imports changes our results very much. The welfare gain from adoption of a consumption tax is between 10 and 20 percent lower under this new formulation. The results for corporate tax integration are virtually identical to those of our standard case. Much greater differences arise as a result of the new models of capital flows. The consumption tax is no longer a very attractive policy under either of the models with capital flows. In the capital service flow version, the consumption tax leads to very substantial losses. The intuition behind these results is that, if the world capital market functions well, a policy such as a consumption tax will not significantly increase the U.S. capital stock.

Whereas the consumption tax no longer leads to large welfare gains under the international capital flow formulations, the efficiency gains implied by corporate tax integration are increased. Integration causes the after-corporate-tax rate of return to capital to increase, thus leading to capital inflows. Under some specifications of the capital service flow model, the welfare gain from corporate tax integration is twice as great as it is with the standard model. However, considerable uncertainty exists about the value of some of the key parameters of the capital flow models. Therefore, we provide fairly detailed sensitivity analyses.

We analyze two types of value-added taxes, each at a 10 percent rate. Value-added taxes of the consumption type lead to substantial welfare gains under all four variants of the model. Income-type VATs lead to considerably smaller welfare gains in most cases. The results for the VAT models are fairly sensitive to the type of equal yield replacement tax, since a 10 percent VAT generates a great deal of revenue.

In sections 11.2 through 11.4 we present our alternative models of the foreign sector. In section 11.5 we discuss the linkage between foreign trade issues and tax policy design. The following section includes the results of simulations using various formulations of the external sector.

These include a brief review of the results from the standard version of the model, as well as sensitivity analyses with respect to the elasticity parameters that control the shape of the offer surface in our basic constant elasticity formulation.

11.2   A Model of Trade with Imperfectly Substitutable Imports

Our first alternative specification of the external sector separates imports into two broad categories, depending on whether they are perfect or imperfect substitutes in production for domestically produced intermediate goods.

In the basic version of the model we treat all imports as perfect substitutes in production for producer goods made in the United States. We then represent these imports as a negative component of final demand. Consequently, every additional unit of import of producer good i reduces the gross output requirement of industry i by one unit. Industries demanding intermediate goods from industry i are assumed to be indifferent as to whether those goods are produced at home or imported.

We now consider a model specification that allows some imports to be imperfect substitutes for domestic goods in production. Under this specification we introduce a single new aggregated import commodity, which enters the production structure as an imperfectly substitutable input. This specification invokes the Armington assumption, since it assumes that a qualitative difference exists between the imported input and any domestic inputs used in production (Armington 1969).

The foreign excess demand equations are now

$$(11.1) \qquad M_i = M_i^0 \left(\frac{P_{M_i}}{e} \right)^\mu, \qquad \begin{array}{l} 0 < \mu < \infty, \\ i = 1, \dots, n; \end{array}$$

$$(11.2) \qquad E_i = E_i^0 \left(\frac{P_{E_i}}{e} \right)^\nu, \qquad \begin{array}{l} -\infty < \nu < -1, \\ i = 1, \dots, n; \end{array}$$

and

$$(11.3) \qquad R = R^0 \left(\frac{P_R}{e} \right)^\mu, \qquad 0 < \mu < \infty;$$

where M_i is the supply of imports in the ith industry, E_i is that industry's export demand, and e is the exchange rate. Equation (11.3) is the supply function for the import commodity. The R in equation (11.3) can be taken to stand for resources. We treat R like the other factors of production, capital and labor. The demand for R is derived from production requirements. We should also note that M_i^0 in equation (11.1) and E_i^0 in equation (11.2) may represent either gross or net trade flows in the base case where all prices and the exchange rate are unity.

The trade balance condition is now

$$(11.4) \qquad P_R R + \sum_{i=1}^{n} P_{M_i} M_i = \sum_{i=1}^{n} P_{E_i} E_i.$$

Let

$$(11.5) \qquad \gamma_1 = (P_R)^{\mu+1} R^0 + \sum_{i=1}^{n} (P_{M_i})^{\mu+1} M_i^0,$$

and

$$(11.6) \qquad \gamma_2 = \sum_{i=1}^{n} (P_{E_i})^{\nu+1} E_i^0.$$

Then, substituting (11.1), (11.2), and (11.3) into (11.4), and using the notation of (11.5) and (11.6), we get

$$(11.7) \qquad e = \left(\frac{\gamma_2}{\gamma_1}\right)^{\frac{1}{\nu-\mu}},$$

and

$$(11.8) \qquad M_i = M_i^0 P_{M_i}^{\mu} \left(\frac{\gamma_2}{\gamma_1}\right)^{\frac{\mu}{\mu-\nu}},$$

$$(11.9) \qquad E_i = E_i^0 P_{E_i}^{\nu} \left(\frac{\gamma_2}{\gamma_1}\right)^{\frac{\nu}{\mu-\nu}},$$

$$(11.10) \qquad R_i = R^0 P_R^{\mu} \left(\frac{\gamma_2}{\gamma_1}\right)^{\frac{\mu}{\mu-\nu}}.$$

As in chapter 3, these are the reduced form or trade-balance-compensated import supply and export demand equations. They provide a constant elasticity set of excess demand functions to describe trade behavior.

With this formulation we also must modify the production structure to incorporate the imported resource. In the previous version of the model, the production function for each sector could be written as

$$(11.11) \qquad Q_j = \min\left[\frac{1}{a_{0j}} VA(K_j, L_j), \frac{x_{1j}}{a_{1j}}, \ldots, \frac{x_{nj}}{a_{nj}}\right],$$

where the a_{ij} ($i = 1, \ldots, n$) are the fixed intermediate input requirements per unit of output, x_{ij} are the intermediate inputs, $VA(\cdot, \cdot)$ is the CES value-added function for sector j with capital (K_j) and labor (L_j) as inputs, and a_{0j} is the requirement of value added per unit of output.

Under this new specification, the production function is

$$(11.12) \qquad Q_j = \min\left[\frac{1}{a_{0j}} J[VA(K_j, L_j), R], \frac{x_{1j}}{a_{1j}}, \ldots, \frac{x_{nj}}{a_{nj}}\right],$$

where J is a CES or Cobb-Douglas function for each sector, and a_{0j} now represents the requirements of the resource/value-added composite per unit of output.

The solution procedure takes advantage of the separability of the production structure, as in the basic version of the model. First, we calculate the cost-minimizing proportions of capital and labor that each industry should use in its value-added function. Using this information we can then find the cost-minimizing proportions of domestic-factor value added (VA) and imported resources (R) for each industry. Except for this, there are no further fundamental differences between our procedures under this version of the model and our procedures in the basic version.

This specification presents us with an additional data requirement. In chapter 4 we described our procedures for using the U.S. input-output tables. In order to install the version of the model with imperfectly substitutable imports, we went back to the input-output tables and identified a row of imports by industry. In table 11.1 we show the quantities of

Table 11.1   **Ordinary (Perfectly Substitutable) Imports and Armington (Imperfectly Substitutable) Imports in 1973 (in millions of dollars)**

Sector	Ordinary Imports	Armington Imports	Total
Agriculture, forestry, and fisheries	3467.3	1240.0	4707.3
Mining	898.5	323.0	1221.5
Crude petroleum and gas	5009.2	181.4	5190.6
Construction	0.0	0.0	0.0
Food and tobacco	756.9	4933.5	5690.4
Textiles, apparel, and leather	3885.0	1856.5	5741.5
Paper and printing	924.6	1245.4	2170.0
Petroleum refining	1189.7	1950.1	3139.8
Chemicals and rubber	984.3	2525.2	3509.5
Lumber, furniture, stone, clay, and glass	0.0	2760.9	2760.9
Metals and machinery	18803.6	6446.7	25250.3
Transportation equipment	1084.2	0.0	1084.2
Motor vehicles	6171.2	4067.7	10238.9
Transportation, communications, and utilities	7917.8	3666.5	11584.3
Trade	0.0	0.0	0.0
Finance and insurance	0.0	0.0	0.0
Real estate	0.0	0.0	0.0
Services	0.0	2309.6	2309.6
Government enterprises	0.0	0.0	0.0
TOTAL	51092.3	33506.5	84598.8

ordinary imports and imperfectly substitutable imports that are used in the 1973 base year. The division of the imports in each industry between ordinary imports and Armington imports seems reasonable. Industries such as food and tobacco, lumber, furniture, and services contain high proportions of Armington imports. (One thinks of Danish furniture and Norwegian sardines, which are qualitatively different from their American counterparts.) On the other hand, industries with more homogeneous outputs, such as crude petroleum and gas and transportation equipment, use ordinary imports for the most part.

We also need to specify a substitution elasticity between U.S. value added and R. For this we use estimates of the aggregate price elasticity of import demand for the United States. As our central case value we use 1.7 to represent the pure substitution effect between domestic value added and imported resources. However, we do not believe that this should be treated as an extremely precise estimate. Therefore, we will perform sensitivity analyses with respect to this parameter by using the values of 0.5, 1.0, and 3.0.

11.3   A Simple Model of International Capital Flows

In our model of international capital flows we add an additional consumer to the model. This consumer is "the foreigner" who is endowed with large quantities of those commodities that the United States imports, and with a large amount of capital services. In the benchmark year the foreigner's endowment of each import commodity is usually set at five times the benchmark level of imports of that commodity by the United States, while the foreigner's capital services endowment is five times the U.S. capital services endowment in the benchmark. In order to analyze the sensitivity of the model, we have varied the magnitudes of the foreigner's endowments of import goods and capital services. We assume that the foreigner "consumes" most of his endowments; that is, most of these import goods and capital services are used by the foreign economy rather than sold or rented to the United States. In the benchmark, in particular, we assume that the foreigner sells just the observed amount of imports (one-fifth of his endowment) to the U.S. economy and rents no capital services to the United States. Thus, the foreigner consumes his entire endowment of capital services. Loosely speaking, this treatment might mean that these capital services are foreign resources that provide output to the foreigner directly.

As U.S. prices change with a tax change, however, the foreigner alters his behavior. If the U.S. rental price of capital increases above the benchmark level, the foreigner will "rent" some of his endowment to be used in U.S. production (i.e., there will be a capital inflow from the perspective of the United States). On the other hand, if the U.S. rental price of capital were to fall below the benchmark level, the foreigner would "rent" U.S. capital for his foreign consumption (i.e., there will be a capital outflow from the U.S. perspective).

This behavior is specified as

$$(11.13) \qquad W_K - X_K = W_K \cdot P_K^{E_K},$$

where W_K is the capital service endowment of the foreigner, X_K is capital services rented to the United States by the foreigner (or rented from the United States if X_K is negative), and E_K is an elasticity parameter controlling capital flow responses in the model. P_K is the rental rate of capital in the United States. Since $P_K = 1$ in the benchmark, the benchmark value of X_K is zero.

The critical parameters in this formulation are the ratio of W_K to the U.S. capital service endowment (5 in our central case analysis) and E_K. E_K should be negative to give the capital service flow responses we require, although there does not seem to be a consensus as to what value to use. We highlight two values of E_K: -1.0 and -0.5. For sensitivity analysis we also use values of 0.0, -0.1, and -4.0 for E_K.

Equation (11.13) thus determines capital service flows in the model, once factor prices are known. A two-stage procedure is involved in determining foreign behavior. We first determine X_K from P_K. Once X_K is known, we can calculate the amount of income the foreigner has left over for expenditure on all other goods. For simplicity we specify a Cobb-Douglas function for the foreigner's expenditure on all other goods. We use benchmark data to determine the weights for this Cobb-Douglas function.

It might be interesting to evaluate the welfare of the foreigner, but we do not do so. As before, our welfare calculations only deal with the U.S. population, corrected for population growth. Even though this version of the model is more complicated than earlier versions, it is still basically true that our treatment of the foreign sector merely closes the model. In this connection it is worthwhile to note that we do *not* derive equation (11.13) from any explicit model of the utility-maximizing behavior of the foreigner. The literature now contains several completely specified multi-country general equilibrium models. In these models the behavior of consumers, producers, and governments in each of several countries is specified explicitly and symmetrically. (For a survey of these models, see Shoven and Whalley 1984).

Our work in this area is motivated in part by the recent debate about the world capital market between Arnold Harberger on one side and Martin Feldstein and Charles Horioka on the other. This debate is important because of its implications for policy evaluation using general equilibrium tax models. In a world with a perfect, frictionless international capital market, the domestic choice between an income and consumption tax would have little effect on the aggregate domestic employment of capital. Despite the fact that an income tax discourages saving by U.S. consumers, and thus tends to discourage capital formation, the rest of the world would provide U.S. industry with capital until its rate of return were equal to the world level. However, an origin-based tax such as the U.S. corporation income tax would still be distortionary, affecting both the amount of capital in the economy and its allocation across industrial sectors. In his 1978 and 1980 papers, Harberger finds that there "seems to be no strong and systematic tendency for rates of return to be high in countries with a low capital stock per worker." He takes this as evidence for the existence of a reasonably well-functioning world capital market. Feldstein and Horioka (1980) observe a high correlation between the saving of countries and their levels of investment. This leads them to argue that there are severe restrictions on the operation of the world capital market. Harberger (1978) challenges these results by showing that this correlation is much lower for less-developed countries than for the OECD countries studied by Feldstein and Horioka. However, Harberger does back away from the position that the world capital market functions with perfect freedom and great speed. In a passage quoted by Feldstein (1982), Harberger says:

> My own intuition does not want to accept the notion that increments of investment activity are in all or nearly all countries effectively 100 percent "financed" by funds flowing in from abroad, and that increments in saving simply spill out into the world capital markets. I find the analogy to a hydraulic system with perhaps a viscous fluid, in which the pipes are partially clogged, and in which some vessels are separated by semipermeable membranes, to be more consonant with my image of the world than the alternative analogy to a hydraulic system where the water flows freely through the system and, essentially instantaneously, finds the same level everywhere. (1980, p. 336)

Thus, in their most recent exchange, Feldstein and Harberger seemed to be converging to the view that, while there is some pressure towards equalizing the rates of return to capital across world markets, this equilibration is incomplete, and even the partial movements observed do not occur instantaneously. The main focus of the debate seems now to be on their differing views about the speed of the adjustment. Feldstein argues that, "the tendency toward equalization must be measured in decades rather than months or even years" (1982, p. 4). Harberger seems to argue that the long run is shorter than this.

We can capture the key aspects of this debate by altering E_K, the elasticity parameter for the demand for capital services by foreigners. We find, unfortunately, that our model results are fairly sensitive to the value of this parameter. Finally, let us note that we always use the basic constant elasticity formulation of foreign trade along with the new models of capital markets described here and in the next section.

11.4 A Model with Capital Purchases

In the model of section 11.3 the foreigner is endowed with a large amount of capital service which he "rents" to the United States if the U.S. offers a higher rental price. If the rental price in the United States falls, the foreigner rents capital from the United States. While this is a step toward including world capital markets in our model, it fails to capture important aspects of foreign investment.

Under this specification a capital inflow involves a financial outflow (the United States must make the rental payments). However, it may be that the more likely response to high rates of return in the United States would be direct foreign investment in the U.S. In this case the foreigner would *purchase* U.S. capital goods, rather than rent them, providing the United States with an immediate financial inflow. Rather than receive immediate financial compensation, the foreigner accumulates a claim on the future earnings of the capital acquired by these purchases.

This behavior can be incorporated in our model by using a somewhat different representation of the foreigner. The initial U.S. capital endowment of the foreigner is taken to be zero. The foreigner, however, can acquire United States capital by purchasing the saving good (the sixteenth consumer good, which is a fixed proportion portfolio of real investment goods). He will do this if the expected rate of return on U.S. investments rises above the benchmark level. The foreigner is interested in the rate-of-return net of the corporation income tax, the corporation franchise tax, and property taxes. If the U.S. rate of return should fall, the foreigner may sell foreign capital to domestic savers. Once again, we do not model the production structure of the rest of the world. Instead, the foreigner simply "consumes" foreign capital, as in section 11.3.

This formulation is reasonably complex in terms of modeling. There are now two kinds of capital goods—foreign and domestic. The two types of capital offer separate (although conceivably identical) rates of return. Initially, domestic consumers own only domestic capital and the foreigner owns only foreign capital. The demand functions are structured such that the foreigners will save in the United States only if the U.S. rate of return rises above the foreign rate, whereas the U.S. consumers will purchase foreign capital service endowments only if the U.S. rate of return falls below the foreign rate. While the U.S. rate of return is endogenous in the model, the foreign rate is usually set at the benchmark rate, although it can be influenced by certain tax policies of the United States.[1]

---

1. For example, in this model the foreign rate of return is affected by a U.S. policy that changes the percentage of U.S. consumers' saving that can be deducted from taxable income. Such a policy alters the after-tax price of saving to U.S. consumers, whether the saving is made at home or abroad. Consequently, the policy affects the foreign rate of return to U.S. consumers of saving abroad.

Saving behavior in the United States stems from the same demand functions as in our standard model, except that it involves not just a domestic saving good but a composite saving good aggregated over domestic and foreign saving goods. For each household,

$$(11.14) \qquad S = \theta S^D + (1 - \theta)S^F,$$

where S is total saving, and S^D and S^F are domestic and foreign saving goods acquired. θ is a distribution parameter that depends on the relation between domestic and foreign rates of return (r^F and r^{US}) according to:

$$(11.15) \qquad \theta = 1, \qquad\qquad \text{if } r^{US} \ge r^F;$$

$$\theta = e^{-Z_1(r^F - r^{US})}, \qquad \text{if } r^{US} < r^F.$$

Here, r^F and r^{US} are rates of return to U.S. consumers. Because of differences in marginal tax rates, r^F and r^{US} each will differ across the twelve consumer groups. We account for these differences in the model, although for convenience we speak of a single r^F and r^{US} in this discussion.

In the benchmark, $r^F = r^{US}$ and $\theta = 1$ (U.S. households buy no foreign capital goods). In the solution of the model, θ for each household is used to form a composite price for saving goods, which enters household budget constraints. Household utility functions only have an interpretation over composite goods, since we do not investigate the real characteristics of assets (such as risk) that would account for a diversified portfolio by savers. Once again, the literature only provides us with a very rough guide as to what a reasonable value of Z_1 might be. After considerable experimentation with different values for this parameter, we have decided to highlight the results from simulations with $Z_1 = 250$ and $Z_1 = 50$. We also provide further sensitivity analyses for values of Z_1 outside of this range.

The foreigner's saving in the United States, S_{US}^F, is given by

$$(11.16) \qquad S_{US}^F = 0, \qquad\qquad \text{if } r_F^{US} \le r_F^F;$$

$$S_{US}^F = Z_2(r_F^{US} - r_F^F)^{Z_3}, \qquad \text{if } r_F^{US} > r_F^F.$$

Here, r_F^{US} and r_F^F are U.S. and foreign rates of return expected by the foreigner. Because U.S. consumers are not treated identically in the tax system, r^{US} generally differs from r_F^{US}, and r^F from r_F^F.

A two-stage procedure similar to that in section 11.3 applies here. First, we determine the foreigner's investment behavior. Then, the foreigner's expenditures on other goods are allocated according to a Cobb-Douglas utility function. In this case our dynamic sequencing of equilibria takes account of previous investment abroad in determining the capital service endowments in each country in each period. In our central case analysis we set Z_2 equal to 50,000 and Z_3 equal to 0.5. We perform sensitivity analyses on the values of Z_2 and Z_3 when we simulate corporate tax integration. The parameters Z_2 and Z_3 are irrelevant to the study of the consumption tax, since the domestic price of capital drops in that case and the foreigner does not save in the United States. Similarly, Z_1 is irrelevant to the case of corporate tax integration, because the domestic rate of return increases in that case and domestic consumers do all of their saving at home.

11.5   Taxes and Foreign Trade

In this section we explore some of the issues linking international trade to the design of taxes and explore how they can be analyzed using the different external sector formulations in the U.S. general equilibrium model. First, we explore the foreign trade linkage to the value-added tax. Next, we consider the difference between broadly based taxes that use the *origin basis* and those that use the *destination basis*. Finally, we discuss some issues connected with factor mobility and tax structure.

11.5.1   The Value-Added Tax and Foreign Trade

Value-added taxes (VATs) have been used in Europe for almost three decades, but have never been used in the United States. Nevertheless, there is a great deal of interest in adopting a VAT in the United States. Much of this interest was sparked by bills introduced by Representative Al Ullman (D-Ore.), the former chairman of the House Ways and Means Committee.

The development of the tax in Europe follows from the difficulties in France, Germany, and other countries with the turnover taxes that existed before the war and in the period immediately following. Under a tunover tax each firm pays a tax on the total value of sales, with no credit given for the taxes already paid on intermediate inputs. Turnover taxes lead to "cascading," with the taxes compounding when the production process involves several stages or market exchanges. The turnover tax provided an incentive for firms to integrate vertically in order to avoid taxes. The turnover taxes were administered on a destination basis, thus it became very difficult to agree on the appropriate way to rebate taxes on export items. European nations were forced to negotiate annually in order to agree on mean tax rates by product. These negotiations were a rough attempt to take account of international differences in the degree of vertical integration.

In the early 1950s the French began to seek ways to avoid these problems of the turnover tax. They were attracted to the value-added tax for administrative reasons.[2] A value-added tax can be administered in a

---

2. *Value added* is simply the summation of returns to labor and capital by industry. We can calculate it as the total value of sales by industry minus all material inputs.

number of different ways. The tax can be applied directly to value added (as a composite payroll and capital income tax) or indirectly as a tax on the total value of sales less the cost of material inputs. Most European countries now administer the tax by the so-called credit method, under which a company is taxable on the total value of sales but receives a credit for all taxes paid on intermediate inputs purchased in earlier stages of the production process. During the initial debate on the VAT in France, it was pointed out that, under a retail sales tax or a turnover tax, tax administrators typically collect the largest fraction of the tax from a large number of relatively small retail outlets. This contrasts with the value-added tax. Since the VAT is collected as the value of the product accumulates through the production process, a significant portion of the tax would be collected from a relatively small number of large primary producers. Thus, the VAT was represented as being administratively more cost efficient than other taxes, since tax administrators found it easier to collect a large amount of tax from a small number of producers.

This type of argument was extended as the European Economic Community (EEC) moved into the field of tax design. In the initial stage of economic harmonization, the nations of the EEC eliminated all tariffs between member countries and adopted a common external tariff. It was then argued that further progress toward economic union would require the member nations to harmonize their tax systems. By the middle 1960s the nations of the EEC became convinced that they should adopt a common system of indirect taxation. The system eventually adopted involved a value-added tax for each member nation.

As administered in the EEC, the VAT is a tax of the consumption type, under which the tax incorporates complete deductibility of products purchased for business use, including capital goods. In its broadly based variant, where all value added is taxed at the same rate, this tax is to be thought of as equivalent to a retail sales tax on consumption.

An alternative form of a value-added tax is what Carl Shoup (1969) calls a VAT of the income type. Under this arrangement the firm can only take deductions for depreciation. The base of this tax is equivalent to that of a flat personal income tax without any exemptions. However, the tax is collected from firms rather than from individuals. Finally, Shoup suggests a VAT of the product type, where there is no deduction for depreciation. The base of this type of VAT is the same as GNP.

11.5.2   The Origin and Destination Basis Issue and International Trade

Another feature of the VAT in Europe is that it is levied on a *destination basis*, under which exports leave the country tax free, while imports are taxed when they enter. This contrasts with the *origin basis*, under which the tax is applied at the site of manufacture. The choice between the origin basis and the destination basis for indirect taxes has attracted a good deal of attention over the last fifteen to twenty years. This issue is a clear example of the link between tax design and foreign trade concerns. Most of the major trading partners of the United States have broadly based indirect taxes that operate on the destination basis. We have already mentioned the VAT in the European Economic Community. In addition, Japan has a commodity tax and Canada has a federally operated manufacturers' sales tax.

A common argument repeated over the years is that the United States is placed at a disadvantage by this tax treatment, since the taxes on American firms are not rebated on export items, whereas import items enter the United States tax free. Such a disadvantage might exist in the very short run. However, we believe that this argument does not stand up to close scrutiny in the context of long-run equilibrium.

One of the prominent themes within the academic literature is that with broadly based taxes, the destination basis and the origin basis do not differ in their effects in long-run equilibrium (provided that no discrimination arises in the tax rates) (see Johnson and Krauss 1970). With flexible exchange rates, a movement between the two bases can be offset by an exchange rate change that leaves the real characteristics (trade flows) unchanged. With fixed exchange rates, changes in domestic price levels (and implied changes in domestic money stocks) preserve the real equilibrium. Thus, in long-run equilibrium, a movement from one tax basis to another is equivalent to a purely monetary phenomenon with no implications for real economic behavior.

This can be shown as follows.[3] As a simplification we consider two countries, each producing a single good, X_1 in 1, X_2 in 2. P_1 and P_2 represent the cost-covering competitive producer prices of products in each country, in domestic currencies. Let e be the exchange rate between currency 1 and 2. Demands for products in each country depend on relative prices in domestic currencies: X_1^2 are exports by 1 to 2; X_2^1 are exports by 2 to 1. For each country, balance in international payments requires that the domestic currency value of outflows equal the domestic currency value of inflows. We consider a single consumer in each country and assume that all tax revenues are redistributed in lump-sum form. We can consider three regimes: (1) no tax, (2) a destination-based tax in country 1, and (3) an origin-based tax in country 1. If we examine the balance-of-payments conditions (from the viewpoint of either country) and relative commodity prices (in domestic currencies) under each of these regimes, we will see that the relative commodity prices that determine consumer behavior remain unchanged and the same real trade flows will satisfy the balance-of-payments conditions in all three cases. The truth of this proposition is independent of the exchange rate regime. The

3. The analytics that follow draw upon the arguments presented in Whalley 1979.

Table 11.2   **Balance-of-Payments Conditions and Relative Prices under Various Tax Regimes**

Tax Regime	Balance-of-Payments Condition for Country 1	Relative Prices Denominated in Domestic Currenty 1
1. No tax	$P_1^{NT} X_1^2 = e^{NT} P^{NT} X_2^1$	$P_1^{NT}/e^{NT} P_2^{NT}$
2. Destination tax (rate t_1)	$P_1^D X_1^2 = e^D P_2^D X_2^1$	$P_1^D(1 + t_1)/e^D P_2^D(1 + t_1)$
3. Origin tax (rate t_1)	$P_1^O(1 + t_1)X_1^2 = e^O P_2^O X_2^1$	$P_1^O(1 + t_1)/e^O P_2^O$

information upon which these conclusions are based is summarized in table 11.2. The superscripts NT, D, and O refer to the no-tax, destination-tax, and origin-tax regimes. Relative prices are unchanged in all regimes, and the same X_1^2, X_2^1 satisfy the balance-of-payments conditions under all regimes if,

$$(11.17) \quad \text{with flexible exchange rates:} \quad \begin{matrix} e^D = e^{NT}, \ P_1^D = P_1^{NT}, \ P_2^D = P_2^{NT}, \\ e^O = (1 + t_1)e^{NT}, \ P_1^O = P_1^{NT}, \ P_2^O = P_2^{NT}; \end{matrix}$$

$$(11.18) \quad \text{or with fixed exchange rates:} \quad \begin{matrix} e^D = e^{NT}, \ P_1^D = P_1^{NT}, \ P_2^D = P_2^{NT}, \\ e^O = e^{NT}, \ P_1^O = P_1^{NT}/(1 + t_1), \ P_2^O = P_2^{NT}. \end{matrix}$$

Thus, the introduction of a broadly based tax or a change in basis is equivalent to a purely monetary change. It does not affect real trade flows and thus does not restrict trade.

A similar argument is sometimes made regarding international tax unions. The argument is that it is necessary for the members of such a union (such as the members of the EEC) to have similar tax rates in order for the tax distortions between them to be removed. However, a careful analysis will show once again that the no-tax equilibrium will be preserved, even when two countries have different tax rates. This is true regardless of whether the origin base or the destination base is used. The same conclusion also holds if one country uses the origin basis and the other uses the destination basis.

We model origin-based taxes as factor taxes and destination-based taxes as sales taxes, because this is the easiest way to capture the difference between an origin-based and a destination-based tax. A factor tax is origin based because it applies to exports but not to imports. A sales tax is destination based because it applies to imports but not to exports. For broadly based taxes the neutrality of movements between the two tax bases applies, since we use a classical general equilibrium approach.

11.5.3   Taxes and International Capital Mobility

Another area of concern is the tax treatment of foreign investment inflows and outflows. The tax laws governing foreign investment are very complex. Typically, profits will originate in one country (the "host" country), and a portion of these profits will be paid through a parent company in another country (the "destination" country) to the stockholders. The profits originating in the host country are usually subject to four separate layers of tax. First, the host country levies a corporate tax. Next, the host country levies a withholding tax on dividends and interest paid. This tax is designed to substitute for personal income tax in the host country. The next tax is the corporate tax in the destination country, followed by the personal income tax in the destination country.

These four layers of tax can be a very heavy burden. As a result, most nations grant some sort of tax relief to the income from foreign investment. Such tax relief can be granted unilaterally or can result from negotiated tax treaties. The United States unilaterally allows corporations a credit for taxes paid abroad. The United States also has a number of treaties that deal symmetrically with profits flowing into or out of the United States. Under these treaties the withholding tax rate on profits paid in either direction is the same.

Now that we have described the existing arrangements for the tax treatment of foreign investments, let us discuss the economic incentives that influence such arrangements. Some of these incentives are described by Koichi Hamada (1966). Figure 11.1 is based on the diagram in Hamada's paper. In this static, two-country model, capital in country 1 is measured from left to right, and capital in country 2 is measured from right to left. Country 1 has a fixed capital endowment of $\bar{K}_1$, and country 2 has a fixed endowment of $\bar{K}_2$. In each country the marginal value product of capital schedule is downward sloping. These schedules are shown as MVP_{K_1} and MVP_{K_2}. The capital endowments will be used most efficiently if the value of the marginal product is equal in both countries. In general,

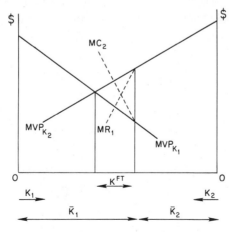

Fig. 11.1   International capital flows in the Hamada model.

this condition will not be met unless there is an international flow of capital. In figure 11.1, this flow is of K^{FT} from country 1 to country 2, in the free-trade situation where there are no taxes or other impediments to the movement of capital.

Hamada's point is that each country has an incentive to use tax policy to interfere with this capital flow. First, let us look at the situation from the point of view of country 1—the capital-exporting country. The marginal cost to country 1 of exporting capital abroad is the foregone marginal value product of capital in 1, given by the MVP_{K_1} curve. However, the marginal revenue obtained by exporting capital is not equal to the marginal value product of capital schedule in country 2. This marginal value schedule determines the average return received by capital sent abroad. Therefore, as more units of capital are exported by 1 to 2, the price received on *all* units sent abroad is bid down. The marginal value product schedule of country 2 is the average revenue schedule to country 1; thus from the point of view of country 1 the marginal revenue schedule MR_1 is more steeply sloped than the marginal value product of capital schedule in country 2.

Thus, if country 1 can restrict the capital flow and, through a tax, extract the differential between the marginal value product in country 1 and country 2, country 1 would be better off than in the free-trade situation. It would then receive a larger share of a smaller total output but would still be better off.

Figure 11.2 conveys much the same information as figure 11.1, except that it uses a separate diagram for each nation. The rate of return at which the marginal products are equalized in the no-tax case is r_0. The total welfare of country 1 is $ABCD + EFG\bar{K}_2$, where $C\bar{K}_1 = \bar{K}_2G$ is the flow of capital. If country 1 then imposes a tax on income received from abroad, the capital flow will be reduced to, say, $H\bar{K}_1 = \bar{K}_2M$. The net-of-tax rate of return in the two countries will be equalized at r_{net}. However, the gross return to capital in country 2 will be greater by the amount of tax. After

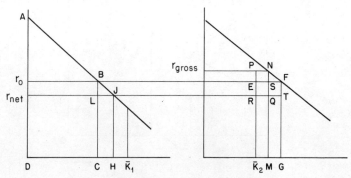

Fig. 11.2   The international allocation of capital.

the imposition of the tax, country 1's total welfare will be $AJHD + PNM\bar{K}_2$. Tax revenue is $PNQR$. Country 1 has given up $SFGM$, but it gains $PNSE + BJHC$. We know that $CH = MG$, because country 1's capital exports must equal country 2's capital imports, both before and after the policy change. Therefore, $LJHC = QTGM$, so country 1's gains outweigh its losses.

If we return to figure 11.1, we can see that similar arguments apply to country 2—the capital-importing country. For the capital-importing country, the marginal value product schedule in country 2 is the relevant marginal revenue schedule. However, the marginal value product of capital schedule in country 1 represents the average cost schedule to country 1, since the price paid for capital is determined by the market price for the last unit of internationally mobile capital. Thus, country 2 faces a marginal cost schedule (MC_2 in figure 11.1), and country 2 also has an incentive to interfere in the capital flow through tax policy. From the point of view of country 2, this tax policy would attempt to extract the differential between the two marginal value product schedules. If country 2 were able to impose a tax with no retaliation from country 1, then the citizens of country 2 would make themselves better off than they were in the free-trade situation.

The typical outcome in this situation is that each country would retaliate to the other's tax, and a postretaliation equilibrium situation would result. Double taxation treaties are appealing because the participants in such treaties act to return the world economy closer to the free-trade situation. It is not always the case, however, that countries are worse off in a postretaliation equilibrium than they would be in the presence of free trade. In the case that Hamada considers, where the marginal schedules are linear, it is always true that both countries are worse off. However, with nonlinear schedules, it may be possible for a country to be better off in the postretaliation equilibrium. Consequently, certain countries may not consider it advantageous to negotiate double taxation treaties with the United States.

Hamada's piece sheds light on the circumstances under which one can make a case for double taxation treaties on capital income received from abroad. In our model we are unable to analyze the issue of retaliation. However, our capital good flow and capital service flow models do capture the incentive for one country to intervene, while abstracting from the issue of retaliation.

11.6 Policy Analyses under Alternative Formulations of the External Sector

In this section we simulate the effects of several policy proposals, using the various formulations of the external sector presented in sections 11.2,

11.3, and 11.4. We consider corporate tax integration (see chapter 8), the consumption tax (see chapter 9), and various forms of the value-added tax.

These analyses involve the same numerical specification we have used throughout. We use the same values for all parameters that do not deal with the external sector. The various external sector formulations are incorporated as separate model extensions.

For the sake of brevity, we refer to the four formulations as follows:

1. *Constant Elasticity, No Armington.* Foreigner's behavior involves constant elasticity excess demand functions; no Armington heterogeneity enters; no capital service or capital good flows are considered.

2. *Constant Elasticity with Armington.* As in (1), except that we also consider Armington product heterogeneity for imported intermediate inputs, as described in section 11.2.

3. *Capital Services Flows.* Flows of capital services take place between the United States and the rest of the world as described in section 11.3.

4. *Capital Goods Flows.* Flows of capital goods take place between the United States and the rest of the world as described in section 11.4.

These formulations are listed in table 11.3, along with the values we have specified for the more critical parameters. In the case of the first formulation, we use values for μ of 0.465 and ν of -10. These were discussed in section 6.4. They jointly imply an export price elasticity of demand of -1.4. For sensitivity analyses in this case, we consider μ and ν set first at 10 and -10 and then at 1 and -1. For the $(10, -10)$ case, the export price elasticity is -5.5. In the two-good case, as ν and μ both become large (in absolute value), the elasticity of the offer curve approaches unity; this specification for the foreigner's behavior would imply that the United States is a small, open, price-taking economy. For the case of $(1, -1)$, the export price elasticity is -1, and in the two-good case the elasticity of the offer curve is ∞. We also consider cases where net trade flows rather than gross flows enter the benchmark calculation.

For the second formulation, the critical parameters are μ, ν, and σ_{VA}^R. We take the same μ and ν values as for the central case in our first formulation. σ_{VA}^R is set at 1.7. In our sensitivity runs, σ_{VA}^R is set at 0.5, 1.0, and 3.0.

For the capital service flow and capital good flow formulations, the critical parameters are E_K, Z_1, Z_2, and Z_3, which control substitution in the two cases. The ratio of the endowment of the foreigner to that of the United States is also an important parameter. Because of our lack of knowledge about the responsiveness of international capital flows to differentials in the rate of return, we provide two sets of central case simulations for each of our formulations with international capital mobility. In the formulation with capital service flows, we set E_K at -0.5 and -1.0 (and we also provide some extra sensitivity analyses, with E_K at 0.0,

Table 11.3   **Characteristics of Alternative External Sector Specifications**

	Constant Elasticity, No Armington	Constant Elasticity with Armington	Capital Service Flows	Capital Good Flows
Described in section	3.6	11.2	11.3	11.4
Brief description	Constant elasticity excess demands; no product heterogeneity; no capital flows; gross trade flows	Constant elasticity excess demands; product heterogeneity for intermediate imports; no capital flows; gross trade flows	Capital service flows, no product heterogeneity; Cogg-Douglas commodity demands; gross trade flows	Capital good flows, no product heterogeneity; Cobb-Douglas commodity demands; gross trade flows
Critical parameters	μ, ν	$\mu, \nu, \sigma_{VA}^{R}$	E_K	Z_1, Z_2, Z_3
Values in central case	$\mu = .465$ $\nu = -10$ (jointly imply U.S. faces export price elasticity of -1.4)	$\mu = .465$ $\nu = -10$ $\sigma_{VA}^{R} = 1.7$	$E_K = -1.0$ or -0.5 Capital service endowment of foreigner = $5 \times$ U.S. endowment	$Z_1 = 250$ or $Z_1 = 50$ $Z_2 = 50,000$ $Z_3 = 0.5$ Capital service endowment of foreigner = $5 \times$ U.S. endowment
Sensitivity cases	$\mu = 10$ $\nu = -10$ $\mu = 1$ $\nu = -1$ gross and net trade flows	$\sigma_{VA}^{R} = 3.0$ $\sigma_{VA}^{R} = 1.0$ $\sigma_{VA}^{R} = 0.5$	Factor of 5 reset at 2, 10 $E_K = 0.0, -0.1, -4.0$ gross-of-tax return to capital rather than net used	Factor of 5 reset at 2, 10 $Z_1 = 1000, 100, 10$ $Z_2 = 100,000$ $Z_3^2 = 0.25, 1.0$

-0.1, and -4.0). Our central case ratio is 5, and in our sensitivity analyses we set the ratio at 2 and 10.

A final and important sensitivity analysis in this case involves the return to capital. In the central case, when foreigners rent to the United States, they receive P_K, the real net-of-tax rental price of capital. P_K is paid to the United States when Americans rent to foreigners. Because of the tax system in the United States, a differential exists between the marginal product of capital (the gross-of-tax price) and the net-of-tax return to capital. Thus, the United States gains if it rents capital services from abroad, since it collects the marginal product of capital but pays the net-of-tax return to capital. Conversely, if the United States rents capital to the foreigner, the United States suffers a loss. To correct for this, we calculate a tax rate that applies to international capital transactions, and we use this new rate in one of our sensitivity cases.

For the capital good flow formulation, we provide sensitivity analyses around two central case values of Z_1, namely, 250 and 50. Our central case values for Z_2 and Z_3 are 50,000 and 0.5, respectively. For sensitivity cases we use Z_1 of 1000, 100, and 10, Z_2 of 100,000 and Z_3 of 0.25 and 1.0. We also vary the foreigner's capital service endowment, so that it equals 2 times and 10 times the endowment of the United States.

11.6.1 Consumption Tax

In table 11.4 we show model results for a single tax-policy—an 80 percent savings deduction—under the different external sector formulations. This policy, described in detail in chapter 9, represents a move from the current income tax system toward a consumption tax system. We adjust marginal income tax rates either additively or multiplicatively so that the total revenue raised by the government is not altered in any period by the policy change. All results reported in this chapter come from sequences of eleven equilibria spaced five years apart.

In our central case, with no Armington good and no capital flows, the gains from the consumption tax are over \$500 billion in present value, or a little over 1 percent of the total discounted welfare stream. The type of replacement tax for equal yield does not greatly affect the results. The Armington formulation does not change things much. The welfare gains are less by about 15 percent under either additive or multiplicative scaling. One reason for the similarity among the welfare gain results is shown in table 11.5. The Armington good does very little to affect the process of capital accumulation, so that the decrease in the relative price of capital is nearly identical in the Armington and non-Armington formulations. The results of simulations using these two formulations are similar in many other ways as well. In each case the decrease in the price of capital leads to a shift toward the more capital-intensive industries. By the final period in a consumption tax simulation under the standard,

Table 11.4   Further Analysis of Adoption of a Consumption Tax

	Welfare Effect	
	Additive Replacement	Multiplicative Replacement
1. Central case—constant elasticity, no Armington	556.1 (1.115)	536.9 (1.077)
2. Central case—constant elasticity with Armington	480.7 (0.964)	457.7 (0.918)
3. Central cases—capital service flow		
A. $E_K = -1.0$	−494.0 (−0.991)	−606.6 (−1.217)
B. $E_K = -0.5$	−288.7 (−0.579)	−380.5 (−0.763)
4. Central cases—capital good flow		
A. $Z_1 = 250$	−36.3 (−0.073)	−52.1 (−0.104)
B. $Z_1 = 50$	233.9 (0.469)	222.5 (0.446)

Note: Dynamic welfare effects in present value of compensating variations over time; all figures in billions of 1973 dollars. The numbers in parentheses represent the gain (or loss) as a percentage of the present discounted value of consumption plus leisure in the base sequence ($49 trillion).

no-Armington version, the prices of the various industrial outputs range from 0.889 for the capital-intensive real estate sector to 0.977 for the labor-intensive transportation equipment sector. With the Armington formulation, the comparable prices are 0.890 and 0.977, respectively. A notable exception under either formulation is the construction industry. This is one of the more labor-intensive sectors, but its output increases by more than 11 percent under either formulation, because it is an important component of investment. The consumption tax causes an increase in investment demand that is nearly the same under either version. In the first period, the increase is about 32.8 percent over the base case. By the eleventh and final period, investment is still 27.9 percent greater than in the base case.

Much greater changes are evident when we compare our standard formulation with either of the models with capital flows. However, we should emphasize that these results are fairly sensitive to the specification of the parameters controlling the capital flows. To highlight this, we present two sets of results in tables 11.4 and 11.5, and we will present further sensitivity analyses in the next subsection. In either the capital service flow or capital good flow formulations, domestic welfare declines as the capital flows become more elastic (i.e., as we specify E_K or Z_1 to be greater in absolute value). In no case are the results very sensitive to the type of replacement tax for equal revenue yield, because the consump-

Table 11.5   Changes in the Relative Price of Capital Services as a Result of
                  Adoption of a Consumption Tax (additive replacement for equal
                  yield)

			Model Variant			
	Constant elasticity, no	Constant elasticity with	Capital service flow		Capital good flow	
Period	Armington	Armington	$E_K = -1.0$	$E_K = -0.5$	$Z_1 = 250$	$Z_1 = 50$
1	.988	.988	.998	997	.992	.989
2	.952	.952	.991	.985	.974	.958
3	.923	.924	.985	.974	.974	.941
4	.902	.902	.979	.966	.973	.931
5	.884	.885	.974	.958	.973	.924
6	.870	.871	.970	.951	.973	.920
7	.859	.860	.967	.946	.973	.917
8	.850	.851	.963	.941	.972	.915
9	.842	.843	.960	.936	.972	.913
10	.836	.837	.958	.932	.972	.912
11	.831	.832	.956	.929	.972	.911

tion tax does not cause as great a revenue loss as, say, corporate tax integration.

For the values of E_K that we highlight here (-1.0 and -0.5), the consumption tax causes the United States to incur substantial service outflows. As a result of this foreign demand for U.S. capital services, the relative price of capital drops much less under this variant of the model than it did in the standard version. Nevertheless, the price of capital does drop somewhat, and as it drops the rate of capital outflow increases. In the first period of a simulation with $E_K = -1.0$, using additive replacement, the capital service outflow is under \$1 billion. By the eleventh period, the outflow has swollen to over \$50 billion, which is nearly 9 percent of that year's saving. This capital service outflow causes a substantial welfare loss for these values of E_K. (In the next subsection we will see that a gain can still occur if E_K is close enough to zero.) The main reason for this loss is that the United States incurs substantial capital service outflows as a result of the policy change, so that the United States foregoes the gross-of-tax return to capital (capital's marginal product), but only receives the net-of-tax return.

An interesting policy prescription from this case is that the United States might gain by having additional taxes on capital income received from abroad by revoking the foreign tax credit. If the first of these policies were adopted, the additional tax rates should equal U.S. capital tax rates. We should note, however, that foreign nations may well retaliate against such a policy change on the part of the United States. The possibility of retaliation reduces the attractiveness of increasing the taxation of capital income received from abroad. We have made no attempt to model the complex issue of retaliation. Of course, it is also true that the capital service flows about which we are concerned are driven by the move toward a consumption tax. The case for a compensatory tax on capital income received from abroad is weak if the U.S. does not undertake a policy of increased stimulus to saving.

Under the first three versions, the domestic capital stock increases very substantially. By the final period of the consumption tax simulations, the domestic capital endowment exceeds the base-case endowment by 22.9 percent in the standard model and the Armington model, and 24.7 percent in the capital service flow model (when $E_K = -1.0$). The domestic economy gains in the first two cases because all of that capital is used at home. In the capital service flow version, a great deal of it is used abroad. The results are somewhat different for the capital good flow version of the model. In this case, the domestic capital stock barely grows at all. By the final period of the sequence, the domestic capital endowment is only 2.7 percent greater than in the base case. The reason for this is that domestic consumers hold a great deal of foreign capital. In the case of $Z_1 = 250$, domestic consumers devote 8 percent of their saving in the first period to saving abroad. By the eleventh period, these purchases of foreign capital have grown to nearly 25 percent of saving, and the rental payments on the accumulated foreign capital amount to 2.6 percent of national income.

These capital flows are very substantial and may strike some readers as being rather high. This is why we have also chosen to highlight the results from simulations with $Z_1 = 50$. In this case, in the first period, domestic consumers only use a bit more than 2 percent of their saving to purchase foreign capital. By the eleventh period, they still only spend about 16 percent of their saving for foreign capital, despite the fact that the differential between foreign and domestic rates of return is much greater than it was in the simulation with $Z_1 = 250$. If the lower value of Z_1 is considered to be more realistic, then the consumption tax is a gaining proposition under the capital good flow formulation.

11.6.2 Sensitivity Analysis for Consumption Tax Results

In table 11.6 we report our sensitivity analyses for our two constant elasticity formulations. Given that the central case versions are rather similar, it may not be surprising that similar results emerge from the sensitivity cases. Neither the choice of the $\mu - \nu$ combination, nor the specification of gross or net trade flows makes very much difference to the no-Armington case. In the model with Armington goods, the elasticity of substitution between value added and the Armington good does not

Table 11.6   Sensitivity Analysis of Consumption Tax for Constant Elasticity
              Formulations

	Welfare Effect	
	Additive Replacement	Multiplicative Replacement
1. Central case—constant elasticity,	556.1	536.9
no Armington, with $\mu = .465$, $v = -10$	(1.115)	(1.077)
2. Constant elasticity, no Armington, with	541.8	527.6
$\mu = 10$, $v = -10$	(1.087)	(1.058)
3. Constant elasticity, no Armington, with	585.2	567.9
$\mu = 1$, $v = -1$	(1.174)	(1.139)
4. Constant elasticity, no Armington, with net	575.5	557.7
rather than gross trade flow analysis,	(1.154)	(1.118)
$\mu = .465$, $v = -10$		
5. Central case—constant elasticity with	480.7	457.7
Armington, $\mu = .465$, $v = -10$,	(0.964)	(0.918)
$\sigma_{VA}^{R} = 1.7$		
6. Constant elasticity, with	446.9	423.1
Armington, with $\mu = .465$, $v = -10$,	(0.896)	(0.848)
$\sigma_{VA}^{R} = 0.5$		
7. Constant elasticity, with	468.3	445.1
Armington, with $\mu = .465$, $v = -10$,	(0.939)	(0.893)
$\sigma_{VA}^{R} = 1.0$		
8. Constant elasticity, with	488.7	466.2
Armington, with $\mu = .465$, $v = -10$,	(0.980)	(0.935)
$\sigma_{VA}^{R} = 3.0$		

Note: Dynamic welfare effects in present value of compensating variations over time; all
figures in billions of 1973 dollars. The numbers in parentheses represent the gain (or loss) as
a percentage of the present discounted value of consumption plus leisure in the base
sequence ($49 trillion).

make much difference. One reason for this is that the imported resource
does not represent a very large proportion of total factor inputs.[4]

In tables 11.7 and 11.8, we report our sensitivity analysis of the consumption tax results for our capital service and capital goods flow formulations. For the capital service flow formulation, we change E_K from
-1.0 to 0.0, -0.1, and -4.0. We also vary the endowment ratios
between 2 and 10. Clearly, our results are very sensitive to the value of E_K
and somewhat sensitive to the size of the endowment ratio. If we believe
that the capital service flow version is the correct model to use, then our
ultimate assessment of the value of adopting a consumption tax will

---

4. When the price of capital decreases, as it does in all of these simulations, the price of
value-added composite also drops. This gives an incentive to substitute away from the
imported resource, with the degree of the response controlled by $\sigma_{VA,R}$. When this elasticity
of substitution is 0.5, very little change occurs. However, in our other cases, the change is
enough to lead to decreases of a few percentage points in the price of the imported resource.

Table 11.7   Sensitivity Analysis of Consumption Tax for the Capital Service Flow Formulation

	Welfare Effect	
	Additive Replacement	Multiplicative Replacement
1. $E_K = -1.0$, endowment ratio = 2	−$207.5	−$292.6
	(−0.416)	(−0.587)
2. $E_K = -1.0$, endowment ratio = 5	−494.0[a]	−606.6[a]
	(−0.991)	(−1.217)
3. $E_K = -1.0$, endowment ratio = 10	−635.6	−764.4
	(−1.275)	(−1.533)
4. $E_K = -1.0$, endowment ratio = 4, foreigner pays gross-of-tax rental rate	452.5	162.5
	(0.907)	(0.326)
5. $E_K = -0.5$, endowment ratio = 2	31.6	−30.8
	(0.063)	(−0.062)
6. $E_K = -0.5$, endowment ratio = 5	−288.7[a]	−380.5[a]
	(−0.579)	(−0.763)
7. $E_K = -0.5$, endowment ratio = 10	−490.0	−603.3
	(−0.983)	(−1.210)
8. $E_K = -0.5$, endowment ratio = 5, foreigner pays gross-of-tax rental rate	544.5	370.9
	(1.092)	(0.744)
9. $E_K = 0.0$, endowment ratio = 5	567.8	548.6
	(1.139)	(1.100)
10. $E_K = -0.1$, endowment ratio = 5	233.5	188.6
	(0.468)	(0.378)
11. $E_K = -4.0$, endowment ratio = 5	−720.8	−863.2
	(−1.446)	(−1.731)

Note: Dynamic welfare effects in present value of compensating variations over time; all figures in billions of 1973 dollars. The numbers in parentheses represent the gain (or loss) as a percentage of the present discounted value of consumption plus leisure in the base sequence.
[a]These results were reported previously in table 11.4.

depend upon the value we choose for E_K. We have highlighted the results for $E_K = -1.0$ and $E_K = -0.5$, under each of which the consumption tax is a losing proportion. However, table 11.7 indicates that if the value is close enough to zero, enough of the new capital stays at home that United States consumers benefit.

As can be seen from rows 4 and 8 of table 11.7, the results change dramatically when the foreigner is required to pay the gross-of-tax rental price of capital. The substantial losses in rows 1 and 5 become substantial welfare gains under this alternative model, as explained above. This result clearly demonstrates the possibility that the United States could gain by instituting a compensatory tax on capital income received from abroad. However, we must repeat three warnings for those who would advocate such a tax. First, these results arise only in this version of the model. Second, they occur only when we study a consumption tax. Third, we have ignored the possibility of retaliation.

For our capital good formulation, we report only sensitivity analyses on Z_1 and the endowment ratio in table 11.8, because under the consumption tax, the United States saves abroad, but no foreign saving occurs in the United States. Consequently, Z_2 and Z_3 are immaterial in this case. However, they have an effect in the integration cases reported below, where the capital good flow is in the opposite direction. Table 11.8 reveals that our results are rather sensitive to the value of Z_1, but are quite insensitive to the endowment ratio values.

The consumption tax results certainly raise the possibility that a tax policy that appears to improve efficiency in a model of a closed economy may reduce efficiency in a model with an open world capital market. The intertemporal efficiency gains implied by the move to a consumption tax are more than offset by the misallocation of capital between the domestic and foreign economies. This result is due to our assumptions that the

Table 11.8   Sensitivity Analysis of Consumption Tax for the Capital Good Flow Formulation

| | Welfare Effect | |
	Additive Replacement	Multiplicative Replacement
1. $Z_1 = 250$, endowment ratio = 2	−$37.5 (−0.075)	−$52.9 (−0.106)
2. $Z_1 = 250$, endowment ratio = 5	−36.3[a] (−0.073)	−52.1[a] (−0.104)
3. $Z_1 = 250$, endowment ratio = 10	−33.9 (−0.068)	−50.7 (−0.102)
4. $Z_1 = 50$, endowment ratio = 2	238.1 (0.477)	225.1 (0.451)
5. $Z_1 = 50$, endowment ratio = 5	233.9[a] (0.469)	222.5[a] (0.446)
6. $Z_1 = 50$, endowment ratio = 10	235.2 (0.472)	218.4 (0.438)
7. $Z_1 = 10$, endowment ratio = 5	466.7 (0.936)	450.7 (0.904)
8. $Z_1 = 100$, endowment ratio = 5	105.6 (0.212)	92.1 (0.185)
9. $Z_1 = 1000$, endowment ratio = 5	−145.6 (−0.292)	−160.9 (−0.323)

Note: Dynamic welfare effects in present value of compensating variations over time; all figures in billions of 1973 dollars. The numbers in parentheses represent the gain (or loss) as a percentage of the present discounted value of consumption plus leisure in the base sequence ($49 trillion).
[a]These results were reported earlier in table 11.4.

capital flows are zero in the base case and that the corporation income tax is left in place. The new saving incentives created by the adoption of a consumption tax induce individuals to save abroad where the social rate of return is lower than for domestic investments. The corporation income tax is the primary cause of this misallocation.

The sensitivity of our open-economy results to our capital flow elasticity parameters argues that these figures should be the subject of econometric investigation. While we have not pursued such a course ourselves, we hope that the profession can narrow the range of reasonable estimates so that the model's predictions can be made with more precision and confidence.

11.6.3   Corporate Tax Integration

In table 11.9 we present further analyses of corporate and personal tax integration in the United States, using the alternative external sector variants. Under the standard variant of the model, this policy produces gains of $418 billion with additive replacement and $311 billion with multiplicative replacement. These gains are between 0.5 and 1 percent of

Table 11.9   Further Analysis of U.S. Corporate and Personal Tax Integration

	Welfare Effect	
	Additive Replacement	Multiplicative Replacement
1. Central case—constant elasticity, no Armington	$418.2 (0.839)	$310.6 (0.623)
2. Central case—constant elasticity with Armington	417.0 (0.836)	314.0 (0.630)
3. Capital service flow version		
A. $E_K = 0.5$	1281.2 (2.569)	1244.8 (2.497)
B. $E_K = -1.0$	1415.2 (2.838)	1386.1 (2.780)
4. Capital good flow version		
A. $Z_2 = 50,000; Z_3 = 0.5$	611.0 (1.225)	514.9 (1.033)
B. $Z_2 = 100,000; Z_3 = 0.5$	794.4 (1.593)	708.0 (1.420)
C. $Z_2 = 50,000; Z_3 = 0.25$	1044.6 (2.095)	971.6 (1.949)
D. $Z_2 = 50,000; Z_3 = 1.0$	431.4 (0.865)	324.5 (0.651)

Note: Dynamic welfare effects in present value of compensating variations over time; all figures in billions of 1973 dollars. The numbers in parentheses represent the gain (or loss) as a percentage of the present discounted value of consumption plus leisure in the base sequence ($49 trillion).

Table 11.10   Changes in the Relative Price of Capital as a Result of Integration of the Corporate and Personal Income Taxes Model Variant

Period	Constant elasticity, no Armington	Constant elasticity with Armington	Capital service flow $E_K = -1.0$	Capital good flow $Z_2 = 50,000$; $Z_3 = 0.50$
1	1.208	1.207	1.029	1.204
2	1.188	1.187	1.027	1.174
3	1.171	1.170	1.025	1.151
4	1.157	1.157	1.023	1.133
5	1.146	1.145	1.022	1.120
6	1.136	1.136	1.020	1.110
7	1.128	1.128	1.019	1.102
8	1.121	1.121	1.018	1.096
9	1.116	1.116	1.017	1.092
10	1.111	1.111	1.016	1.088
11	1.107	1.107	1.016	1.086

Note: All results based on additive replacement for equal revenue yield.

the total present discounted value of welfare. The results are virtually identical for the Armington version of the model. This is true not only for the aggregate welfare measure, but also for many of the detailed results. One can see from table 11.10 that the paths for the relative price of capital are very similar in the two cases.

Once again, it is the capital service flow version of the model that is the least similar to the other versions. With capital service flows, the welfare gains from integration are very large, in excess of 2.5 percent of total welfare. In this case the United States rents capital services from abroad, because integration results in an increase in the price of capital. This contrasts with the consumption tax case. Residents of the United States gain significantly from this transaction, since they pay the net-of-tax return. These rentals are very large. By the final equilibrium period, they amount to nearly $100 billion, compared with the rental value of the domestic capital stock of about $660 billion. These substantial supplies of capital from abroad are the reason that the relative price of capital services increases so much less under this version of the model than under all of the other versions. However, this does not appear to affect domestic capital accumulation very greatly. The incremental saving brought about by the policy change is about 80 percent as great in the capital service flow version as in the standard version. (In each case, the incremental saving is less than half as great for the policy of integration as for the consumption tax.)

Because the price of capital services does not rise as far under the capital service flow version, there are some differences among the model variants in the sectoral allocation of production. Under the standard version of the model, the relative outputs of lightly taxed, capital-intensive industries such as agriculture and real estate are reduced for two reasons. First, these industries are less attractive after the tax changes because they now shoulder a relatively greater portion of the tax burden. Second, they suffer because of the relative increase in the price of capital services. Under the capital service flow version of the model, the second of these effects is greatly reduced, such that agriculture retains its share of output almost completely, and real estate only suffers about two-thirds as great a relative drop as under the standard version of the model. Similar reasoning would imply that heavily taxed, labor-intensive industries would increase their relative output and that the increase would be greater under the standard version of the model. Indeed, this occurs in many industries.

In table 11.9 we also provide sensitivity analysis on the welfare gains from corporate tax integration in the capital goods flow model. The parameters Z_2 and Z_3 control the strength of the capital inflow response to the increase in the price of capital in the United States. For values of Z_2 and Z_3, which seemed to us to provide believable responses by the foreigner, integration always causes a large welfare gain. Our reading of table 11.9 is that, despite some sensitivity to the values of these parameters, integration under the capital good version seems to yield gains in the neighborhood of 1 percent of the total present value of welfare.

11.6.4 Value-Added Tax

In table 11.11 we present results from our analyses of four different forms of value-added tax for the United States. We model an origin-based VAT as an equal-rate factor tax on both primary factors and a destination-based tax as an equal-rate final sales tax on expenditures in the United States. Under the income-type VAT, all goods are taxed, while only current consumption goods are taxed under the consumption-type VAT. We model the latter feature through a saving deduction for the origin-based VAT of the consumption type. In the case of the destination-based VAT, we model an income-type tax as a tax on all sixteen consumer goods and a consumption-type tax as a tax on the fifteen consumer goods other than saving. We impose equal revenue yield through additive or multiplicative scaling of the income tax. Since the VAT leads to an increase in revenue, the equal yield tax changes are *decreases* in personal tax rates. Therefore, the gains from the various types of VAT are greater (or the losses smaller) under multiplicative replacement. This contrasts with both integration and the consumption tax, under which tax increases were necessary in order to preserve yield equality. Not only does multiplicative replacement lead to better outcomes than additive replacement for the VAT, but the differences are substantial. This is because for the 10

Table 11.11   Welfare Effects of Introducing 10 Percent VAT of Differing Types

Income-Type VAT

	Central case— constant elasticity, no Armington (1)	Central case— constant elasticity with Armington (2)	Capital service flow (3) $E_K = -0.5$	$E_K = -1.0$	Capital good flow (4)
Origin basis					
Additive	−34.8	−35.4	230.6	278.4	−515.3
	(−0.070)	(−0.071)	(0.463)	(0.558)	(−1.033)
Multiplicative	192.3	186.2	390.6	425.7	−372.6
	(0.386)	(0.373)	(0.783)	(0.854)	(−0.747)
Destination basis					
Additive	−34.8	−35.4	209.8	253.5	−461.4
	(−0.070)	(−0.071)	(0.421)	(0.508)	(−0.925)
Multiplicative	192.3	186.2	374.3	406.8	−320.7
	(0.386)	(0.373)	(0.751)	(0.816)	(0.643)

Consumption-Type VAT

Origin basis					
Additive	268.6	251.8	127.5	93.9	136.4
	(0.539)	(0.505)	(0.256)	(0.188)	(0.274)
Multiplicative	489.3	464.1	265.3	219.8	284.7
	(0.981)	(0.931)	(0.532)	(0.441)	(0.571)
Destination basis					
Additive	268.6	251.8	136.2	108.4	130.6
	(0.539)	(0.505)	(0.273)	(0.218)	(0.262)
Multiplicative	489.3	464.1	284.3	242.7	278.2
	(0.981)	(0.931)	(0.570)	(0.487)	(0.558)

Note: Dynamic wefare effects in present value of compensating variations over time; in billions of 1973 dollars. The numbers in parentheses represent the gain (or loss) as a percentage of the present discounted value of consumption plus leisure in the base sequence ($49 trillion).

percent VAT that we consider here, the tax reductions for equal yield are very substantial. In the case of the income-type VATs, marginal income tax rates are reduced by about 40 percent (for multiplicative replacement) and about ten percentage points (for additive replacement). For the consumption-type VATs, the rate reductions are about 35 percent and nine percentage points. This is the general order of magnitude of the tax changes for equal yield in all periods for all formulations of the model. Of course, if we were to consider a smaller VAT, the rate reductions would be smaller and the difference between additive and multiplicative replacement would not be as great. We restrict our attention here to 10 percent VATs for purposes of simplicity.

The changes in welfare resulting from the VAT are relatively small when compared with the results of corporate tax integration or the consumption tax. Whereas the latter changes remove some of the most heavily distortionary portions of the tax system, the VAT is designed to be a nondistortionary tax, except for the effects on labor supply and saving. Therefore, in the versions of the model with no international capital flows, the main welfare improvements come from the reductions in marginal income tax rates or from the reduction in intertemporal distortion resulting from the consumption-type VAT. The neutrality between the origin basis and the destination basis holds exactly for the formulations with no capital goods, and nearly so for the other cases.

In the versions of the model with no international capital flows, and in the capital good flow case, the welfare gains resulting from the income-type VAT runs are generally smaller than those resulting from the corresponding consumption-type VAT simulations. The gains are smaller because the income-type VAT inefficiently distorts individuals' consumption-saving decisions more than the consumption-type VAT, since the former tax applies to investment goods (as well as consumption goods) and in effect taxes saving. For instance, in the standard version of the model with additive replacement, the consumption-type VAT leads to a 6.6 percent increase in saving in the first period, while the income-type VAT causes a 7 percent decrease. These patterns continue in later periods. These changes in saving behavior lead to predictable changes in the relative price of capital. In the case of the income-type VAT, this price rises from about 1.009 in the first period to about 1.054 in the eleventh equilibrium. The consumption-type VAT causes the price of capital to fall from 1.004 to 0.965. These changes are small compared to those caused by the consumption tax on corporate tax integration but they do help explain the welfare results in the VAT simulations.

There is one exception to this general result. In the capital service flow case, the gains under an income-type VAT are larger than under the consumption-type VAT. Because of the movements of the relative price of capital, capital is rented to the United States under the income-type tax and from the United States under the consumption-type tax. Since, as discussed earlier, those offering capital overseas receive only the net-of-tax price of capital as compensation, the direction of the capital service flow is favorable to the United States under the income-type VAT, and unfavorable to the United States under the consumption-type VAT. The favorable effect under the income-type tax more than compensates for any adverse impact related to the tax's distortion of consumption-saving decisions.

The results of table 11.11 show that a consumption-type VAT is welfare improving in the open capital markets formulations, whereas earlier we saw that a consumption tax implemented as an 80 percent savings deduction reduces welfare in the same environment. The difference in results can be attributed to the fact that saving is still taxed under the VAT (although at a reduced rate after the equal yield adjustments), and to the fact that the incidence of a VAT differs from that of an expenditure tax. The high-bracket households, those who do most of the saving, have far more incentive to increase savings with the expenditure tax, given our specifications of the two experiments. Therefore, our VAT simulations entail much smaller capital outflows and social loss.

We view the value-added tax as it exists today as a particular European response to European problems of tax administration and the structural objectives of international economic integration in the EEC. What is not clear is whether the European experience is especially relevant to the problems of the United States. It does not seem that foreign trade concerns provide a legitimate reason for the United States to introduce a VAT. We have seen that the concern over the difference between origin-based and destination-based taxes is somewhat misplaced. In addition, there is no need to tie an origin or destination basis to a particular type of tax. For example, if the United States wanted to countervail the destination-based VAT in the EEC with a destination-based tax in the United States, that could be done equally well with a destination-based retail sales tax. Nevertheless, the results in table 11.11 indicate that a consumption-type VAT leads to welfare gains under every one of the foreign trade formulations. They indicate that a broadly based VAT that replaces existing distortions is worth considering.

11.7 Conclusions

In this chapter we have described four alternative external sector formulations that can be used to represent external sector behavior in our general equilibrium tax model for the United States. We consider two formulations of merchandise trade behavior using constant elasticity excess demand functions for the behavior of the foreign sector. We also consider internationally mobile capital service and capital goods.

Under these different formulations, we reinvestigate two policy alternatives considered in earlier chapters: consumption tax and integration of the personal and corporate income taxes.

Our results indicate that the different external sector formulations make some difference to the results of our model. The most pronounced changes result from the capital service flow formulations. Each of the policies that we investigated appears to have the potential to generate substantial capital service flows between the United States and abroad. When the net flow is from the U.S. to foreigners, the United States is adversely affected since those offering capital receive only the net-of-tax rental price.

12   Concluding Remarks

Any attempt to evaluate national tax policy must deal with at least three major problems. First, when looking at a particular tax or proposed reform, we must account for interactions among different tax instruments. The distributional and efficiency effects of one tax reform depend fundamentally on other taxes that might be levied on other transactions or by other units of government. Second, if the reform applies to a broad-based tax, we must account for other reactions of economic agents. A particular excise tax might be evaluated in a partial equilibrium framework, for example, but the corporate income tax requires a general equilibrium model. Third, if the reform is more than incremental, we must calculate a whole new counterfactual equilibrium rather than rely upon local approximations around the initial equilibrium.

This book presents the structure of a numerical general equilibrium model designed to deal with these problems. The model includes many features of the U.S. economy, including all major taxes, savings and investment behavior, production, consumption, government transactions, and trade. The model can be used to evaluate particular proposals or to study other more general tax issues. Production is disaggregated in the model in order to capture the efficiency effects of factor reallocations, and consumers are disaggregated in order to capture distributional effects. The book contains considerable detail on all of these specifications and on all of the data used. We also provide results from a number of applications.

This modeling activity is part of a broader range of developments, both within public finance and within the applied general equilibrium literature. Most recent tax policy evaluations have been based on the pioneering work of Arnold Harberger (1962, 1966), who first included both efficiency and distributional considerations in a general equilibrium model. Many applications and extensions of this approach are described in the survey by Charles McLure (1975). These analytical models were limited to few production sectors, however, and can only consider incremental changes. With the development of computer methods and techniques such as the algorithm of Scarf (1973), more detailed and sophisticated models began to appear. These models have been applied not only to U.S. tax policy, but to other countries and other issues such as trade or development policy. Some of these models are reviewed in Fullerton, Henderson, and Shoven (1984), and in Shoven and Whalley (1984). This book fits squarely into this public finance and modeling literature.

The original Harberger approach considered the allocation of fixed factor supplies in a single equilibrium period. In our model, we disaggregate production in order to capture more of these static effects, and we allow for endogenous supply of labor in each period. One of the major features of our model, however, is its capability of analyzing dynamic effects through a sequencing of equilibria. An endogenous supply of savings in any one period is added to the capital stock for the next period, and a time profile for the economy is calculated. Welfare implications proceed from the comparison of alternative intertemporal consumption profiles that are generated by alternative tax regimes. This approach has the further advantage that it does not just compare steady-state growth paths, but considers the transition from one to another.

12.1   Results from the Model

One of the major applications of our model involves the integration of corporate and personal income taxes (chapter 8). In fact, many features of the model were designed with this application in mind. We include in our model the personal factor tax, described in section 3.5 above, because the features of the corporate tax which discriminate among industries might be offset or exacerbated by the industry-discriminating features of personal taxes on interest, dividends, and noncorporate income. We find that significant welfare gains can be obtained by undertaking this kind of reform, and that the size of this gain depends on the specifics of the policy. Also in chapter 8 we discuss the distributional effects of corporate tax integration.

Other features of the model were designed in order to evaluate the move to a progressive consumption tax. Labor/leisure choices are required for second-best evaluation of a comprehensive consumption tax, as is consideration of intertemporal effects. Chapter 9 shows that the welfare gain from this reform is of the same order of magnitude as the gains arising from corporate tax integration. Moreover, in this model, either reform could provide individual welfare gains to every one of our twelve income classes. We do not capture possible redistributions among groups based on age or other demographic characteristics, but this Pareto improvement for our twelve income groups is still a significant finding. Other distributional considerations are discussed below.

Besides particular policy proposals, the model can be used to evaluate more conceptual tax policy problems. In chapter 10, for example, we use the model to plot the total government revenue that results from each possible tax rate on labor income. The resulting Laffer curve, for our standard elasticity parameters, is sharply upward sloping for our estimate of the existing tax rate on labor, and it continues to increase up to a 70 percent overall marginal tax rate. Higher labor supply elasticities imply that the curve peaks at lower marginal tax rates, but the aggregate elasticity would have to be unreasonably high (about 3.0) before existing tax rates would put us on the downward-sloping segment of the curve.

All of the results can be sensitive to assumptions and specifications in the model. One of our most important assumptions, however, is that the United States has a fixed supply of capital. If instead capital is internationally mobile, as many have argued, then the impact of taxes could be substantially different. For this reason, chapter 11 goes on to investigate four alternatives. In the specification where capital services are highly mobile across boundaries, investment incentives (such as corporate tax integration) can be associated with additional investment, capital inflows, and welfare gains to the United States, while savings incentives (such as the switch to a consumption tax) can be associated with additional savings, capital outflows, and welfare losses to the United States.

Elsewhere, the model has been used to evaluate many other policy problems. Fullerton and Henderson (1983), for instance, examine the major features of President Reagan's tax policy program, including both the Economic Recovery Tax Act of 1981 and the Tax Equity and Fiscal Responsibility Act of 1982. Ballard, Shoven, and Whalley (1985) measure the overall efficiency effects of every United States tax instrument. For each instrument they simulate its complete removal in order to measure average excess burden (the ratio of total excess burden to total revenue), and they simulate a small change in the rate in order to measure the marginal excess burden (the ratio of the change in excess burden to the change in revenue). One of the main themes to emerge from this analysis involves highlighting the efficiency costs of the tax system in general. Whereas Harberger first suggested that some of these costs were about one-half of 1 percent of GNP, the results from this model indicate that the costs are more significant. Ballard, Shoven, and Whalley find that excess burden is in the range of 20 percent of total revenue, but can easily approach 50 percent of marginal revenue.

We emphasize that these results are not specific forecasts of the U.S. economy under alternative policy regimes. Rather, the model should be viewed as providing a numerical approach to economic theory and policy.

We use the numerical equilibrium model to provide the same kind of economic insight that a theoretical model would provide for a simpler problem that could be solved analytically. We do not use it to predict actual responses. We look at tax changes with a strong ceteris paribus assumption, so we do not consider any of the myriad possible nontax changes that can affect the actual development of the economy.

12.2   Strengths and Weaknesses of the Approach

On many occasions throughout this book we have discussed the strengths and weaknesses of the computational general equilibrium approach, as well as of our particular model. At this point it is appropriate to review these strengths and weaknesses, and mention some others. This will help to place our results in perspective.

As a part of this discussion we will refer to many authors who have relaxed certain assumptions and explored issues that we have not addressed directly in this book. The field of computational general equilibrium (CGE) has grown enormously in recent years, probably because of a widespread feeling that it has many important advantages. The greatest advantage of these models is that they are able simultaneously to consider all interactions in a complex model economy, without ignoring income effects. This allows us to obtain quantitative answers to questions that cannot even be posed in a partial equilibrium framework. Policy analysts who use partial equilibrium techniques are often forced to make a large number of ceteris paribus qualifications to their results. The CGE approach allows us to reduce the number of such qualifications that must be made.

Further advantages of the CGE approach can be seen when it is compared with the simpler model of general equilibrium popularized, in the public finance field, by Harberger. As pointed out in chapter 2, the Harberger model can only be used to analyze changes within a very small number of sectors, and, strictly speaking, its results are only valid for small changes in the relevant parameters. The CGE approach allows us to consider model economies with many dimensions, and it allows us to look at a tremendously wide range of tax policy changes.

As with any form of economic analysis, our applied general equilibrium analysis has its difficulties. These range from general problems implicit in competitive analysis to specific problems in the choice of functional form. Let us consider these problems, beginning with the broader, more general ones.

We assume that all markets are perfectly competitive, that all economic agents have complete information about current prices, and that production is characterized by constant returns to scale. Obviously, each of these assumptions is contrary to many of our everyday observations about the real-world economy. However, we feel that they can be defended in three ways. First, our model is designed to investigate long-run questions of economic efficiency. There may be long-run tendencies toward perfect competition and complete information, even if at any moment these assumptions do not hold throughout the economy. Second, these assumptions give us analytical and computational tractability—the capability to work with a structure that incorporates the main elements of the economic system but at the same time provides a mechanism for analyzing policy issues. Third, these assumptions are used widely in the theoretical literature. Our model stands in clear relation to the existing theoretical literature, and its results can be better understood in light of that theory.

We also assume full employment of productive factors in a long-run equilibrium, without any money supply or macroeconomic fluctuations. This approach seems patently unrealistic, but it allows us to concentrate on real allocation and distribution problems. Our results are not predictions of any near-term effects or even of long-run occurrences. Instead, our results should be seen as indicating the effects of one important set of economic forces that operate in the long run (namely, taxes), while abstracting from a number of other forces that might be felt in the interim. In this sense our results are clearly counterfactual. The only macroeconomic effects that might be relevant would be those that somehow affect long-run tendencies.

In general, an important difficulty is the problem of *model preselection*, that is, the need to select a particular form for the model before the analysis can proceed. The results depend crucially on these choices, but no systematic method exists for making them. The literature simply does not provide clearly defined specification tests for discriminating among alternative model variants.

An example of this difficulty arises when we have to choose an assumption about consumer expectations regarding future prices and tax rates. Expectations might be myopic, as in this model, or perfectly accurate as in Auerbach and Kotlikoff (1983). Ballard and Goulder (1982) investigate the importance of this issue by varying the degree of consumer foresight in an otherwise unchanged version of the model in this book, and they find reasonable robustness in our results.

Another example of model preselection involves the assumption about international capital flows. In analyzing the incidence of the corporate tax, Harberger (1962) assumed a fixed domestic capital stock. He found that, in spite of intersectoral differences in tax rates and the ability of capital to shift between sectors, capital bears the full burden of the tax. Other authors have pointed out, however, that alternative assumptions can totally change the conclusion. If we assume that capital is internationally mobile and that the economy under consideration is small relative to world capital markets, then the supply function for capital is perfectly elastic. The price of capital cannot change as taxes are reformed, so domestic capital owners are unaffected. Tax burdens are borne instead by internationally immobile factors such as labor.

We place our model in the original Harberger tradition by assuming that capital is immobile between nations but perfectly mobile among sectors. The first assumption is relaxed in chapter 11, and we find sensitivity in the results as suggested above. The second assumption, about intersectoral mobility, is relaxed by Fullerton (1983). The welfare gain from corporate tax integration is somewhat diminished in this alternative model where capital takes time to relocate, but the basic results are fairly robust.

Some particularly important structural problems involve the ways in which the various taxes are modeled. Any particular tax must be represented in model-equivalent form, and there are generally several acceptable ways to do this. In our model we represent each tax as an ad valorem tax, and these rates are built into the model structure. Yet the public finance literature generally suggests alternative analyses of nearly all of the major taxes that make up our tax system. The corporate income tax, for example, has been treated as a partial factor tax by Harberger (1962), as a lump-sum tax by Stiglitz (1973), and as an instrument of risk sharing by Gordon (1981). Whichever of these treatments is adopted will influence the conclusions from the model. When Fullerton and Gordon (1983) build the risk-sharing view into a model that is otherwise identical to the one in this book, they obtain substantially different results. Instead of providing welfare gains, the integration of corporate and personal taxes results in a net welfare loss. (More discussion of this alternative is provided in section 3.2.)

The property tax, as another example, has been viewed as an excise tax on housing and more recently as a tax on the return to capital employed in particular industries. We adopt this new view of the state and local property tax, and our equilibrium model allows the partial factor tax to have excise effects on the price of output in any industry where the property tax is higher than average (e.g., the housing industry). However, the tax may be systematically related to benefits. If individuals and firms are mobile among a large number of local jurisdictions, and if local public goods provide no spillover benefits to other jurisdictions, as in a Teibout (1956) equilibrium, then tax payments would be exactly matched by benefits received. The tax in this analysis is a payment for services, not a distorting wedge.

In spite of these many difficulties, it still is necessary to analyze the tax system so that tax policies can be formulated more intelligently. We believe that a major contribution of this book is the explicit discussion of the various modeling choices. The reader can then consider these choices in evaluating our conclusions.

Even more specific are the problems involved in choosing functional forms and parameter values. We have chosen CES functions because they are analytically tractable and because they allow us to incorporate key elasticity parameters easily. In the absence of substantial agreement in the literature about the values of some of these parameters, we want to be able to vary them in sensitivity analysis. The best we are able to do is to use the existing literature to choose a single best-guess value, as well as a wider range of values that might be deemed reasonable. Through the use of alternative values, we assess whether the policy conclusions are robust.

For many tax reforms, such as corporate tax integration, we find that the welfare gains are an upward-sloping function of the assumed saving elasticity (described in section 6.4.3). No single reform always dominates all other reforms when we compare them on the basis of the welfare gain. Fullerton and Lyon (1983) find that, even within a fairly narrow range, the choice for the saving elasticity parameter value is directly linked to the choice of reform (if that choice is based on welfare gains).

It might be argued that the range of estimates for some of the parameters is so great that our model can only be of limited use as a guide to policy. We would respond to this claim in two ways. First, the main themes of our results are not altered by changes in the elasticities. Corporate tax integration and the consumption tax generate substantial welfare gains, regardless of the saving elasticity. Second, the need to make policy decisions leads us to do the best we can, given currently available estimates and techniques. We would very much like to have improved elasticity values on which to base our calculations, but in the absence of more reliable estimates, our sensitivity analyses give a good feel for the likely range of responses to the policy change.

12.3 Directions for Future Research

The ultimate value of a model such as this one hinges both on the believability of the calculations and on their usefulness to policy analysts. It is easy to dismiss such exercises as worthless on the grounds that the assumptions are crude, the data are poor, and the model is preselected (i.e., the particular treatment of each policy instrument has been adopted before the calculations have been made). Nevertheless, we are faced with a policy environment where decisions must be made. If little or no modeling activity takes place, then the analytical structure of conventional economic theory is not being brought to bear fully in making policy decisions. We suggest that our model, and other models like it, have an important role in the policy-making process.

Still, much is left to be done. For example, the numerical specifications of these models are unpalatable to many econometricians. The models are not estimated with any statistical techniques, and no tests apply to the choice of specification. As a consequence, one major contribution would be the econometric estimation of a complete model of this type. Jorgenson (1984) has embarked on one such econometric specification of a general equilibrium model. Mansur and Whalley (1984) discuss this estimation issue, and they conclude that it may well be impossible to estimate an applied general equilibrium model of large dimension using a complete estimation procedure that incorporates all restrictions on parameters. They suggest that such models will never be estimated without some partitioning of the parameter values. As a consequence, the state of the art will probably continue to include some recourse to extraneous parameter estimation or specification through literature search.

The dynamic structure of these models is another area in which considerable research is now taking place. The models developed thus far have predominately been static. Although we have gone further in this book in examining sequenced general equilibrium models, we still assume a world in which consumers live forever. Adoption of an explicit life-cycle structure would be a welcome addition to the analysis of many intertemporal issues. The work of Auerbach and Kotlikoff (1983) provided this type of structure for the first time. Ballard (1983) has continued by extending the model used in this book to include overlapping generations of life-cycle consumers. Each generation receives inheritances, and each gains utility from bequests. The generations are of different sizes, reflecting the baby boom phenomenon. Ballard finds that the consumption tax leads to welfare gains for every cohort, although the gains are generally somewhat less than the gains found in this book. Although Auerbach-Kotlikoff and Ballard differentiate among consumers of different ages, no CGE model has yet differentiated among consumers of the same age across different levels of income or wealth.

Another important research priority is to improve the specification of tax rate parameters, since these can affect the results crucially. A more complete incorporation of recent work on effective tax rates would therefore be an advance. (A summary review of such studies is provided in Fullerton 1984).

Finally, at this point, we note a number of researchers who are currently suggesting areas for further study. Feltenstein (1984), for example, is working on a general equilibrium model with money and bonds. Many researchers find bonds to be a useful addition to an otherwise real equilibrium model, because their existence allows the government to spend more real resources than it collects in real taxes. An example is the model of Mexico by Serra-Puche (1984), a model that also includes unemployment of labor. Willig (1983) has begun to investigate imperfect competition in an equilibrium model, and Bovenberg (1983) is working further on a model of imperfectly mobile capital with installation costs.

Even within the competitive equilibrium framework, one can learn from the disaggregation of productive factors, as in Keller (1980), or of sectors, as in Dixon, Parmenter, and Rimmer (1984). Other studies have emphasized detailed treatments of particular sectors such as the energy sector in Jorgenson (1984) or Borges and Goulder (1984). One could proceed to study the allocative significance of particular deductions in the personal tax, public goods that are nonrival in consumption, or externalities as additional distortions in production or consumption. In addition, we are always in need of more recent data or evidence on producer behavior, consumer behavior, saving behavior, and expectations.

This is only a partial list of the many avenues along which research is now being carried out. Many more exciting areas of research have not yet been explored. Ultimately, these models will prove worthwhile if they shed light on economic questions previously not well understood, and if they contribute to the rational formulation of economic policy. We believe that these models have been successful on both counts, and that the use of these models not only will continue but will expand.

References

Aaron, Henry J. 1973. *Why is welfare so hard to reform?* Washington, D.C.: Brookings Institution.

Anderson, Robert, and Ballentine, J. Gregory. 1976. The incidence and excess burden of a profits tax under imperfect competition *Public Finance* 31:159–76.

Andrews, William D. 1974. A consumption-type or cash flow personal income tax. *Harvard Law Review* 87 (April):1113–88.

Armington, Paul S. 1969. A theory of demand for products distinguished by place of production. International Monetary Fund *Staff Papers* 16:159–76.

Arrow, Kenneth J., and Debreu, Gerard. 1954. Existence of an equilibrium for a competitive economy. *Econometrica* 22 (June):265–90.

Ashenfelter, Orley, and Heckman, James J. 1973. Estimating labor supply functions. In *Income Maintenance and Labor Supply*, ed. Glen G. Cain and Harold W. Watts. Chicago: Rand McNally.

———. 1974. The estimation of income and substitution effects in a model of family labor supply. *Econometrica* 42 (January):73–85.

Auerbach, Alan J. 1979a. Share valuation and corporate equity policy. *Journal of Public Economics* 11 (June):291–306.

———. 1979b. Wealth maximization and the cost of capital. *Quarterly Journal of Economics* 93 (August):433–46.

Auerbach, Alan J., and Jorgenson, Dale W. 1980. Inflation-proof depreciation of assets. *Harvard Business Review* 58 (September–October):113–18.

Auerbach, Alan J., and Kotlikoff, Laurence J. 1983. National savings, economic welfare, and the structure of taxation. In *Behavioral simulation methods in tax policy analysis*, ed. Martin Feldstein. Chicago: University of Chicago Press.

Auerbach, Alan J.; Kotlikoff, Laurence J.; and Skinner, Jonathan. 1983. The efficiency gains from dynamic tax reform. *International Economic Review* 24 (February):81–100.

Bacharach, Michael. 1971. *Bi-proportional matrices and input-output change*. Cambridge: Cambridge University Press.

Bailey, Martin J. 1969. Capital prices and income taxation. In *The taxation of income from capital*, ed. Arnold C. Harberger and Martin J. Bailey. Washington, D.C.: Brookings Institution.

Ballard, Charles L. 1983. Evaluation of the consumption tax with dynamic general equilibrium models. Ph.D. dissertation, Stanford University.

Ballard, Charles L., and Goulder, Lawrence H. 1982. Expectations in numerical general equilibrium models. Research paper no. 31, Stanford Workshop in the Microeconomics of Factor Markets. Department of Economics, Stanford University.

Ballard, Charles L.; Shoven, John B.; and Whalley, John. 1982. The welfare costs of distortions in the U.S. tax system: A general equilibrium approach. Working paper no. 1043, National Bureau of Economic Research.

———. 1985. General equilibrium computations of the marginal welfare costs of taxes in the United States. *American Economic Review* 75 (March).

Beck, John H. 1979. An analysis of the supply-side effects of tax cuts in an IS-LM model. *National Tax Journal* 32 (December):493–99.

Berglas, Eitan. 1981. Harmonization of commodity taxes: Destination, origin, and restricted origin principles. *Journal of Public Economics* 16:377–88.

Berndt, Ernst R. 1976. Reconciling alternative estimates of the elasticity of substitution. *Review of Economics and Statistics* (February):59–68.

Bernheim, B. Douglas. 1981. Dissaving after retirement. Massachusetts Institute of Technology. Mimeo.

Blechman, Barry M.; Gramlich, Edward M.; and Hartman, Robert W. 1975. *Setting national priorities: The 1976 budget*. Washington, D.C.: Brookings Institution.

Blinder, Alan S. 1974. *Toward an economic theory of income distribution*. Cambridge: Massachusetts Institute of Technology Press.

———. 1981. Thoughts on the Laffer curve. In *The supply-side effects of economic policy*, ed. Laurence H. Meyer. St. Louis: Center for the Study of American Business, Federal Reserve Bank of St. Louis, and Washington University.

Blinder, Alan S.; Gordon, Roger H.; and Wise, Donald E. 1980. Reconsidering the work disincentive effects of social security. *National Tax Journal* 33 (December):431–42.

———. 1981. Social security, bequests, and the life cycle theory of saving: Cross-sectional tests. Working paper no. 619, National Bureau of Economic Research.

Boadway, Robin, and Treddenick, John M. 1978. A general equilibrium computation of the effects of the Canadian tariff structure. *Canadian Journal of Economics* 11:424–46.

Borges, Antonio M., and Goulder, Lawrence H. 1984. Decomposing the impact of higher energy prices on long-term growth. In *Applied general equilibrium analysis*, ed. H. E. Scarf and J. B. Shoven. New York: Cambridge University Press.

Borjas, George J., and Heckman, James J. 1978. Labor supply estimates for public policy evaluation. *Proceedings* of the Industrial Relations Research Association, 320–31.

Boskin, Michael J. 1973. The economics of the labor supply. In *Income maintenance and labor supply*, ed. Glen G. Cain and Harold W. Watts. Chicago: Rand McNally.

———. 1978. Taxation, saving, and the rate of interest. *Journal of Political Economy* 86, part 2 (April):S3–S27.

Bovenberg, Lans. 1983. Capital immobility, capital accumulation, and financial assets: q theory in an applied general equilibrium framework. University of California, Berkeley, Department of Economics. Mimeo.

Bradford, David F. 1980. The case for a personal consumption tax. In *What should be taxed: Income or expenditures?*, ed. Joseph A. Pechman. Washington, D.C.: Brookings Institution.

———. 1981. The incidence and allocation effects of a tax on corporate distributions. *Journal of Public Economics* 15, no. 1 (February):1–22.

Bradford, David F., and Fullerton, Don. 1981. Pitfalls in the construction and use of effective tax rates. In *Depreciation, inflation, and the taxation of income from capital*, ed. Charles R. Hulten. Washington, D.C.: Urban Institute Press.

Brittain, John. 1980. Comment on Howrey and Hymans. In *What should be taxed: Income or expenditures?*, ed. Joseph A. Pechman. Washington, D.C.: Brookings Institution.

Brouwer, L. E. J. 1910. Über ein eindeutige, stetige transformationen von flächen in sich. *Mathematische Annalen* 67:176–80.

Brown, E. Cary. 1981. The 'Net' versus the 'Gross' investment tax credit. In *Depreciation, inflation, and the taxation of income from capital*, ed. Charles E. Hulten. Washington, D.C.: Urban Institute Press.

Browning, Edgar K. 1976. The marginal cost of public funds. *Journal of Political Economy* 84 (April):283–98.

Bulow, Jeremy I., and Summers, Lawrence H. 1984. The taxation of risky assets. *Journal of Political Economy* 92 (February):20–39.

Burkhauser, Richard V., and Turner, John. 1981. Can twenty-five million Americans be wrong?—A response to Blinder, Gordon, and Wise. *National Tax Journal* 34 (December):467–72.

Burtless, Gary, and Hausman, Jerry A. 1978. The effect of taxation on labor supply: Evaluating the Gary negative income tax experiment. *Journal of Political Economy* 86 (December):1103–30.

Caddy, Vern. 1976. Empirical estimation of the elasticity of substitution: A review. Preliminary Working Paper OP-09, IMPACT Project. Industrial Assistance Commission, Melbourne, Australia.

Canto, Victor A.; Joines, Douglas H.; and Laffer, Arthur B. 1978. An income expenditure version of the wedge model. University of Southern California. Mimeo.

Canto, Victor A.; Joines, Douglas H.; and Webb, Robert I. 1979. Empirical evidence on the effects of tax rates on economic activity. *Proceedings* of the Business and Economic Statistics Section, American Statistical Association, Washington, D.C.

Caves, Richard E., and Jones, Ronald W. 1973. *World trade and payments*. Boston: Little, Brown.

Christensen, Laurits R. 1971. Entrepreneurial income: How does it measure up? *American Economic Review* 61:575–85.

Christensen, Laurits, and Jorgenson, Dale W. 1973. U.S. income, saving, and wealth, 1929–69. *Review of Income and Wealth*, series 19, no. 4 (December):329–62.

Coen, Robert M. 1980. Alternative measures of capital and its rate of return in U.S. manufacturing. In *The measurement of capital*, ed. Dan Usher. Chicago: University of Chicago Press.

Council of Economic Advisers. 1973. *Economic Report of the President*. Washington, D.C.: Government Printing Office.

David, Paul A., and Scadding, John L. 1974. Private saving: Ultrarationality, aggregation, and 'Denison's law'. *Journal of Political Economy* 82, no. 2, part 1, 225–49.

Debreu, Gerard. 1959. *Theory of value*. New York: John Wiley.

Denison, Edward F. 1958. A note on private saving. *Review of Economics and Statistics* 40 (August):261–67.

Deran, Elizabeth. 1967. Industry variations in the social security tax: Effects on equity and resource allocation. *Quarterly Review of Economics and Business* 7 (Autumn):7–18.

Dixon, Peter B.; Parmenter, B. R.; and Rimmer, Russell J. 1984. Extending the ORANI model of the Australian economy: Adding foreign investment to a miniature version. In *Applied general equilibrium analysis*, ed. Herbert E. Scarf and John B. Shoven. New York: Cambridge University Press.

Dupuit, Jules. 1969. On the measurement of the utility of public works.

In *Readings in welfare economics*, ed. Kenneth J. Arrow and Tibor Scitovsky. Homewood, Ill.: Richard D. Irwin, Inc.

Eaves, B. Curtis. 1972. Homotopies for the computation of fixed points. *Mathematical Programming* 3:1–22.

Ebrill, Liam, and Hartman, David G. 1982. On the incidence and excess burden of the corporation income tax. *Public Finance* 37:48–58.

Evans, Owen J. 1983. Tax policy, the interest elasticity of saving, and capital accumulation: Numerical analysis of theoretical models. *American Economic Review* 73 (June):398–410.

Feenberg, Daniel, and Rosen, Harvey S. 1983. Alternative tax treatment of the family: Simulation methodology and results. In *Behavioral simulation methods in tax policy analysis*, ed. Martin Feldstein. Chicago: University of Chicago Press.

Feldstein, Martin S. 1974a. The incidence of a capital income tax in a growing economy with variable savings rates. *Review of Economic Studies* 41:505–14.

———. 1974b. Tax incidence in a growing economy with variable factor supply. *Quarterly Journal of Economics* 88:551–73.

———. 1974c. Social security, induced retirement and aggregate capital accumulation. *Journal of Political Economy* 82:905–26.

———. 1978. The welfare cost of capital income taxation. *Journal of Political Economy* 86, no. 2, part 2, S29-S51.

———. 1982. Domestic saving and international capital movements in the long run and the short run. Working paper no. 947, National Bureau of Economic Research.

Feldstein, Martin, and Feenberg, Daniel R. 1983. Alternative tax rules and personal saving incentives: Microeconomic data and behavioral simulations. In *Behavioral simulation methods in tax policy analysis*, ed. Martin Feldstein. Chicago: University of Chicago Press.

Feldstein, Martin, and Green, Jerry. 1983. Why do companies pay dividends? *American Economic Review* 73 (March):17–30.

Feldstein, Martin S., and Horioka, Charles. 1980. Domestic savings and international capital flows. *Economic Journal* 90:314–29.

Feldstein, Martin S., and Slemrod, Joel. 1978. Inflation and the excess taxation of capital gains on corporate stock. *National Tax Journal* 31:107–18.

———. 1980. Personal taxation, portfolio choice, and the effect of the corporation income tax. *Journal of Political Economy* 87 (October):854–66.

Feldstein, Martin S.; Slemrod, Joel; and Yitzhaki, Shlomo. 1980. The effects of taxation on the selling of corporate stock and the realization of capital gains. *Quarterly Journal of Economics* 94 (June):777–91.

Feldstein, Martin S., and Summers, Lawrence. 1978. Inflation, tax rules, and the long run interest rate. *Brookings Papers on Economic Activity*, no. 1, 61–99.

Feltenstein, Andrew. 1984. Money and bonds in a disaggregated open economy. In *Applied general equilibrium analysis*, ed. Herbert E. Scarf and John B. Shoven. New York: Cambridge University Press.

Finegan, T. Aldrich. 1962. Hours of work in the United States: A cross-sectional analysis. *Journal of Political Economy* 70 (October):452–70.

Fisher, Irving. 1942. *Constructive income taxation*. New York: Harper Publishing Co.

Fleisher, Belton M.; Parsons, Donald O.; and Porter, Richard D. 1973. Asset adjustment and labor supply of older workers. In *Income maintenance and labor supply*, ed. Glen G. Cain and Harold W. Watts. Chicago: Rand McNally.

Flow of funds accounts, 1946–75. 1976. Washington, D.C.: Board of Governors of the Federal Reserve System.

Fraumeni, Barbara M., and Jorgenson, Dale W. 1980. The role of capital in U.S. economic growth, 1948–1976. In *Capital, efficiency, and economic growth*, ed. George von Furstenberg. Cambridge, Mass.: Ballinger.

Fullerton, Don. 1982. On the possibility of an inverse relationship between tax rates and government revenues. *Journal of Public Economics* 19 (October):3–22.

———. 1983. Transition losses of partially mobile industry-specific capital. *Quarterly Journal of Economics* 98 (February):107–25.

———. 1984. Which effective tax rate? *National Tax Journal* 37 (March):23–41.

Fullerton, Don, and Gordon, Roger H. 1983. A reexamination of tax distortions in general equilibrium models. In *Behavioral simulation methods in tax policy analysis*, ed. Martin Feldstein. Chicago: University of Chicago Press.

Fullerton, Don, and Henderson, Yolanda K. 1983. Long run effects of the accelerated cost recovery system. Discussion paper in economics no. 20, Woodrow Wilson School of Public and International Affairs, Princeton University.

Fullerton, Don; Henderson, Yolanda K.; and Shoven, John B. 1984. A comparison of methodologies in general equilibrium models of taxation. In *Applied general equilibrium analysis*, ed. Herbert Scarf and John B. Shoven. New York: Cambridge University Press.

Fullerton, Don; King, A. Thomas; Shoven, John B.; and Whalley, John. 1980. Corporate and personal tax integration in the U.S.: Some preliminary findings. In *Microeconomic simulation models for public policy analysis*, ed. Robert H. Haveman and Kevin Hollenbeck. Madison, Wis.: Institute for Research on Poverty.

————. 1981. Corporate tax integration in the United States: A general equilibrium approach. *American Economic Review* 71 (September):677–91.

Fullerton, Don, and Lyon, Andrew B. 1983. Uncertain parameter values and the choice among policy options. Working paper no. 1111, National Bureau of Economic Research.

Fullerton, Don; Shoven, John B.; and Whalley, John. 1978. General equilibrium analysis of U.S. taxation policy. In *1978 Compendium of tax research*, 23–55. Office of Tax Analysis, U.S. Treasury Department. Washington, D.C.: Government Printing Office.

————. 1983. Replacing the U.S. income tax with a progressive consumption tax. *Journal of Public Economics* 20 (February):3–23.

Galper, Harvey, and Toder, Eric. 1982. Transfer elements in the taxation of income from capital. Paper presented at the National Bureau of Economic Research Conference on Income and Wealth, Madison, Wis.

Gordon, Roger H. 1981. Taxation of corporate capital income: Tax revenue versus tax distortions. Working paper no. 687, National Bureau of Economic Research.

Goulder, Lawrence H.; Shoven, John B.; and Whalley, John. 1983. Domestic tax policy and the foreign sector: The importance of alternative foreign policy formulations to results from a general equilibrium tax analysis model. In *Behavioral simulation methods in tax policy analysis*, ed. Martin S. Feldstein. Chicago: University of Chicago Press.

Gravelle, Jane G. 1981. The social cost of nonneutral taxation: Estimates for nonresidential capital. In *Depreciation, inflation, and the taxation of income from capital*, ed. Charles R. Hulten. Washington, D.C.: Urban Institute Press.

Greenberg, David H., and Kosters, Marvin. 1973. Income guarantees and the working poor: The effect of income maintenance programs on the hours of work of male family heads. In *Income maintenance and labor supply*, ed. Glen G. Cain and Harold W. Watts. Chicago: Rand McNally.

Grieson, Ronald E. 1980. Theoretical analysis and empirical measurements of the effects of the Philadelphia income tax. *Journal of Urban Economics* 8 (July):123–37.

Grieson, Ronald E.; Hamovitch, William; Levenson, Albert M.; and Morgenstern, Richard D. 1977. The effect of business taxation on the location of industry. *Journal of Urban Economics* 4 (April):170–85.

Grossman, Gene M. 1980. Partially mobile capital: A general approach to two-sector trade theory. Princeton University. Mimeo.

Grubel, Herbert G., and Lloyd, P. J. 1975. *Intra-industry trade: The theory and measurement of international trade in differentiated products*. New York: John Wiley and Sons.

Hall, Robert E. 1968. The implications of consumption and income taxation for economic growth. *Proceedings* of the National Tax Association.

Hall, Robert E., and Jorgenson, Dale W. 1967. Tax policy and investment behavior. *American Economic Review* 57 (June):391–414.

Hamada, Koichi. 1966. Strategic aspects of international taxation of investment income. *Quarterly Journal of Economics* 80:361–75.

Hansen, Terje. 1968. On the approximation of a competitive equilibrium. Ph.D. dissertation, Yale University.

Harberger, Arnold C. 1959. The corporation income tax: An empirical appraisal. In *Tax revision compendium*, vol. 1. House Committee on Ways and Means. Washington, D.C.: Government Printing Office.

———. 1962. The incidence of the corporation income tax. *Journal of Political Economy* 70 (June):215–40.

———. 1964. Taxation, resource allocation, and welfare. In *The role of direct and indirect taxes in the Federal Reserve System*. Princeton: Princeton University Press.

———. 1966. Efficiency effects of taxes on income from capital. In *Effects of corporation income tax*, ed. M. Krzyzaniak. Detroit: Wayne State University Press.

———. 1974. *Taxation and welfare*. Chicago: University of Chicago Press.

———. 1978. Perspectives on capital and technology in less developed countries. In *Contemporary economic analysis*, ed. M. J. Artis and A. R. Nobay. London: Basil Blackwell.

———. 1980. Vignettes on the world capital market. *American Economic Review* 70 (May):331–37.

Harberger, Arnold C., and Bruce, Neil. 1976. The incidence and efficiency of taxes on income from capital: A reply. *Journal of Political Economy* 84:1285–92.

Hausman, Jerry A. 1981. Labor supply. In *How taxes affect economic behavior*, ed. Henry J. Aaron and Joseph A. Pechman. Washington, D.C.: Brookings Institution.

———. 1983. Stochastic problems in the simulation of labor supply. In *Behavioral simulation methods in tax policy analysis*, ed. Martin S. Feldstein. Chicago: University of Chicago Press.

Heller, Walter. 1978. The Kemp-Roth-Laffer free lunch. *Wall Street Journal*, July 12, p. 20. Reprinted in *The economics of the tax revolt: A reader*, ed. Arthur B. Laffer and Jan P. Seymour, 46–49. New York: Harcourt, Brace, Jovanovich, 1979.

Hill, C. Russell. 1973. The determinants of labor supply for the working urban poor. In *Income maintenance and labor supply*, ed. Glen G. Cain and Harold W. Watts. Chicago: Rand McNally.

Howrey, E. Philip, and Hymans, Saul H. 1978. The measurement and determination of loanable-funds saving. Brookings Papers on Economic Activity No. 3, 655–85. Also in *What should be taxed: Income or expenditure?*, ed. Joseph A. Pechman. Washington, D.C.: Brookings Institution, 1980.

Hulten, Charles R., and Wykoff, Frank C. 1981a. Economic depreciation and accelerated depreciation: An evaluation of the Conable-Jones 10-5-3 proposal. *National Tax Journal* 34 (March):45–60.

———. 1981b. The measurement of economic depreciation. In *Depreciation, inflation, and the taxation of income from capital*, ed. Charles R. Hulten. Washington, D.C.: Urban Institute Press.

Johnson, Harry G. 1953. Optimum tariffs and retaliation. *Review of Economic Studies* 21:142–53.

———. 1961. *International trade and economic growth*. London: Allen and Unwin.

Johnson, Harry G., and Krauss, Melvyn. 1970. Border taxes, border tax adjustments, comparative advantage, and the balance of payments. *Canadian Journal of Economics* 3 (November):595–602.

Jorgenson, Dale W. 1984. Econometric methods for applied general equilibrium modeling. In *Applied general equilibrium analysis*, ed. H. E. Scarf and J. B. Shoven. New York: Cambridge University Press.

Jorgenson, Dale W., and Sullivan, Martin A. 1981. Inflation and corporate capital recovery. In *Depreciation, inflation, and taxation of income from capital*, ed. Charles R. Hulten. Washington, D.C.: Urban Institute Press.

Kalachek, Edward D., and Raines, Fredric Q. 1970. Labor supply of lower income workers. In *President's commission on income maintenance programs, technical studies*, 159–86. Washington, D.C.: Government Printing Office.

Kaldor, Nicholas. 1957. *An expenditure tax*. London: Allen and Unwin.

Kay, John A. 1980. The deadweight loss from a tax system. *Journal of Public Economics* 13 (February):111–19.

Kehoe, Timothy, and Whalley, John. 1982. Uniqueness of equilibrium in a large scale numerical general equilibrium model. University of Western Ontario. Mimeo.

Keller, Wouter J. 1980. *Tax incidence: A general equilibrium approach*. Amsterdam: North Holland.

Kendrick, John. 1976. *The national wealth of the United States: By major sectors and industry*. New York: Conference Board.

Kiefer, Donald W. 1978. An economic analysis of the Kemp/Roth tax cut bill H.R. 8333: A description, an examination of its rationale, and estimates of its economic effects. *Congressional Record*, August 2, H7777–H7787. Reprinted in *The economics of the tax revolt: A reader*, ed. Arthur B. Laffer and Jan P. Seymour, 13–27. New York: Harcourt, Brace, Jovanovich, 1979.

Killingsworth, Mark R. 1983. *Labor supply*. New York: Cambridge University Press.

King, Mervyn A. 1974. Taxation and the cost of capital. *Review of Economic Studies* 41, no. 1, 21–36.

———. 1977. *Public policy and the corporation*. London: Chapman and Hall.

Kinsley, Michael. 1978. Alms for the rich. *The New Republic* 179, 19 August, 19–26. Reprinted in *The economics of the tax revolt: A reader*, ed. Arthur B. Laffer and Jan P. Seymour, 35–43. New York: Harcourt, Brace, Jovanovich, 1979.

Kotlikoff, Laurence J. 1979. Testing the theory of social security and life cycle accumulation. *American Economic Review* 69 (June):396–410.

Kuhn, Harold W. 1968. Simplicial approximation of fixed points. *Proceedings* of the National Academy of Sciences, U.S.A. 61:1238–42.

Kuhn, Harold W., and MacKinnon, James G. 1975. The sandwich method for finding fixed points. *Journal of Optimization Theory and Application* 17:189–204.

Laffer, Arthur B. 1977. Statement prepared for the Joint Economic Committee, May 20. Reprinted in *The economics of the tax revolt: A reader*, ed. Arthur B. Laffer and Jan P. Seymour, 75–79. New York: Harcourt, Brace, Jovanovich, 1979.

———. 1980. An equilibrium rational macroeconomic framework. In *Economic issues in the eighties*, ed. Nake M. Kamrani and Richard Day. Baltimore: Johns Hopkins University Press.

Lawrence, Robert Z. 1980. Comment on Howrey and Hymans. In *What should be taxed: Income or expenditure?*, ed. Joseph A. Pechman. Washington, D.C.: Brookings Institution.

Lemke, C. E., and Howson, J. T. 1964. Equilibrium points of bi-matrix games. *SIAM Journal of Applied Mathematics* 12:413–23.

Leuthold, Jane H. 1968. An empirical study of formula income transfers and the work decision of the poor. *Journal of Human Resources* 3 (Summer):312–23.

Lucas, Robert E., Jr. 1969. Labor-capital substitution in U.S. manufacturing. In *The taxation of income from capital*, ed. Arnold C. Harberger and Martin J. Bailey. Washington, D.C.: Brookings Institution.

Lucas, Robert E., and Rapping, Leonard A. 1970. Real wages, employment, and inflation. In *Microeconomic foundations of employment and inflation theory*, ed. Edmund S. Phelps. New York: W. W. Norton.

McCloskey, Donald N. 1983. The rhetoric of economics. *Journal of Economic Literature* 21 (June):481–517.

MaCurdy, Thomas E. 1981. An empirical model of labor supply in a life-cycle setting. *Journal of Political Economy* 89, no 6 (December):1059–85.

McGuire, Timothy W., and Rapping, Leonard A. 1968. The role of market variables and key bargains in the manufacturing wage determination process. *Journal of Political Economy* 76 (September–October):1015–36.

———. 1970. The supply of labor and manufacturing wage determination in the United States: An empirical examination. *International Economic Review* 11 (June):258–68.

McLure, Charles E., Jr. 1969. The inter-regional incidence of general regional taxes. *Public Finance* 24:457–83.

———. 1970. Tax incidence, absolute prices, and macroeconomic policy. *Quarterly Journal of Economics* 84:254–67.

———. 1971. The theory of tax incidence with imperfect factor mobility. *Finanzarchiv* 30:27–48.

———. 1975. General equilibrium incidence analysis: The Harberger model after ten years. *Journal of Public Economics* 4:125–62.

———. 1979. *Must corporate income be taxed twice*. Washington, D.C.: Brookings Institution.

Mansur, Ahsan, and Whalley, John. 1984. Numerical specification of applied general equilibrium models: Estimation, calibration, and data. In *Applied general equilibrium analysis*, ed. Herbert E. Scarf and John B. Shoven. New York: Cambridge University Press.

Maxwell, J. A., and Aronson, Richard. 1977. *Financing state and local governments*. Washington, D.C.: Brookings Institution.

Meade, James E. 1978. *The structure and reform of direct taxation*. Report of a committee chaired by Prof. J. E. Meade. London: Allen and Unwin.

Merrill, O. H. 1972. Applications and extensions of an algorithm that computes fixed points to certain upper semi-continuous point-to-set mappings. Ph.D. dissertation, University of Michigan.

Mieszkowski, Peter. 1967. On the theory of tax incidence. *Journal of Political Economy* 75:250–62.

———. 1969. Tax incidence theory: The effects of taxes on the distribution of income. *Journal of Economic Literature* 7:1103–24.

———. 1972. The property tax: An excise or a profits tax? *Journal of Public Economics* 1 (March):73–96.

Mirer, Thad W. 1979. The wealth-age relation among the aged. *American Economic Review* 69 (June):435–43.

Musgrave, Richard A. 1959. *The theory of public finance*. New York: McGraw-Hill.

Musgrave, Richard A., and Musgrave, Peggy B. 1980. *Public finance in theory and practice*. New York: McGraw-Hill.

Owen, John D. 1971. The demand for leisure. *Journal of Political Economy* 79 (January–February):56–76.

Parrish, Evelyn M. 1974. U.S. balance of payments developments: Third quarter and first nine months of 1974. *Survey of Current Business* 54 (December):22–43.

Pechman, Joseph A., and Okner, Benjamin. 1974. *Who bears the tax burden?* Washington, D.C.: Brookings Institution.

Piggott, John R., and Whalley, John. 1976. General equilibrium investigations of U.K. tax subsidy policy: A progress report. In *Studies in modern economic analysis*, ed. M. J. Artis and A. R. Nobay. Oxford: Basil Blackwell.

————. 1985. *Applied general equilibrium analysis: An application to U.K. tax policy*. New York: Cambridge University Press.

Prest, A. R., and Barr, N. A. 1979. *Public finance in theory and practice*. London: Weidenfeld and Nicholson.

Projector, D. S., and Weiss, G. S. 1966. *Survey of financial characteristics of consumers*. Washington, D.C.: Board of Governors of the Federal Reserve System.

Ritz, Philip M. 1979. The input-output structure of the U.S. economy, 1972. *Survey of Current Business* 59 (February):34–72.

Ritz, Philip M.; Roberts, Eugene P.; and Young, Paula C. 1979. Dollar-value tables for the 1979 input-output study. *Survey of Current Business* 59 (April):51–72.

Rosen, Sherwin. 1969. On the interindustry wage and hours structure. *Journal of Political Economy* 77 (March–April):249–73.

Rosenberg, Leonard G. 1969. Taxation of income from capital, by industry group. In *The taxation of income from capital*, ed. A. C. Harberger and M. J. Bailey. Washington, D.C.: Brookings Institution.

Samuelson, Paul A. 1951. Abstract of a theorem concerning substitutability in open Leontief models. In *Activity analysis in production and allocation*, ed. Tjalling Koopmans. New York: John Wiley and Sons.

Sato, Kazuo. 1967. A two-level constant-elasticity-of-substitution production function. *Review of Economic Studies* 34:201–18.

Sato, Ryuzo. 1963. Fiscal policy in a neoclassical growth model: An analysis of the time required for equilibrating adjustment. *Review of Economic Studies* 30 (February):16–23.

Scarf, Herbert E. 1967. The approximation of fixed points of a continuous mapping. *SIAM Journal of Applied Mathematics* 15:1328–43.

Scarf, Herbert E. (with collaboration of Terje Hansen). 1973. *The computation of economic equilibria*. New Haven: Yale University Press.

Scarf, Herbert E. 1981. The computation of equilibrium prices: An exposition. In *The handbook of mathematical economics*, vol. 2, ed. K. J. Arrow and M. D. Intriligator. New York: North Holland.

————. 1984. The computation of equilibrium prices. In *Applied general equilibrium analysis*, ed. H. E. Scarf and J. B. Shoven. New York: Cambridge University Press.

Serra-Puche, Jaime. 1984. A general equilibrium model for the Mexican economy. In *Applied general equilibrium analysis*, ed. H. E. Scarf and J. B. Shoven. New York: Cambridge University Press.

Shoup, Carl S. 1969. *Public finance*. London: Weidenfeld and Nicolson.

Shoven, John B. 1976. The incidence and efficiency effects of taxes on income from capital. *Journal of Political Economy* 84:1261–83.

Shoven, John B., and Bulow, Jeremy I. 1975. Inflation accounting and nonfinancial corporate profits: Physical assets. Brookings Papers on Economic Activity No. 3, 557–98.

Shoven, John B., and Whalley, John. 1972. A general equilibrium calculation of the effects of differential taxation of income from capital in the U.S. *Journal of Public Economics* 1:281–322.

———. 1973. General equilibrium with taxes: A computation procedure and an existence proof. *Review of Economic Studies* 40:475–90.

———. 1974. On the computation of competitive equilibrium in international markets with tariffs. *Journal of International Economics* 4:341–54.

———. 1977. Equal yield tax alternatives: General equilibrium computational techniques. *Journal of Public Economics* 8:211–24.

———. 1984. Applied general equilibrium models of taxation and international trade: An introduction and survey. *Journal of Economic Literature* 22:1007–1051.

Slemrod, Joel. 1982. Tax effects on the allocation of capital among sectors and individuals: A portfolio approach. Working paper no. 951, National Bureau of Economic Research.

———. 1983. A general equilibrium model of taxation with endogenous financial behavior. In *Behavioral simulation methods in tax policy analysis*, ed. Martin S. Feldstein. Chicago: University of Chicago Press.

Smith, Adam. [1776] 1976. *An inquiry into the nature and causes of the wealth of nations*. Chicago: University of Chicago Press.

Starrett, David A. 1982. Capital taxation and accumulation in a life cycle growth model: Comment. Stanford University. Mimeo.

State tax handbook. 1974. Chicago: Commerce Clearing House.

Stern, Robert M.; Francis, Jonathan; and Schumacher, Bruce. 1976. *Price elasticities in international trade: An annotated bibliography*. London: Macmillan Publishers for the Trade Policy Research Center.

Stiglitz, Joseph E. 1973. Taxation, corporate financial policy, and the cost of capital. *Journal of Public Economics* 2, no. 1, 1–34.

———. 1976. The corporation tax. *Journal of Public Economics* 5, no. 3, 303–11.

Stuart, Charles. 1981. Swedish tax rates, labor supply, and tax revenues. *Journal of Political Economy* 89 (October):1020–38.

———. 1984. Welfare costs per dollar of additional tax revenue in the U.S. *American Economic Review*.

Summers, Lawrence H. 1981. Capital taxation and accumulation in a life cycle growth model. *American Economic Review* 71 (September): 533–44.

Taylor, Lester. 1971. Saving out of different types of income. Brookings Papers on Economic Activity No. 2, 383–407.

Thirsk, Wayne. 1972. The economics of farm mechanization in Colombia. Ph.D. dissertation, Yale University.

Tiebout, Charles M. 1956. A pure theory of local government expenditures. *Journal of Political Economy* 64:416–24.

U.S. Congress. 1977. *1976 tax expenditures*. Washington, D.C.: Government Printing Office.

United States Department of Commerce, Bureau of Census, 1973, *Statistical Abstract of the United States*. Washington, D.C.: Government Printing Office.

U.S. Department of Commerce. Bureau of Economic Analysis (BEA). 1971. U.S. national income and product accounts, 1967–70. *Survey of Current Business* 51 (July):5–45.

———. 1975. *Summary of input-output tables of the U.S economy 1968, 1969, 1970*. BEA-SP 75-027. Washington, D.C.: Government Printing Office.

———. 1976a. The national income and product accounts of the United States: Revised estimates, 1929–74. *Survey of Current Business*, 56, part 1 (January).

———. 1976b. U.S. national income and product accounts, 1973 to second quarter 1976. *Survey of Current Business* 56 (July):22–69.

———. 1979. The detailed input-output structure of the U.S. economy, 1972. Washington, D.C.: Government Printing Office.

———. Interindustry Economics Division. 1974. The input-output structure of the U.S. economy, 1967. *Survey of Current Business* 54 (February):24–56.

———. Office of Business Economics (OBE). 1954. *National income, 1954*. Supplement to the *Survey of Current Business*. Washington, D.C.: Government Printing Office.

United States Department of Labor, Bureau of Labor Statistics (BLS). 1978. Consumer expenditure interview survey, 1972–73. *BLS Bulletin 1985*. Washington, D.C.: Government Printing Office.

U.S. Department of the Treasury. Internal Revenue Service (IRS). 1974. *Annual report of the Commissioner of Internal Revenue*. Washington, D.C.: Government Printing Office.

———. 1977a. *Statistics of income—Business income tax returns, 1973*. Washington, D.C.: Government Printing Offiice.

———. 1977b. *Statistics of income—Corporation income tax returns, 1973*. Washington, D.C.: Government Printing Offiice.

———. Office of Tax Analysis. 1977. *Blueprints for basic tax reform*. Washington, D.C.: Government Printing Offiice.

Uzawa, Hirofumi. 1962. Production functions with constant elasticities of substitution. *Review of Economic Studies* 29:291–99.

Vandendorpe, Adolf L., and Friedlaender, Ann F. 1976. Differential incidence in the presence of initial distorting taxes. *Journal of Public Economics* 6:205–29.

van der Laan, Gerardus, and Talman, A. J. J. 1979. A restart algorithm for computing fixed points without an extra dimension. *Mathematical Programming* 17:74–83.

Weber, Warren E. 1970. The effect of interest rates on aggregate consumption. *American Economic Review* 60 (September):591–600.

———. 1975. Interest rates, inflation, and consumer expenditure. *American Economic Review* 65 (December):843–71.

Whalley, John. 1973. A numerical assessment of the April 1973 tax changes in the United Kingdom. Ph.D. dissertation, Yale University.

———. 1975. A general equilibrium assessment of the 1973 United Kingdom tax reform. *Economica* 42:139–61.

———. 1977. A simulation experiment into the numerical properties of general equilibrium models of factor market distortions. *Review of Economics and Statistics* 59 (May):194–203.

———. 1979. Uniform domestic tax rates, trade distortions, and economic integration. *Journal of Public Economics* 11:213–21.

———. 1980. Discriminating features of domestic factor tax systems in a goods mobile-factor immobile trade model. *Journal of Political Economy* 88, no. 6 (December):1177–1202.

Whalley, John, and Yeung, Bernard. 1984. External sector closing rules in applied general equilibrium models. *Journal of International Economics* 16 (February):123–38.

Willig, Robert D. 1983. Sector differential capital taxation with imperfect competition and inter-industry flows. *Journal of Public Economics* 21 (July):295–316.

Winston, Gordon C. 1966. An international comparison of income and hours of work. *Review of Economics and Statistics* 48, no. 2, 28–39.

Wright, Colin. 1969. Saving and the rate of interest. In *The taxation of income from capital*, ed. Arnold C. Harberger and Martin J. Bailey. Washington, D.C.: Brookings Institution.

Index

Tax (*cont.*)
  treatment of U.S., system in model,
    29–32
  value-added, 5, 204, 213–14, 231–34
  witholding, 217
Thirsk, Wayne, 7n
Tiebout, Charles M., 31, 240
Toder, Eric, 158
Turner, John, 32n.3

Units convention, 114, 123–24

Value added, definition, 55
Vandendorpe, Adolf L., 7n

Van der Laan, Gerardus, 21

Walras's Law, 10, 15, 18, 20
Webb, Robert I., 192
Weiss, G. S., 99n
Whalley, John, 4, 9, 14, 20–21, 45n.13,
    113, 209, 215n, 236, 237, 242
Williamson, Jeffrey, ix
Willig, Robert D., 242–43
Winston, Gordon C., 137 (table 6.12)
Wise, Donald E., 32n.3

Yeung, Bernard, 45n.13
Yitzhaki, Shlomo, 192